EMANUEL'S CHILDREN

Ron Seckinger

Ron Seckinger

EMANUEL'S CHILDREN

Stories of a Southern Family

To Vinny —
Best wishes,
— Ron —

ISBN: 978-1-09836-839-5 eBook 978-1-09836-840-1

Ron Seckinger

To

THE MEMORY OF MY GRANDMOTHER
JESSIE MAE STROUD FIELDS
THE BRAVEST PERSON I EVER KNEW

Ron Seckinger

*The common day and night - the common earth
and waters,*

Your farm - your work, trade, occupation,

*The democratic wisdom underneath, like solid
ground for all.*

— FROM "THE COMMONPLACE," BY WALT WHITMAN

INTRODUCTION

THESE ARE THE true stories of eight Southerners, the sons and daughters of Richard James ("Jim") Stroud and Ella Sherrod, and of some of their relatives and associates. Born into rural poverty in Emanuel County, Georgia between 1888 and 1913, the Strouds scattered across the eastern United States in their separate quests for security or survival.

The eldest of the eight was my grandmother, Jessie Mae Stroud Fields. Although my mother passed on some tales of her childhood, a saga of hard work, deprivation, and sparse expectations, I can't remember asking my grandmother to talk about her life. Her experiences, and those of her siblings, were not the stuff of history books. None occupied a high public office, amassed a fortune, starred in movies, or discovered the cure for a disease. They occasionally crossed paths with the famous but rarely attracted attention beyond their small circles of family, friends, and acquaintances.

Yet drama filled their lives. Most of them knew squalor or tragedy or both. Some displayed incomparable strength of character and achieved modest triumphs under exceptionally trying circumstances. Others surrendered to alcoholism or despair.

The rural world they inhabited has vanished little by little and barely remains within living memory. As the collective memory of a generation is lost, these stories pay homage to ordinary but nonetheless complex men

Ron Seckinger

and women who demonstrated courage daily and who usually, but not always, remained true to their better natures.

To know their lives is to understand an essential part of the great changes that have transformed the South and the nation.

Ron Seckinger

Contents

Ron Seckinger

Contents

CAST OF CHARACTERS

THE STROUD FAMILY

> **Richard James ("Jim") Stroud** (b. 1870)
> **Ella E. Sherrod** (b. 1872)

Jessie Mae Stroud (b. 1888)

- James Duncan ("J.D.") Fields, Jr. (b. 1907)
- Rosa Lee Fields (b. 1908)
- John Argyle ("John A.") Fields (b. 1911)
- Ralph Henry Fields (b. 1913
- Leila Ella Fields (b. 1915
- Romie Delle ("Ronnie") Fields (b. 1918)
- Lucy Fields (b. 1921)
- Rachael Wynelle Fields (b. 1923)
- Novis Kenneth ("Knob") Fields (b. 1925)

Jewel Stroud (b. 1892)

- Vera Mae Hooks (b. 1910)
- Thelma Gertrude Hooks (b. 1912)
- Melema Hooks (b. 1915)
- Freddie Barbara Hooks (b. 1920)

Emmit Lee Stroud (b. 1894)

- Hilma Frances Stroud (b. 1925)
- Penny Stroud (b. 1941)

Denver Wallace Stroud (b. 1897)

- Lillian Bernice Stroud (b. 1924)

Marjorie ("Margie") Stroud (b. 1903)

- Ellie Julian Scott (b. 1920)

Kermit George ("Little Son") Stroud (b. 1906)

- Carolyn Jean Stroud (b. 1935)
- Denver Julian Stroud (b. 1937)

Alice Susie Stroud (b. 1911)

- Patrick Wise Mitchell (b. 1934)
- Virginia Gail Mitchell (b. 1939)

Maude Stroud (b. 1913)

- Billy Moreno (b. 1933)

OTHERS

- John Ashley, *Everglades desperado*
- Tyrus Raymond ("Ty") Cobb, *baseball player*
- Floyd Collins, *Kentucky caver*
- William C. Dracy, *paramour of Maude Stroud Moreno*
- Hannah Fields Dyson, *sister of James Duncan Fields*
- Joseph Ehrlich, *owner of dry goods store and farmland*
- Rebecca Smolensky Ehrlich, *wife of Joseph Ehrlich*
- Garry B. Fields, *brother of James Duncan Fields*
- Henry Fields, *brother of James Duncan Fields*
- James Duncan Fields, *husband of Jessie Mae Stroud*

- J.W. Fields, *father of James Duncan Fields*
- Joseph Fields, *brother of James Duncan Fields*
- Rosa Lee Smith Fields, *mother of James Duncan Fields*
- White Temples Fields, *brother of James Duncan Fields*
- Willie Fields, *Swainsboro policeman, cousin of James Duncan Fields*
- R.A. ("Ell") Flanders, *banker and landowner*
- R.N. Hardeman, *judge of Circuit Court in Swainsboro*
- Charles Harmon, *friend of Maude Stroud*
- Bertha Frances Harrison, *grandmother of Frances Winwood Bell Stroud*
- Claude High, *husband of Lillian High*
- Lillian High, *employer of Alice and Maude Stroud in Miami*
- Annie Lee Ducker Hooks, *second wife of Frederick Bryan Hooks*
- Delma Hooks, *brother of Frederick Bryan Hooks*
- Gloria Vivian Hooks, *daughter of Frederick Bryan Hooks*
- Frederick Bryan Hooks, *husband of Jewel Stroud*
- John White Hooks, *father of Frederick Bryan Hooks*
- Lillian Flanders Hooks, *mother of Frederick Bryan Hooks*
- Nell Horn Hooks, *wife of Delma Hooks*
- Seaboard ("Seab") Johnson, *convicted murderer*
- Ouida Kirkland Fields, *wife of J.D. Fields*
- Claude McLendon, *friend of Ellie Scott*
- Will McMillan, Jr., *friend of Ellie Scott*
- Archie Moreno, *husband of Maude Stroud*
- Dion O'Banion, *Chicago gangster*
- Walter Pheanious, *childhood friend of J.D. Fields*
- Louis Proctor, *co-owner of movie theater in Swainsboro*
- Jonathan Carol ("Pete") Rich, *friend of Ellie Scott*
- Nesbit Rogers, *friend of Maude Stroud*
- Richard B. Russell, *Georgia Governor and Senator*
- Bernice Register Stroud, *wife of Denver Stroud*

- Frances Winwood Bell Stroud, *wife of Emmit Stroud*
- Rosa Lee Jean ("Rose") Walker Stroud, *wife of Kermit Stroud*
- Sudie Scott Stroud, *second wife of Richard James Stroud*
- Eugene Talmadge, *Georgia Governor*
- Laura Upthegrove, *paramour of John Ashley*
- Gladys Waller, *friend of Maude Stroud*

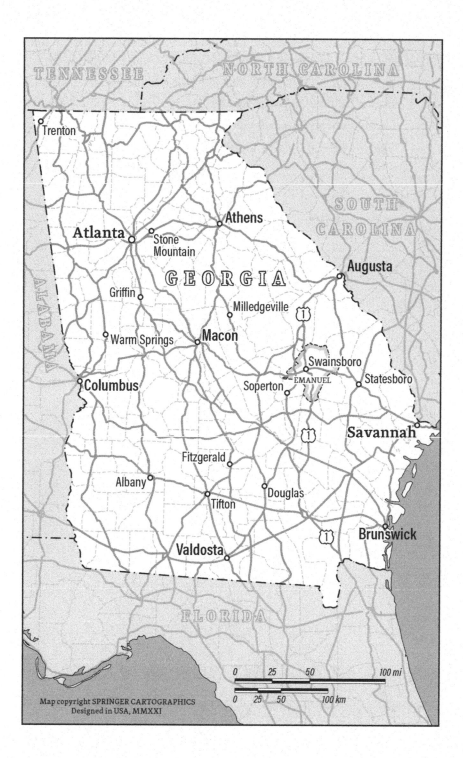

Trenton

Atlanta

Stone
Mountain

Athens

GEORGIA

Augusta

Griffin

Milledgeville

①

Warm Springs

Macon

Swainsboro

Soperton EMANUEL

Statesboro

Columbus

①

Savannah

Fitzgerald

Albany

Douglas

Tifton

①

Brunswick

Valdosta

TENNESSEE

NORTH CAROLINA

SOUTH
CAROLINA

ALABAMA

FLORIDA

0   25   50   100 mi

0   25   50   100 km

Map copyright SPRINGER CARTOGRAPHICS
Designed in USA, MMXXI

Ron Seckinger

ORIGINS

AS DUSK GATHERED on a December evening, a young woman sat on a bed in a city far from her place of birth and prepared to take her own life. Her family and friends would have said she had much to live for, but her trajectory from rural poverty to big city to faded dreams had depleted her courage, and she'd persuaded herself that her options had narrowed to this final one.

She and her siblings, the children of Richard James ("Jim") Stroud and Ella Sherrod, descended from Scots-Irish pioneers who filtered into the frontier areas of central and western Georgia during the 19th century. They settled among the Rountrees, Durdens, Boatrights, Youmans, Colemans, Overstreets, Youngbloods, Keas, and other families, mingling and proliferating like honeysuckle along the country roads. Within a few generations, only the eldest members of each clan could pick their way through the genealogical tangle.

Like other White settlers, the Strouds claimed free land made available by the forced displacement of native Creeks and Cherokees and distributed through lotteries. As the European population grew, the state government created new counties to provide the rudiments of administration. Emanuel County, established in 1812 and named after Revolutionary War hero David Emanuel, embraced some 1,800 square miles of east-central Georgia, later reduced to 690 square miles as the state carved out other counties. It perched on the northern edge of "wiregrass" country, after a ubiquitous ground cover, and within the Pine Barrens, the broad crescent of wooded territory sweeping from the Mississippi River to the Chesapeake Bay. Tall, ancient pines blanketed the monotonous terrain with a green canopy broken only by the brown waters of swamps and twisting creeks.

The early settlers, who with their slaves numbered fewer than 3,000 in 1820, exploited the county's timber resources or raised hogs, cattle, and sheep. As they cleared the land, corn, cotton, sugar cane, and vegetable gardens claimed the eroding, stump-dotted fields.

Save a handful of wealthy planters, the population lived a stark existence. The relatively few slaves suffered harsh treatment here as elsewhere in the South, and White farm families fared poorly. Poverty, endless labor, and casual justice were the lot of most country people, their routines enlivened only by visits to neighboring farms, church services performed by circuit-riding preachers, occasional dances, and liquor-inspired brawls. Life in Emanuel probably resembled the frontier vignettes in Augustus Baldwin Longstreet's *Georgia Scenes*, first published in 1835.

Jim Stroud and an unidentified Black man hold cured hams, ca. 1915.

Ron Seckinger

Decades passed before Swainsboro, founded as the county seat in 1822, offered more than a few residences and stores. Boosters temporarily changed the name to Paris in 1854, but less pretentious folk prevailed, and the settlement's name reverted to Swainsboro.

Like the other men of Emanuel County, the Strouds fought for the Confederacy. John Stroud, for example, enlisted as a private in McLeod's Volunteers, a unit of the 48th Georgia Infantry and the Army of Northern Virginia. Captured at Mine Run, Virginia in November 1863, he spent 14 months in Old Capitol Prison in Washington and went south in a prisoner exchange in late February 1865. After a few days in Richmond's General Hospital, he received a 30-day furlough and apparently missed the fall of the city and the surrender of Lee's army at Appomattox Courthouse. He turned himself in to federal authorities in Augusta, Georgia in May.

The world to which the soldiers returned differed greatly from the one they'd departed four years earlier. One wing of Sherman's army had passed through the northern part of the county, loosing scouts and foragers who confiscated crops and livestock while putting the torch to homes, barns, sawmills, and other structures. Drought in 1866 and excessive rains the following year made the immediate postwar period in Emanuel, as in most of Georgia, a time of near famine. Never really prosperous before the war, the county would be long in recovering.

Into this stark environment came Jim Stroud, the son of veteran John Stroud, in 1870, and Ella E. Sherrod two years later. Raised on farms north of Swainsboro, the two undoubtedly knew each other as children and, like most everyone, married young, about 1887. In May 1888, at the age of 16, Ella delivered their first-born, Jessie Mae.

For a time, the young family apparently lived on a 200-acre parcel originally part of John Stroud's plantation. But in 1889 Jim sold his land for $200 and became, for the rest of his life, a sharecropper.

Stroud's descent from smallholder to tenant presumably followed a pattern all too common throughout the South. Immediately after the war, sharecropping and other forms of tenancy--the use of land in exchange for a portion of the crop or, more rarely, a cash payment--had emerged as a means of controlling the labor of newly freed slaves.

Ella Stroud with Marjorie (standing) and Kermit, ca. 1908.

As the decades passed, a growing proportion of White farmers found themselves in similar circumstances. The low ratio of land to population dictated that most farms would be small, undercapitalized enterprises operating at the margin and easily forfeited.

Many smallholders resorted to the crop lien system, mortgaging their crops to local merchants or wealthy landowners for enough cash to cover seeds, fertilizer, and sustenance. The creditor set the interest rate as well as the prices for goods advanced and stipulated the crop--almost always cotton.

If he were lucky, the farmer, Black or White, would earn enough to pay off the lien and purchase clothes, livestock, or other needs. If not, his

Ron Seckinger

debts carried over to the next year. The fluctuating price of cotton added to his vulnerability.

Landless, the Strouds and their baby daughter settled on a tenant farm near Blun, a tiny community where a single general store provided the sum total of commerce. More children followed: Jewel, Emmit, Denver, Majorie, Kermit, Alice, and Maude, eight live births in all by the time Ella turned 41 in 1913.

Faculty members and students of Hale Chapel School, date unknown.

She took them to Hawhammock Baptist Church every Sunday and sent them to Hale Chapel School, which offered instruction through the sixth grade for five--later extended to nine--months each year. In 1911, the school had 85 students, and some 1,000 family members and well-wishers attended closing ceremonies in May. Although Denver and Emmit's names appeared on the honor roll that year, the Stroud children obtained only the rudiments of learning. As adults, Jessie, Jewel, and Denver wrote in a cramped style with little regard for spelling, punctuation, and capital-ization. Only the two youngest, Alice and Maude, had the opportunity to attend high school.

They were so poor, Emmit would tell his wife years later, that finding an orange on the hearth on Christmas morning sparked great excitement. The children worked in the fields, gathered vegetables from the garden, helped with the canning, and performed chores necessary to keep the farm running.

When time permitted, they played drop-the-handkerchief, hide-and-seek, or red-light with kids from nearby farms. At frequent parties, they took turns cranking the ice-cream machine until it became too hard and a grown-up had to finish. The older girls and their beaus chatted under the adults' watchful gaze, well aware they were not allowed to wander out to the well in the dark.

The Stroud children, ca. 1908. From left: Denver, Kermit (in chair), Jewel, Marjorie, Emmit.

Ron Seckinger

Life for the Stroud children differed little from that of their parents 20 years earlier. But despite the apparent timelessness of the farm, changes in the outside world would soon give them opportunities beyond the dreams of their grandparents.

RUFFIANS

SEVENTEEN-YEAR-OLD Jessie, eldest of the Stroud children, a pretty young woman with long brown hair, married James Duncan Fields in 1906. Tall, wiry, and seven years her senior, Duncan cut a fine figure, despite his jug ears. He played guitar--or "tried to," as a contemporary recalled decades afterwards--at cane grindings and parties, with his brother Henry and other local men.

At the time of their wedding, the Swainsboro *Forest-Blade* characterized Jessie as "a young lady of many noble graces" and Duncan as "a young man of sterling worth and business qualifications. He is very popular and his friends are numbered by his acquaintances." The newspaper wished them all good things:

> Here's to you and yours, Duncan, and may life's journey
> be one continuous honeymoon and may the pathway
> along which you go be strewn with the rarest flowers
> as together you and yours wend your way through this
> life, which after all is but a preparation for that greater
> life to come.

As Jessie would soon discover, the *Forest-Blade* had no gift for prophecy.

Ron Seckinger

*A country band. From left: Bob Rich, Duncan Fields, Henry
Fields, Press Rich, Jordan Sammons, R.H. Hicks.*

The Fields clan might have sprung from one of William Faulkner's novels. Not all of them shared Duncan's almost mythic propensity for self-destruction, but many had run-ins with the law or met untimely deaths. Duncan's uncle and cousin, Fuller and Miles Fields, stood trial for murder in 1896 but escaped with an acquittal. In 1913 a jury found Fuller innocent of charges of rape.

Duncan's older brother Henry settled a dispute with firearms. Engaged in a feud with a married man who forced his attentions on Henry's daughter, Henry encountered the man in a drugstore in Soperton and shot him at point-blank range. At a preliminary hearing, three justices issued a ruling of justifiable homicide, and Henry never stood trial.

Duncan himself was charged with public drunkenness in 1910 and 1915, and in 1913 a grand jury indicted him, along with his brothers Henry and Garry B., for assault and battery. Apparently, the case never went before a judge.

J.W. Fields and family posing beside their farmhouse north of Swainsboro, ca. 1895-1896. From left: Garry B., Hannah, John E., Henry D., James Duncan, White Temples, Rosa Lee Smith, J.W. The last child, Joe, was born in 1897.

Duncan's parents, J.W. and Rosa Lee Smith Fields, raised their seven children on a 182-acre farm inherited or purchased from her father, White Roster Smith. In 1904, J.W. declared himself a candidate for county sheriff--"Not so much because of being so strongly solicited but because I am [in] need of the coin." Elected twice, he served four years. His salary, along with a $200 reward for capturing an accused murderer from South Carolina, allowed J.W. to amass at least another 269 acres. In 1910 he deeded about 50 acres to each of four sons, including Duncan.

For the next 20 years, Duncan and his family resided on this small farm, located about five miles north of Swainsboro, off the dirt road between Blun and Dellwood. On occasion, they leased it out and lived elsewhere.

If Jessie harbored girlish notions of her future, they didn't survive the discovery that her husband was a drunkard and no-account. Well-known and popular, Duncan was invariably the first to offer help when a neighbor was in need. But he showed his wife and children another, darker side. "He was the type of fellow that you'd like out there," Mabel Screws recalled, "but inwardly there was something hid, [something] he didn't bring out to the outside world."

Jessie became pregnant almost immediately. James Duncan, Junior--known all his life as J.D.--came in February 1907, and Rosa Lee, named for Duncan's mother, in April 1908. Until the children grew big enough to work in the fields, Duncan and Jessie couldn't handle all the chores by themselves. In 1910, a young Black man named John Williams resided on the farm as a hired hand, and this arrangement probably lasted for some years longer.

White Roster Smith, 1880s.

Duncan often disappeared for days. As suppertime passed and the babies fell asleep, Jessie sat in the farmhouse, the night outside as dark as homemade sin. She started at every noise, prey to her imagination, until fear egged her to hitch the horse to the wagon and flee with the children to a neighbor's home, retracing her steps after sunup.

Eventually she grew accustomed to nights alone, save when Duncan stumbled in, drunk and abusive. Then she took her babies to the nearby Coleman farm for the night. In the morning, she returned to resume her chores while her husband slept in alcoholic stupor.

Duncan came home often enough to keep Jessie pregnant. More children followed as regularly as the seasons—John Argyle, named after a local preacher and known as John A., in 1911, Ralph Henry in 1913, Leila Ella in 1915, and Romie Delle in 1918. An old Black woman they called "Aunt Mandy," who claimed to have delivered Duncan himself, served as midwife.

If the cotton crop demanded attention, Jessie's convalescence lasted only about a week. She'd return to the fields, placing the new baby in a quilt-lined washtub under a shady tree, close enough that she could hear its cries. She labored till dark and then trudged home to prepare supper.

Often the children fell asleep, sprawled behind the woodstove or under the table, before she could put a meal before them. Rosa took over the cooking and housework at age nine, so small she had to stand on a stool to reach the pots on the stove. This freed Jessie to concentrate on wresting a living from the earth.

Duncan Fields, ca. 1910.

Jessie cared not only for her children but also for a number of relatives, mostly her husband's kin. Duncan's cousin Willie Fields lived on the farm for a while and worked with plow and hoe like the rest of them.

Ron Seckinger

Jessie allowed him to name Leila because he was first to enter the house after the baby's birth. Another of Duncan's brothers, Garry B., resided with them after his wife decamped to Augusta with their three children. And Joe Fields made himself a favored guest, leaving Jessie and her children devastated when he died before his 30th year.

Duncan's father earned no one's favor. After his wife's death in 1913, J.W. rotated among his sons' homes, and his periodic, month-long stays were particularly onerous. An invalid and foul-mouthed curmudgeon, he took out his frustrations on anyone at hand. He beat his hound Johnson and constantly cursed Joe, who carried the old man from porch to table to bed. Joe and Henry sometimes paid Henry's son Jack a quarter to baby-sit their father so they could take in a baseball game. One night, J.W. got into such a state that Jessie, unable to calm him, hitched up the wagon to bring Duncan back from the home of his brother Temples.

One might say that the Fields men were too mean to die. But death waits for everyone. When the old terror J.W. passed away in 1915, no one lamented his passing.

PROGRESS

THE RAILROAD, principal engine of the new era, transformed the wiregrass region of southeastern Georgia after 1880. Largely financed by Northern entrepreneurs, the railroads traversed the sandy, sparsely populated flatlands, reinvigorating the timber and turpentine industries. Agriculture took on new life as trainloads of commercial fertilizers magically increased the yields of the formerly sterile soils. The railroad companies, which amassed vast tracts along the right-of-way, advertised cheap land in an unsuccessful effort to divert the floodtide of humanity then surging from Europe to the northeastern and midwestern United States.

Few immigrants took the bait--in 1910, barely 15,000 foreign-born Whites lived in Georgia, and only 21 in Emanuel County--but others did. White farmers from the mountains of northern Georgia and African American farmers from the "Black Belt" of rich farmland across the center of the state took advantage of cheap acreage to establish themselves in the wiregrass counties. Some 100,000 new settlers arrived during the last decade of the century, and some who started as tenants eventually managed to buy their own land.

Emanuel County benefited from this boom, even though it had no direct rail line until 1910. The Civil War and the impoverishment that followed interrupted the efforts of local entrepreneurs to link Swainsboro to Midville by a spur line. The expansion of the timber industry during the

1870s, however, provided the necessary impetus. The owners of booming sawmills, no longer content to float their logs downriver to the coast, began to construct tram roads to the nearest railheads.

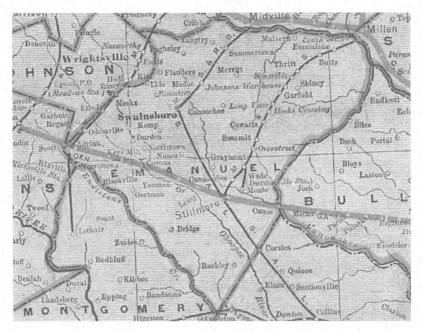

This detail from a Central of Georgia Railway map of Alabama and Georgia, dated 1899, shows the principal east-west lines through Midville and Stillmore with connections to Swainsboro and other towns in Emanuel County.

The earliest tram road in Emanuel County ran south from Midville to Summertown and later to Modoc. This served as the basis for a primitive line called the Midville, Swainsboro & Red Bluff Rail Road, connecting the county seat to the Central of Georgia after its 1888 charter and used mostly for hauling logs. Other tram lines built by the timber barons also became railroads--from Adrian to Stillmore across the southwestern part of the county, north from Stillmore through Garfield in the east, and from Stillmore to Swainsboro.

By 1906, when the railway craze had not yet crested, the loggers had largely depleted Emanuel's once seemingly inexhaustible pine forests. In that year, the owners of two of the largest sawmills announced their intentions of relocating to virgin tracts, one in southern Alabama and the other in Florida.

Workers at Swainsboro Lumber Company, 1935. Courtesy,
Georgia Archives, Vanishing Georgia Collection, emn052.

The Swainsboro *Forest-Blade,* in noting the passing of the timber era, thankfully pointed out that "our numerous railroads, now here to stay and to play so important a part in our future, are the handiwork of the saw-mill men."

These lines only slowly overcame their origins as logging trains. Their engines and tracks were unreliable, and their passenger coaches, Spartan.

As early as 1904, the intrepid could take Sunday excursions to the beach at Tybee Island east of Savannah via the Midville & Swainsboro Railroad (MSRR)--the line never reached Red Bluff--with connections to the Central of Georgia. The passengers who detrained in Midville, their eyes red from smoke and their clothes streaked with soot and singed by sparks from the firebox, claimed that the initials MSRR stood for "Miserable, Sorry, and Rough Road." Farmers and merchants, loath to trust the shipment of goods to such perilous means of transport, preferred to travel the 20 miles to Midville by wagon.

Discriminatory rates, overcharging, and other abuses made the railroads a mixed blessing, and at the turn of the century reformers in Georgia

Ron Seckinger

and other Southern states battled to bring the rail companies to heel. The *Forest-Blade* and the entrepreneurial interests it represented saw no merit in such negatives. The newspaper, which exhorted its readers to "Pull for Swainsboro or pull out," seized on the necessity of a through line as the key that would unlock the county's potential.

The railroad gave Emanuel County residents the means to escape to locales such as Tybee Beach at Savannah. This ad appeared in the Forest-Blade on June 1, 1911. Courtesy, Forest-Blade Publishing Co.

After years of false hopes, the citizens of Swainsboro secured the elusive through line by subscribing $20,000 and 20 miles of right-of-way to the Georgia & Florida Railway. This would link the county not only to the nation's expanding rail network but also, as the *Forest-Blade* pointed out in February 1910, to the burgeoning trade expected in the ports of Florida following the completion of the Panama Canal.

The great event soon came to pass. On July 1, 1910, the first train passed through Swainsboro en route from Augusta to Madison, Florida, "greeted by thousands along the rail-route of triumph." Swainsboro's entrepreneurs immediately formed a Chamber of Commerce.

The coming of the railroad allowed locals to export their products more expeditiously and to import goods from the outside more cheaply. The eight daily passenger trains also gave them a previously inconceivable freedom of movement. Little Margie Stroud, just seven or eight years old and carrying her clothes in a shoebox, rode alone from Blun to Summertown to visit a cousin, and even greater adventures were available.

Excursions took Emanuel's citizens to the opening game of the South Atlantic ("Sally") Baseball League in Augusta; a music festival in Atlanta; Mardi Gras in New Orleans, Mobile, Pensacola, or Knoxville; the Southern Baptist Convention in Jacksonville; the Confederate Veterans' Reunion in Little Rock; or the University of Virginia summer session in Charlottesville. Even New York, Chicago, and San Francisco lay within the reach of those with cash and a thirst for travel.

The motor car contributed to the new mobility. At the turn of the century, businessmen and civil leaders established Good Roads Associations in most of the Southern states and pressed for highways suitable for automobile traffic. The notion caught on in Emanuel County as cars became more common. By 1907, even the small community of Graymont claimed three autos, and three years later two Swainsboro entrepreneurs opened an agency to sell Cartercars.

The county government purchased a grading machine in 1904, but Black convicts, leased to the county by the state, did most of the work with shovels. Between 1904 and 1909, convict labor doubled the mileage of improved roads in Georgia. After the abolition of convict leasing, the state legislature took up a proposal to establish a chain-gang system using both Black and White prisoners on the roads. According to the *Forest-Blade*, "Officials of every county are averse to working white men if possible," but the bill passed in 1909.

Charley Cheatham in one of the first automobiles in Swainsboro, ca. 1910. In 1918 an auto seriously injured Cheatham's three-year-old daughter as she crossed the street in front of her home. Courtesy, Georgia Archives, Vanishing Georgia Collection, emn050.

Some found this solution too slow. A Swainsboro man who favored a bond issue wrote in 1910 that the convicts had laid clay on only 70 miles of roadbed in 17 months. He calculated that finishing the 1,240 miles of public roads in the county would require 26 years. Concerned citizens formed the Emanuel County Good Roads Association the following year to press for quick improvements. In early 1911, two local men set a new record by driving a Maxwell the 106 miles from Swainsboro to Savannah in just six hours. They stopped only once to light the headlamps.

EMANUEL'S CHILDREN

Progress had its costs. Ten days after the Georgia & Florida opened service to Swainsboro, the 2:20 train struck a horse-drawn wagon at the Main Street crossing, seriously injuring the driver. The town's first auto fatalities occurred less than a year later, in April 1911, when a car traveling at 40 miles per hour collided with a buggy, killing a woman and her three children. "The whole town is indignant," reported the *Forest-Blade.* "Automobile racing and the death-rush of pleasure will now have to stop! It has taken this stack of deaths to do it."

The newspaper would continue to rail against speeders over the coming decades, without noticeable effect. Progress listened to its own counsel.

BASEBALL

SLENDER AND dark-featured, Jewel Stroud reigned as the family beauty, with luminous brown eyes that conveyed a haunting sense of sadness. In January 1909, at the age of 17, she married Frederick Bryan Hooks in Louisville, the seat of Jefferson County to the north of Emanuel. The two had known each other since attending school together as children.

Two years older, Fred was almost six feet tall, with curly blond hair and fine features. Born in 1890 in Wrightsville, in neighboring Johnson County, he was the eldest son of John White Hooks and Lillian Flanders.

John Hooks stood six-feet-four and weighed 240 pounds, a strong, big-boned man. His diminutive wife never reached five feet or budged the scales past 100 pounds. As a young woman, she'd accompanied her preacher-father on the Methodist circuit, riding a mule to remote congregations where she played the piano or organ while the faithful sang. Serving in a rural schoolhouse, she met and married fellow teacher John Hooks.

Around the turn of the century, John purchased 196 acres of farmland and forest a few miles north of Swainsboro. He felled dozens of pines and floated logs downstream to Darien, near Brunswick, and had them cut into boards and brought back to Emanuel County. With them he built a sprawling farmhouse to shelter his growing family. He also operated a general store and served as postmaster. The tiny community that grew up around his establishment became known as Hooks Crossing.

Jewel and Fred Hooks with daughter Mae, ca. 1911.

His clan loved baseball, and the community once fielded an entire team with the Hooks surname. No other sport contested baseball's status as the national pastime. Practically every community in the country, no matter how small, fielded at least one team.

The caliber of play often was as shabby as the participants' makeshift uniforms and homemade gloves, but the friends and neighbors of the players nonetheless flocked to the local diamond, almost as central to community life as church and school.

Family lore has it that Fred and the legendary Ty Cobb were teammates. As Fred's younger brother Delma told the story 80 years later, the two played together in Cobb's first game in Augusta--Fred as pitcher and Cobb as catcher. Subsequently, the two friends were examining a pistol that accidentally discharged and ruined one of Fred's knees. As a result, he gave up baseball while Cobb went on to the major leagues and sports history.

So goes the story. But the truth, like a pebble on a riverbed, changed shape with the passage of time.

Many still consider Tyrus Raymond Cobb of Royston, Georgia the greatest baseball player ever. His strong-willed father wanted him to study law or medicine, but the 17-year-old boy had a mind of his own. Writing to the six teams of the newly formed South Atlantic ("Sally") League, Cobb won a tryout and a spot with the Augusta Tourists. He took center field on opening day in April 1904 but was cut after just two games. Rather than return home, he played with a semi-professional team in Anniston, Alabama until recalled by the Tourists in August.

Despite his unimpressive .237 batting average, the team brought Cobb back the following year, and the young man from Royston quickly established himself as the league's premier player. Before season's end the Detroit Tigers bought Cobb's contract from the Tourists for $900, and on August 27, 1905 he played the first of more than 3,000 games in the majors.

Nicknamed "the Georgia Peach," Ty Cobb dominated the sport. After 1920, baseball would become the realm of power hitters, best exemplified by George Herman ("Babe") Ruth of the Boston Red Sox and the New York Yankees. But in Cobb's heyday, the game hinged on strategy and finesse. He mastered all of the chief offensive weapons—bunt, steal, and hit-and-run. Moreover, he brought a recklessness to the base paths that unnerved opposing teams and delighted the fans. He'd try to take second on his own bunt, score from first on a fly ball to the outfield, or steal home, always doing the unexpected and somehow managing to pull off the most improbable stunts. A sports legend, he set dozens of records, many of which stood for decades, and his remarkable lifetime batting average of .367 appears untouchable.

Despite his undeniable athletic skills, as a human being Cobb batted poorly. He had a reputation as a virulent racist, although some claimed he hated everyone, not just Blacks. His penchant for using his spikes on opposing players and a betting scandal in 1927 further marred his career. A brawler on and off the diamond, he easily ranked as the least popular player in baseball.

Ty Cobb of the Detroit Tigers at spring training in Augusta, Georgia, 1906. Courtesy, National Baseball Hall of Fame, Cooperstown, New York.

Although Ty Cobb's path probably crossed Fred Hooks's, the story passed down in the Hooks family doesn't square with the known facts. Cobb usually played in the outfield; although he sometimes took a position in the infield and on rare occasions pitched as a novelty, no evidence suggests he ever squatted behind the plate.

Moreover, Fred Hooks was only 13 years old at the time of Cobb's debut in Augusta and didn't appear on the Tourists' roster. Indeed, judging by the box scores published in the Augusta *Chronicle*, no one named Hooks played for the Tourists or any other Sally League team during 1904-1909.

Finally, the accident that crippled Fred--the bullet entered his thigh and lodged behind the kneecap--occurred in Emanuel County on June 4, 1909, a day when Cobb went 0-for-3 against the Red Sox in Boston.

Chances are that Hooks knew the famous ballplayer, as he later told his second wife, and they may even have played on the same diamond. Cobb maintained his off-season residence in Augusta for some years and owned an automobile dealership there. In 1906 and 1907, moreover, the Tigers held spring training in Augusta, where they played games with local teams. After the season, Cobb usually toured the Southeast with other players, demonstrating his skills in a series of exhibition games, some of which may have involved the less fortunate Fred Hooks.

So Cobb attained fame and glory while Fred Hooks remained behind in Emanuel County. Other disappointments would follow.

TOWN AND COUNTY

BY 1910, EMANUEL County claimed some 25,000 persons, up from 6,000 in 1870. During the same 40 years, annual cotton production had soared from fewer than 1,400 bales to more than 59,000. Most people still worked the soil or cut timber, relying exclusively on human and animal power. The population covered the landscape, and more than a dozen thriving communities catered to the needs of families in the surrounding areas.

Stillmore, for example, located at the intersection of two rail lines, had large machine shops where "anything can be done to a locomotive except to manufacture it." Adrian, divided by the boundary that separated Emanuel and Johnson Counties, boasted its own newspaper, hotel, cotton gin, saw and shingle mill, turpentine still, and an assortment of general stores, millineries, and groceries. A factory in Garfield produced cottonseed oil, and entrepreneurs exploited Emanuel's pine forests at sawmills, turpentine stills, crosstie businesses, and naval stores concerns in Aline, Blun, Blundale, Covena, Dellwood, Gertman, McLeod, Modoc, Nunez, Oak Park, Rackley, Summertown, Summit, Von, and Wade. Huge mounds of sawdust dotted the county, a hazard to unwary children who jumped on them despite their parents' warnings. Other communities included Kemp, Norristown, Lexsy, Graymont, Maceo, Merritt, and Nell. A few had banks, and many had druggists, liveries, blacksmiths, dry goods stores, and other establishments.

Ron Seckinger

With some 1,300 souls, and as the county seat, Swainsboro was the largest and most prosperous community, although the *Forest-Blade* surely exaggerated when it declared in 1910 that "the magic touch of Southern enterprise has stripped her of her swaddling clothes and developed her into one of Wiregrass Georgia's fairest debutantes—a belle among cities." The same newspaper had complained six years earlier that Swainsboro would need two marshals and a dog to keep hogs and cows off the streets. And, in the absence of a city water works, outdoor privies studded backyards throughout the town.

Gentry Brothers' Circus was one of many attractions available
to Swainsboro residents at the turn of the 20th century.

Still, improvements kept coming. In 1904, Swainsboro gained an electric light plant and a new school building for White children with a 1,000-seat auditorium. In 1918, Black children obtained their own school building, constructed not by the city or county but by Julius Rosenwald, philanthropist and founder of Sears Roebuck. The Rosenwald Foundation provided matching funds to build 5,300 schools for Black children in the South and Southwest between 1917 and 1932.

In 1906, the Southern Bell Telephone and Telegraph Company established telephone service for 73 customers in Swainsboro. An operator known as "Central" connected callers and located doctors if needed. Central would even contact other operators to investigate weather and road conditions for a subscriber planning a trip.

An ice factory appeared the same year, and by 1910 the town claimed 12 general stores, two druggists, a photographer's studio, five grocers, a butcher, a hotel, two blacksmiths, two livery stables, a hardware-furniture store, two jewelers, a turpentine still, a sawmill, a planing mill, a naval stores company, a Coca-Cola bottling plant, and two banks--which between them had a total capitalization of $70,400.

Brick buildings began to replace wooden ones along the courthouse square. Several physicians practiced locally, and a dentist and an optician from other counties visited periodically--usually during Superior Court session, when they could count on finding many farmers in town. Residential neighborhoods mushroomed as new thoroughfares pushed out from the center. By 1911, local women had founded the Civic Improvement Club to clean up the streets, cemeteries, and other public spaces.

When not beautifying the town, citizens could choose from a growing list of leisure activities. In 1907 a druggist inaugurated a roller-skating rink above his store on Main Street, and the sport quickly became a fad among young people. Baseball games marked summer afternoons; Swainsboro had two teams for Whites and one for Blacks, and practically every other community had at least one team for each race. Men could participate in the activities of various lodges and secret societies, including the Masons, the Odd Fellows, and the Knights of Pythias. Nearly every year, Confederate veterans held a camp meeting to reminisce about the war and bask in the adulation of their fellow citizens. Some families owned pianos--a tuner periodically visited from Augusta--and even a few "talking machines" or phonographs.

Performances by traveling artists, who had long enlivened the boredom of backwoods communities and tempted children to run away from home, became more frequent with the expansion of the railroads.

From the appearance of the first posters, all of Swainsboro buzzed with anticipation. During a 14-month stretch in 1909-1910, the town hosted the Gentry Brothers' Circus, the Mighty Haag Railroad Shows-- featuring a somersaulting elephant—the K.G. Barkoot Carnival Company, Howe's Great London Shows, and John H. Sparks' World Famous Shows. Medicine shows, films, and vaudeville acts rolled into town. Opera houses presented a variety of entertainments, such as the 1904 performance of the melodrama "Only a Woman's Heart"--prices 25, 35, and 50 cents.

African Americans watched these spectacles from separate seating areas. Numbering nearly 10,000 in 1910, Blacks accounted for two of every five residents of Emanuel County but shared little in the new prosperity. Only 162 African American families owned their own farms, while 941 worked as tenants. Almost half of all Black males of voting age couldn't read, according to the federal census of 1910, compared to 12 percent of White males.

Not that Blacks were allowed to vote. The turn of the century witnessed the enactment of Jim Crow laws that segregated and disenfranchised African Americans throughout the South. Georgia voters had paid poll taxes since 1877, and in 1892, the Democratic Party began staging Whites-only primaries to select candidates for general elections. Emanuel County held its first in 1904. In 1907, Governor Hoke Smith, elected the previous year on a platform calling for Black disenfranchisement, secured a state constitutional amendment stipulating that each registrant meet one of five requirements, such as pass a literacy test or pay the poll tax six months before the election.

In daily interactions. Whites and Blacks often maintained an easy familiarity. But the descendants of slaves knew where they stood. The *Forest-Blade*--like Hoke Smith's newspaper, the Atlanta *Journal*--poked fun at Blacks, patronized those whose behavior it considered exemplary, and expressed outrage at the real and imagined depredations of others.

African American women wash chitterlings during a hog-killing day in Emanuel County, date unknown. Courtesy, Georgia Archives, Vanishing Georgia Collection, emno382.

Frequent acts of violence buttressed White supremacy. Georgia's 505 recorded lynchings led the nation during the period 1882-1923, and the number rose annually while remaining steady or declining in most other states. Moreover, the violence extended to every region of Georgia. By 1930 lynchings had occurred in 119 of the state's 159 counties. In 1906 alone, Georgian vigilantes murdered 73 persons, all but three of them Blacks.

One of the victims, a young man named Ed Pierson, met his death at the hands of an Emanuel County mob. Masked men seized Pierson, allegedly discovered under the bed of a White woman, during his transfer from the Swainsboro jail to Savannah, and the murderers dumped his bullet-riddled body in the Canoochee River.

Ron Seckinger

Poor Whites like the Strouds had much in common with poor Blacks, but the efforts of Populist leaders like Tom Watson in the 1890s to forge a biracial coalition dedicated to achieving political power and enacting policies favorable to Southern farmers had come to naught. White supremacy prevailed, and even those Whites uninfected by blind hatred generally assumed their own superiority and expected deference from Blacks.

Beneath the fabric of Whites' daily life lay a propensity for violence, visited not only on African Americans but also on other Whites. Every rural family had hunting weapons, and many men carried pistols. Locals often settled disputes, particularly those initiated under the influence of alcohol, with guns.

For example, a feud between Tom Moxley and Jim Stroud's older brother John culminated in a shootout in 1901. Moxley, John Stroud's nephew and brother-in-law, had threatened, cursed, and libeled his relative, according to the Swainsboro *Pine Forest*. When the two men met on a public road and exchanged words, Moxley reportedly pulled a revolver and took two shots at Stroud, who returned fire with his rabbit gun, killing his nephew. A jury found Stroud not guilty, presumably on grounds of self-defense.

Casual violence soon gave way to the organized kind. Dozens of Emanuel County youths would fight for the United States when the country joined the ongoing conflagration in Europe.

WAR

EMMIT, THE THIRD of the Stroud children, abandoned farm life about 1913, at the age of 19. He found a job as boilermaker with the Atlanta, Birmingham & Atlantic (AB&A) Railroad and would pursue no other profession during the rest of his life.

He was working in the AB&A yards in Fitzgerald, Georgia when the United States entered the Great War in April 1917. The country had remained aloof from the carnage that followed the outbreak of hostilities in Europe in August 1914, even though most Americans sympathized with Great Britain and France. Relations with Germany steadily worsened, particularly after Berlin resumed unrestricted submarine warfare in January 1917 and sank passenger ships with American citizens on board. On April 2, President Woodrow Wilson asked Congress for a declaration of war.

William Jennings Bryan, one of the nation's best-known politicians and three-time Democratic Party candidate for the Presidency, had earlier agreed to deliver a public address at the Ben Hill County courthouse in Fitzgerald on April 7. Known as the "Great Commoner" for his populist defense of ordinary folk, Bryan emerged as a strong advocate of isolationism while serving as Wilson's Secretary of State. Unhappy with the President's hardening attitude toward Germany, Bryan resigned in mid-1915 and devoted his energies to promoting a mediated settlement. He also sought to mobilize public opposition to involvement in the European conflict.

Ron Seckinger

William Jennings Bryan. Public domain.

But the crowd at the courthouse in Fitzgerald--merchants and town fathers in their black coats and string ties, farmers reeking of the barnyard, railroad workers with their cloth caps and grimy hands--heard a different message. Departing from his prepared text on peace, "The European War and Its Lesson to Us," the country's finest orator rallied behind Wilson's call to arms. One of the local newspapers reported:

> The great Commoner stated that while he had done everything in his power to avert hostilities between this country and Germany, that he was now squarely behind the president and was willing to do everything to push the war to a successful end. His patriotic utterances were greeted with the deafening applause by his hearers, especially when he made mention of his telegram to President Wilson offering his services as a private if the country needed him.

The United States had no need for a 57-year-old private--Wilson instead sent Bryan to tour the country promoting Liberty Loan bonds, the principal means of financing the war--but it did need millions of younger men in uniform. Congress passed a conscription law in May, and on June 5 more than 9.6 million men registered for the draft. In each community, registrants received numbers, and a lottery held by the War Department on July 20 established the order of induction.

Emanuel County did its part. Registration Day at the courthouse attracted a horde of young men and their families. Duncan Fields and his older brother Temples registered in September 1918, but the signing of the Armistice two months later meant they owed no service. Instead, it was Joe Fields, youngest of Duncan's brothers, who put on a uniform and served in the field artillery.

At least 22 men from the county died, some in combat and some of illness. Ten perished in a single incident, when the British transport ship HMS Otranto, part of a US-British convoy, collided with a sister ship and sank off the coast of Scotland in October 1918.

Denver Stroud as a sailor, 1918-1919.

In Fitzgerald, Emmit Stroud registered on June 5, 1917. He held number 370 out of 1,223 registrants, but the lottery placed him near the bottom. He and the other railroad men who stayed behind did their part in the war effort. AB&A employees raised $13,000 in the first Liberty Loan subscription in July 1917, and Emmit bought $100 in each of the third and fourth subscriptions the following year.

For Emmit's younger brother Denver, the fourth of the Stroud children, who had followed Emmit to a job with the AB&A, ponying up $100 for the Third Liberty Loan in April 1918 didn't seem enough. On July

17, he enlisted for the duration of the war at the Navy Recruiting Station in Atlanta.

Sent home to await orders, Denver returned to Atlanta on September 16 and transferred to the Naval Training Station at Hampton Roads, Virginia.

Federal officials had long considered Hampton Roads, situated at the mouth of the Chesapeake Bay, for the site of a naval base. President Theodore Roosevelt in 1907 had used the locale to bid farewell to the Great White Fleet on its two-year, 'round-the-world tour to demonstrate that the United States had become a major sea power.

Two months after the declaration of war on Germany, Congress appropriated $1.2 million to purchase the site for a naval training station, an aviation station, a supply center, and a submarine base. Work began in July 1917, and the first recruits were processed in October. By the time Denver Stroud arrived the following year, the station could handle 5,000 sailors at once, and a second facility nearing completion would double the capacity.

After two months of training, Denver emerged as a Seaman Second Class assigned to the *USS South Carolina,* a battleship laid down in Philadelphia in 1906 and commissioned in 1910. In September, she'd joined the escort of a convoy to France. But the guns in Europe had fallen silent a few days before Denver ascended the gangplank. He would see no action and spent the next six weeks in gunnery practice.

On New Year's Eve, the bosun piped Denver aboard another battleship, the *USS Wisconsin,* which had sailed with the Great White Fleet and passed in review before President Roosevelt in 1909. She and her crew spent the winter of 1919 in Cuban waters with the Atlantic Fleet.

At the end of June 1919, Denver transferred to the *USS Nansemond,* probably serving on at least one of the ship's round-trip voyages to Europe to return troops and convalescents of the American Expeditionary Force. After the ship's decommissioning in New York at the end of August,

Denver was discharged in Atlanta on September 17, 1919, 14 months to the day since his enlistment. His severance package bulged his pocket--a $60 war gratuity, $98.08 in back pay, and a $9.60 travel allowance to get him to Swainsboro.

Joe Fields in his Army uniform, 1917-1918.

Joe Fields survived the carnage of France to return home a dashing figure in uniform. Several young women set their caps for him, but their longings came to naught. Joe had contracted syphilis--not in a European brothel but from a prostitute who serviced clients in a tent at Coleman's Lake. He died in 1927, still a young man. He never married.

Ron Seckinger

STRIKE

EVEN AS AMERICANS celebrated the end of the war in Europe, troubles were brewing at home. Workers who'd tolerated the erosion of their purchasing power by wartime inflation wanted better wages and a bigger voice for labor in the workplace. Labor actions in the turbulent year of 1919 included a general strike in Seattle and walkouts by textile workers in Lowell, Massachusetts, the police in Boston, and steelworkers and miners throughout the country. More than 4 million workers participated, an unprecedented 20 percent of organized labor.

A wave of anti-Black violence, a series of bombings attributed to labor radicals, and a growing fear of subversion in the wake of the Bolshevik Revolution in Russia contributed to the atmosphere of crisis. Before year-end, the Justice Department, in a spasm of activity subsequently known as the "Red Scare," rounded up and deported 249 foreign nationals considered threats to public order. The unrest sharpened public and government suspicions of labor.

As a member of the International Brotherhood of Boilermakers, Iron Ship Builders and Helpers of America, Emmit Stroud shared the sentiments of other union men. The railroads had provided his ticket out of rural poverty, and he probably would have endorsed the sentiments of a man who commented after 50 years as water boy, fireman, and yard engineer, "As my daddy used to say, once a railroad man, never worth a cuss at nothing else."

At the AB&A machine shops in Fitzgerald, Emmit repaired the boilers that produced steam to power the locomotives. Once the firebox was emptied and the water drained, he crawled into the still-hot boiler with his tools to adjust bolts and seal cracks. He often had to remove his leather gloves for precision work. His hands were always scarred and nicked, and a particularly severe burn fused the ring and little fingers on one hand. Frequently the boilers' hot plates seared the legs of his heavy overalls.

Compared to other workers, the railroad trades had won considerable security and benefits. The Adamson Act of 1916 guaranteed the operating brotherhoods—locomotive engineers, firemen, brakemen, and conductors, known as the "Big Four"—a reduction in daily hours from 10 to eight, with no cut in pay, and time-and-a-half for overtime. Moreover, the federal government took over the lines the following year as a wartime measure; wages rose for all of the unions, and the principle of collective bargaining was firmly established. In 1919, the 14 railroad unions, representing some 2.2 million workers, pushed for Congressional approval of the Plumb Plan, which called for permanent government ownership of the rail lines.

While Congress considered the legislation, the railroad shopmen, who had demanded a pay hike since the Armistice, decided to force the issue. Although the "Big Four" constituted the elite of organized labor, the other railroad crafts had lagged behind. The owners had long isolated the shopmen—machinists, boilermakers, blacksmiths, sheet-metal workers, carmen, and electricians—by locating repair barns in rural areas or on the outskirts of towns, limiting their contact with better-organized workers.

Claiming that all other rail employees had received wage increases that year, the six shop crafts threatened a strike in July 1919. They asked the government, still operating the lines, to authorize a 17-cent increase for top workers, then earning a maximum of 68 cents an hour, and lesser raises for helpers and apprentices, retroactive to January 1.

Striking workers at the Atlanta, Birmingham & Atlantic Railroad machine shops in Fitzgerald, Georgia, October 1919. Emmit Stroud is fifth from the left in the second row (wearing a hat, over the left shoulder of the man seated in front). Denver Stroud is third from the left in the back row.

On August 1, with no settlement in sight, shopmen began walking off the job and forming strike committees throughout the South and the Midwest. A workers' meeting in Fitzgerald that night failed to muster enough votes for the walkout, but strike committees from other shops lobbied with the faint-of-heart, and a second ballot closed the AB&A repair barns the following day. Nationally, some 250,000 shopmen, almost half the total, participated.

At first the strikers seemed immoveable. They rejected a plea from the unions' national leaders to return to work pending a poll of the entire membership, and they also spurned President Wilson's proposal that Congress establish a committee to resolve the wage issue. Although the railroads tried to keep the lines open, the rapid deterioration of rolling stock quickly affected operations.

By the sixth day of the strike, state officials in Atlanta, fearing that a shutdown would cut off food supplies to the city, began taking steps to prevent hoarding and profiteering. They also looked into purchasing foodstuffs from War Department stocks.

After a week, Wilson referred the wage dispute to the Director General of Railroads, who promised a settlement once the men had returned to their jobs. Strikers began to comply. In Fitzgerald, the shopmen who had reluctantly walked out proved equally hesitant to return, but the AB&A shops reopened on August 14. Throughout the country, the former strikers labored at night and on Sundays to restore the rolling stock to peak condition. In early September, the unions accepted the government's offer of a four-cent raise.

Grumpy but without recourse, the 300 AB&A shopmen in Fitzgerald made do with their meager wage hike. Within two months, however, they walked out again, this time over purely local grievances.

In late October, the workers demanded that the railroad dismiss a foreman who had violated their contract by inspecting boilers rather than assigning the work to a journeyman boilermaker. When AB&A officials refused, the shopmen--who now included Denver Stroud, recently returned from his Navy duty--struck on October 28. The national leadership of the affiliated shop crafts declared the strike unauthorized, and the men took up their tools again after four days. The railroad, apparently protected by the illegality of the labor action, retaliated by firing a number of the strikers.

The two Stroud brothers found themselves unemployed. Packing their belongings, Emmit and Denver shook hands and parted company, leaving Fitzgerald to seek their livelihoods elsewhere.

JEWEL

FOR 14 YEARS after the shooting accident that ruined his knee, Fred Hooks tried in vain to find his niche as barber or businessman in several towns and cities. After failing to establish himself in Augusta, the inland port on the Savannah River 80 miles north of Swainsboro, he returned to Emanuel County. In early 1914, he accepted a job with a barbershop in Waynesboro, but bad luck followed. Once he disobeyed doctor's orders and went to work in bad weather while recuperating from the measles. As a consequence, he contracted pneumonia and almost died.

Subsequently, following a misdiagnosis of tuberculosis, Fred spent a season in Colorado Springs, leaving Jewel and his children on his parents' farm in Emanuel County. By mid-1918 the family again resided in Augusta, where Fred cut hair in a basement shop. In November of that year, he was working in Asheville, North Carolina when Jewel fell ill. Returning to Asheville as soon as she was on the mend, he intended to settle his family there, but again his plans came to naught.

In 1919, the Hooks moved once more to Augusta, where Fred tried his hand as a traveling salesman for a commercial house. They occupied a yellow, two-story house on Watkins Street, shared with two boarders.

During these years of drift and uncertainty, Jewel gave her husband three daughters. Vera Mae was born in February 1910, when her mother was 18 years old. Thelma Gertrude followed in August 1912, and Melema in November 1915. Mae and Melema had blonde hair and blue eyes like their father, while Thelma inherited her mother's dark looks.

Jewel Hooks, ca. 1912.

Jewel worked hard, raising her children and keeping house. When visiting her in-laws at Hooks Crossing for two or three weeks each summer, she took her place in the fields with the others. Like her sister Jessie, she had a reputation as one of the fastest cotton-pickers in Emanuel County.

Jewel's relatives believed that Fred Hooks mistreated her. His daughter Vera later claimed he chased women and did her mother wrong.

Whatever the truth, the difficulty Fred experienced in making a living no doubt strained their relationship. Like Jessie, Jewel made the best of her lot and remained with her husband, either by choice or for lack of an alternative.

In 1919, Jewel became pregnant again. She was in poor health, perhaps never having recovered fully from the illness that had laid her low the previous year, and the pregnancy proved complicated. For some time before coming to term, she lay in bed, and her mother-in- law came to help with the delivery.

At 7:30 on the morning of April 12, 1920, after a long and difficult labor, she gave birth to a 12-pound girl. Exhausted, Jewel asked, "Is she marked?"

Jewel with Melema, Mae, and Thelma, ca. 1916.

Lillian Hooks looked at the baby, who bore an enormous purple stain on her right cheek and throat. "No," she lied.

Jewel developed "milk leg," or phlebitis, and her strength faded quickly. Back in Emanuel County, the younger Fields children went to the train station at Modoc to see Jessie off on a farewell visit. She returned from Augusta after two days to report that Jewel looked bad and likely wouldn't survive. Denver also came to his sister's bedside and donated blood in a fruitless effort to save her life.

As death approached, Jewel decided she didn't want her husband to take the baby, christened Freddie Barbara. Instead, she asked her mother-in-law to keep the child, and Lillian consented.

At 1:00 on Tuesday morning, May 11, 28-year-old Jewel died at the hospital in Augusta. Fred shipped her body to Emanuel County, where her in-laws hosted services at their home in Hooks Crossing. Mae, Thelma, and Melema were led forward to kiss their mother's cold cheek. When the casket was closed, the Hooks and Fields clans with other relatives and friends traveled to Moore's Cemetery on the outskirts of Swainsboro, and Jewel was buried in an unmarked grave.

In later years, Jessie and her surviving sisters often talked of erecting a headstone, but they never did. Today no one remains who can identify the concrete slab under which Jewel rests.

DRY GOODS

IN 1917, DUNCAN Fields accepted a position as overseer on a neighboring farm owned by Joseph Ehrlich. The intersection of the Ehrliches and the Fields marked wholly different trajectories--in one case, an immigrant family rising from penury to plenty, and in the other, a clan of old pioneer stock sliding toward ruin.

Joe Ehrlich was among the hundreds of thousands of Jews who emigrated from Europe to the United States between 1880 and 1900. The Russian tsars had long confined Jews to peripheral regions known as the Pale of Settlement and subjected them to various forms of discrimination. Following the assassination of Alexander II in 1881, they became the target of riots tolerated if not encouraged by the imperial authorities. In Odessa, Yelizavetgrad, Kiev, and other locales, mobs assaulted Jewish homes and shops, stealing or destroying property and beating, raping, and murdering those found within.

The emigration sparked by these events swelled after 1883, when the introduction of a school quota system denied educational opportunities to most Jewish youths. By 1890, some 50,000 Russian Jews departed annually. The following year the government's expulsion of all Jews from Moscow prompted a mass exodus from the entire empire, and more than 111,000 arrived in the United States in 1891 alone. Most came from Lithuania and the Polish provinces. By the turn of the century, Eastern European Jews numbered 2 million in the United States.

The Polish-Russian émigrés included Joe Ehrlich, who crossed the Atlantic in 1890, and his future wife, Rebecca Smolensky, who came the following year. Both became citizens in 1896. Why they settled in Georgia is unknown, but economic opportunity is the most likely explanation. Although many Jews went no farther than New York or Brooklyn after clearing immigration, others scattered across the continent.

Wedding photo of Joseph Ehrlich and Rebecca Smolensky, 1896. Courtesy, Southern Historical Collection, Wilson Library, University of North Carolina.

Like many Jewish emigrants--such as Adam Gimbel and Benjamin Bloomingdale, to cite two of the most prominent examples--Ehrlich started out as an itinerant peddler. He bought goods on credit and carried a heavy backpack along the country roads, selling small items such as pins, needles, and spools of thread to farm families. Soon he amassed enough cash to purchase a mule and wagon, which allowed him to carry a larger inventory.

He had regular customers who looked forward to his visits and made him feel welcome, inviting him to share their meals. Since he observed Jewish dietary laws, he refused to eat pork and also rejected meat prepared with milk, accepting only a boiled egg, a glass of milk, or a cup of tea. Once an entire family ran out to greet him as he arrived, telling him excitedly that they had just cooked a chicken in butter. He had to find a gracious way to decline their hospitality.

By early 1896, Ehrlich had saved enough to open a store, which required only $500 to $2,000 in startup capital. He located his first retail operation in Manassas, a tiny community in Tatnall County, about 45 miles west of Savannah. About a year later, he moved his store to Milledgeville, the seat of Baldwin County. In 1896, he also married Rebecca Smolensky.

By 1900, the couple resided in Swainsboro with Bessie and Benjamin, the first of their four children. Leon and Frances followed by 1905.

Lewis Pizitz, Rebecca's brother-in-law, had operated a general store in Swainsboro since at least 1894. Deciding to open a retail outlet in Birmingham, Alabama, Pizitz offered his store on Swainsboro's courthouse square to Ehrlich, who bought him out during the first half of 1903. Thereafter, the *Forest-Blade* noted Rebecca's twice-annual trips to New York to select the latest in women's fashions.

By 1917, the Ehrlich family ranked among the most prominent in Emanuel County. Joe's dry goods establishment enjoyed a total capitalization of $50,000 to $75,000 as well as a good credit rating bestowed by R.G. Dun and Company, the forerunner of Dun & Bradstreet. The following year, he bought a controlling interest in, and became president of, one of the largest packing plants in Savannah. On the corner of Pine and Green Streets in Swainsboro, he built a large colonial home with white columns, selecting the trees from his timber stands and then choosing the best boards at the sawmill.

The home Joe Ehrlich built in Swainsboro, ca. 1910. Courtesy, Southern Historical Collection, Wilson Library, University of North Carolina.

Inside the Ehrlich dry goods store, Swainsboro, ca. 1907. Left to right: Rebecca and Joe Ehrlich, Della Newby, Sue Tolbert, Bennie Ehrlich, and Libby Smolian. Courtesy, Frances Rabhan.

The Ehrliches took a leading role in backing the war effort. The United States had given him opportunities unavailable in his homeland, and Joe believed everyone should do his part to support his adopted country. At the time of the conclusion of the Second Liberty Loan issue in November 1917, the *Forest-Blade* noted, "Mr. Joseph Ehrlich was the largest subscriber, and it was he that made Emanuel County keep pace with other counties." The following year Ehrlich asked that every farmer donate to the Red Cross one to five pounds from every bale of cotton.

Rebecca Ehrlich, ca. 1920. Courtesy, Southern Historical Collection, Wilson Library, University of North Carolina.

For her part, Rebecca sold more bonds than any woman in Georgia. In May 1918, she appealed to every citizen to donate one day's wages--and every merchant, 10 percent of a day's sales--to the war effort. She started the Junior Red Cross in Swainsboro, encouraging children to contribute 10 cents in exchange for a clip-on emblem and recruiting them to roll bandages and help out in other ways. The Ehrliches invited every White soldier from the county to their home for a punch-and-cake reception before their guests shipped out to Europe.

As his wealth increased, Joe Ehrlich became a landowner. Between 1913 and 1916, he purchased almost 300 acres from Duncan Fields' brothers John, Temples, and Garry B. Except for a large grove of pecan trees, the Ehrlich farm was divided into strips worked by sharecropper families, all of them Black until Homer and Ida Screws moved there with their three daughters in 1919.

Jessie Fields, a gentle woman by nature, was close to Lownie Pheanious, one of the African American women on the Ehrlich farm, and occasionally took meals with her. She often commented to her children that she would rather eat at Lownie's table than in the homes of some of the nearby White women. When Jessie and Duncan went out in the evening, they carried their children to the Pheanious household, where Lownie put them in one of her beds for the night. The White and Black children of similar ages played and ate together.

Returning from fishing or hunting forays, Duncan frequently shared his catch with the Black families. But as overseer he treated the men roughly, yelling and striking them when dissatisfied with their work. Once he caught one urinating in another man's well--a serious matter in the country. Duncan asked the offender whether he preferred a beating or the chain gang. The man chose the beating. He took off his shirt and lay across a barrel. Four other Black men held his arms and legs while Duncan whipped him with a leather strap, raising blisters with one blow and popping them with the next.

Duncan's tenure as overseer ended at the close of the 1920 harvest. Yet the Ehrlich and Fields families enjoyed a long association. As long as Joe Ehrlich owned a store on the courthouse square, Jessie Fields never shopped at another dry goods establishment

RASCALS

J.D. FIELDS, Duncan and Jessie's eldest, had as his constant companion Lownie Pheanious's son Walter. Walter and J.D. celebrated their 10th birthdays in 1917. Big enough to handle lots of chores, they broke the soil together in the spring, J.D. behind a red mule called Sun and Walter behind a gray one named Ada. They fought to keep the furrows straight, kicking up dust as the plow sliced through the earth with a metallic *hiss*. They planted cotton, corn, or peanuts, hauled water, rounded up the cows, and performed the dozens of other tasks of farm life. But mostly they got into as much devilment as their imaginations allowed.

From the Fields' barn, they loaded three or four sacks of cottonseed in the wagon and drove to Warren Kea's general store in Modoc, where they traded their pilfered goods for cheese and crackers. They also ate peanuts--intended for spring planting--from the storage house. They always found the key wherever Duncan hid it, and they refused to give up when he eventually threw the key into the creek. The door to the storage house had a hole through which cats could pursue mice, and through this "cat crack" the boys used a stick to hook the bag of peanuts and pull it within reach. When Duncan broke the lock and opened the door in the spring, he found an empty five-bushel sack.

Country stores, like this one in Norristown, Emanuel County, ca. 1910, still dotted the landscape in the 1920s and 1930s. Courtesy, Georgia Archives, Vanishing Georgia Collection, emn003.

J.D. and Walter also tossed chickens into the vat where cows were dipped for protection against ticks. The chickens, squawking in protest, would swim around in the dark, vile-smelling liquid until the boys lifted them out with a dipper. Neither Jessie's switchings nor Duncan's threats to "break you all up" deterred them.

In fact, doing what they were told not to do seemed to hold a special fascination. Duncan allowed them to use his shotguns for rabbit-hunting but warned them to stay away from two new ones. In the absence of the grown-ups one day, Walter grabbed a pump model and J.D. a new automatic. Down in the fields, with dogs running all around, J.D. fired the unfamiliar automatic and, since he kept his finger on the trigger, unintentionally fired a second time, blowing the head off one of the dogs.

He threw the gun down and both boys fled in terror. Stud, one of the older Black children, listened to their story and accompanied them back to the fields. At length, he persuaded them the gun wouldn't fire unless they pulled the trigger, so they picked it up, dusted it off, and returned it to its rightful place. They disposed of the dog, which fortunately was not Duncan's, and he never found them out.

Ron Seckinger

Duncan told them not to ride one of the horses, Warrior, who had served in battle and became undone by loud noises. Naturally, on a Saturday when the adults had gone into town, J.D. said, "I'm gonna ride old Warrior."

They saddled up. Walter followed with a bullwhip on Duncan's favorite mount, Dixie. At the crack of the whip, Warrior leapt into the air and bolted. He sideswiped a fence, where J.D. lost a shoe, and lit out across the fields, with the terrified boy hanging on, crying and looking over his shoulder for help from Walter, who couldn't keep up. Warrior halted only when he reached the feedlot, and J.D., still sobbing, finally got his feet back on the ground.

Back at the barn, the boys climbed on the hay rack, and J.D. lashed the unfortunate horse with the whip to vent his fear and anger. Eventually, they trudged back to recover the shoe wedged in the fence. Losing something so valuable would have been a greater transgression that disobeying his father.

In the spring of 1919, J.D. and Walter begged for a chance to see an airplane on display in Swainsboro. "No, y'all ain't goin'," Duncan told them. "Y'all get up the cows, and what y'all do is stay here."

Of course, they hitched up the buggy as soon as he left and went anyway. At the fairgrounds they lay on the ground not far from Duncan, half drunk and oblivious to their presence, and watched the aircraft--the first they had ever seen--roll lazily through the sky.

Every summer when the crops were laid by, Duncan took the two boys, his younger brother Joe, and another Black or two on a week-long excursion to Coleman's Lake, a popular camping and fishing spot on the Ogeechee River. They slept in a tent and cooked over an open fire.

Fishing ranked high on Duncan's list of favorite activities, and he pursued bream and catfish all year. He often shared his catch with the Pheanious family or other sharecroppers on the Ehrlich farm. At some point, the owners of Coleman's Lake gave him the use of a cabin in exchange for a steady supply of fish for their restaurant.

Duncan loved hunting, too, which allowed him to spend time with his dogs. He owned five or six, with names like Sharp, Belle, and Prince. He took pride in his hounds, ran them in races, and sometimes traded them with his cronies. In the fall, he took his favorites into the woods after quail, moving cautiously forward once the dogs pointed, waiting for the sudden *whirr!* of a covey exploding into the air, quickly firing one or two shells from his shotgun before the birds disappeared. Or he might sit beneath a tree in a field and wait for doves to fly overhead, languidly blowing them from the sky. Invariably he returned home with a bag full of birds for the cooking pot.

Duncan also loved fox hunting, which had become popular in the county around the turn of the century. Periodically, he would organize a chase and invite Fess Kirkland, John A. Bell, and other friends.

Once Duncan kept a fox in a cage for two months in preparation for a hunt. On the appointed Saturday he instructed J.D. and Walter to set the animal free at five in the evening. Because they wanted to go riding rather than wait, the boys secretly let the fox go three hours early. They returned to find the men gathering for the chase.

Preparing for a fox hunt in Pickens County, 1920s. Note the chained fox in the left foreground. Courtesy, Georgia Archives, Vanishing Georgia Collection, pck124-82.

Ron Seckinger

"That fox done gone," J.D. whispered to Walter. "They ain't gonna jump him."

But the fox had killed a rabbit and stayed to feast, so the dogs struck him after all. Then the hunters were off across the fields and along the roads--a couple of dozen dogs yelping, the men on horseback, yelling and laughing and spitting tobacco juice over their shoulders. The two boys kept up as best they could in a wagon. The party chased the fox all the way to Swainsboro and beyond, till he ran into a burnt-out patch of woods and the dogs lost his scent. Still excited, the men talked and laughed some more while the lathered horses cooled down, and then they began a leisurely ride back for a drink or other Saturday-night diversion before returning home.

J.D. and Walter brought up the rear, ignored by the men. They had their own laugh, celebrating the fact that, once again, they'd gotten away with something.

SWAINSBORO

SWAINSBORO'S population stood at 1,578 in 1920, when Margie Stroud left the farm for good. She'd had plenty of opportunities to evaluate suitors at church services and socials, parties, and other community events, including a chaperoned excursion by train to Tybee Beach. Henry Rich appeared to lead the pack, but eventually she settled on Ellie Waitus Scott, a young man who worked on his parents' farm near Dellwood. Tall and broad-shouldered, he towered over the diminutive daughter of Jim Stroud when they married on Christmas Day, 1918. He was 21, and Margie, 15.

They farmed on shares for a year, working side by side in the fields, but soon they moved to town. Waitus, like Margie's brother-in-law Fred Hooks, had taught himself to cut hair. He took a job in Kimberly's Barber Shop on the courthouse square, and the young couple rented a house on Green Street. Waitus's career change spared them the sickening slide to disaster suffered by farmers and sharecroppers when crop prices plummeted later in 1920. They had hardly settled in when Margie gave birth to a son, christened Ellie Julian.

The amenities of town life represented a welcome change from country living. In 1918, electricity had become available in Swainsboro during the day as well as at night. The initiation of a water works that same year to accommodate new public restrooms at the courthouse promised the eventual banishment of backyard privies. The general stores owned by

Joe Ehrlich and John C. Coleman faced competition from seven similar establishments, and the town supported three auto dealerships and two professional photographers. The opening of a cold-storage plant, another of Joe Ehrlich's enterprises, allowed families to serve fresh beef on their tables more frequently, and in 1920 great fanfare attended the opening of a Chero-Cola bottling operation that, like the existing Coca-Cola plant, provided jobs and boosted civic pride.

Margie Stroud, ca. 1920.

The city judge--George Kirkland, Ella Sherrod's cousin, who had named many of the Stroud children--enforced state "blue laws" that prohibited commerce on Sundays and a statute requiring "pistol toters" to obtain gun permits.

Some resisted the intrusion of civilized ways. In 1921, the *Forest-Blade* lamented that, despite notices advising of a law against "expectorating on the sidewalks or in public buildings," the hall floor of the new courthouse--built after the previous one burned in 1919--was "disgracefully marred" with tobacco juice.

Waitus, Ellie, and Margie Scott, ca. 1923.

Entertainment abounded. In 1913, a few prominent citizens had underwritten a campaign to put Swainsboro on the Chautauqua circuit. The week-long educational festivities had included programs by the Chicago Ladies Orchestra, the Lyric Glee Club of Chicago, and the Iroquois Indian Orchestra. Also on the playbill: "My Conquest of the North Pole," by the controversial Dr. Frederick A. Cook, and a performance by Professor Pamahasika's trained pets, "consisting of educated birds, dogs and cats." The Chautauqua experiment proved a financial failure and was soon abandoned.

Yet the townsfolk could still count on the usual traveling circuses, minstrel shows, and vaudeville acts, as well as baseball games, high-school football and basketball contests, the annual county fair at harvest time, and revival meetings in the summer. Churches, lodges, associations, and private citizens held oyster suppers, box suppers, cakewalks, barbecues, "tacky" parties, and Tom Thumb weddings. Card-players had the Rook and Bridge Clubs. Families could dine at the White House Café and might catch a glimpse of Ty Cobb at the Marguerite Hotel during the baseball great's annual off-season hunting excursion to Emanuel County. After

1923, when Judge Kirkland granted a petition from numerous children, adults had to dodge roller-skating youngsters on the sidewalks surrounding the courthouse, the only paved surfaces in town.

The motion picture, without question, proved the preferred form of entertainment. The locals, who occasionally had seen movies exhibited by the traveling shows, ecstatically welcomed the establishment of Louis Proctor's movie house in September 1916. With showings nightly except Sunday, plus a Saturday matinee, the theater bid fair to become the community's most popular locale. Townspeople and farmers flocked to watch Charlie Chaplain, Lillian Gish, Buster Keaton, and the other stars of the era while a pianist provided suitable music. More than the novels of Zane Grey and Edgar Rice Burroughs, more than the radio, which arrived about 1925, the motion picture gave county residents a portal beyond the small towns and rural expanses of their own limited universe.

During the theater's first week of operation, the public-school principal, by order of the board of trustees, forbade pupils from attending the movies from Monday through Thursday, because they "cannot do justice to themselves in their studies if they go to places of entertainment at night."

The children, not surprisingly, contrived to evade the prohibition; some boys even dressed as girls to conceal their identities. In February 1917, the *Forest-Blade* reported that students routinely flaunted the principal's order. On a recent Tuesday night, for example, 26 schoolchildren had attended the theater. Nine of the older boys, sent home from school the following day as punishment, held an "indignation meeting" under the oak tree in front of the courthouse to vent their suspicions about the identity of the informer.

By this time, Franc Magnum and theater-owner Louis Proctor had petitioned the Superior Court to enjoin the principal from suspending their daughters, regular patrons of the forbidden entertainment. Through their four attorneys, the petitioners charged that "the rule is illegal, unreasonable, and is depriving them of their rights as parents." The two men had arranged for a teacher to provide after-hours instruction to their first graders, but the school board retaliated by prohibiting her from doing so.

Judge R.N. Hardeman of the Circuit Court, who had refused to issue a temporary injunction at the outset, also ruled out a permanent injunction when he heard the case in late February. The judge nonetheless allowed an appeal.

Emanuel County Courthouse, ca. 1894-1914, where Judge R.N. Hardeman ruled in 1917 that children couldn't patronize Swainsboro's movie theater on school nights. Courtesy, Georgia Archives, Vanishing Georgia Collection, emn113.

Ron Seckinger

The Georgia Supreme Court declined to issue an injunction in March, pending a hearing of the arguments in May. In January 1918, the justices handed down their decision, sustaining Judge Hardeman and ruling that the prohibition on pupils' attending the movie theater on school nights was "not an unreasonable one." The court rejected an appeal for a rehearing the following month, putting an end to the legal phase of the controversy. Careful readers could discern the disappointment of the *Forest-Blade*'s editors:

> The decision is not only of great interest locally, but inasmuch as it lays down a new principle of law which affects the relative rights of parents and school authorities in the control of children attending the public school, is of great interest to every school board and every parent in Georgia. It is regarded as being wholly in keeping with modern tendency and modern thought, which tends to lessen individual responsibility. It is also regarded that school authorities may determine what a pupil shall do and what they shall not do after they have returned to their homes after school hours.

With the court's backing, the school authorities' tough policy had won out. But lots of folks could've told them that dog wouldn't hunt. Many parents agreed with the *Forest-Blade* that the school board had no business trying to dictate pupils' behavior outside school hours. In April, when the principal expelled six senior boys for violating the regulation, four of them transferred to Stillmore High School and graduated on schedule six weeks later. Enforcement of the "not unreasonable" rule became lax, and children, with their parents' permission, were free to enjoy the films as often as they liked.

During the fall of 1918 and into the next year, Swainsboro's movie theater frequently closed its door to all patrons for a more serious reason--the influenza pandemic then sweeping the world. Apparently originating in Kansas, the lethal virus spread to Army camps, where hundreds of thousands of farm and city men congregated in overcrowded barracks during the coldest winter yet recorded east of the Rockies.

Wagons and motor vehicles mingle on Swainsboro streets, 1920s.
Courtesy, Georgia Archives, Vanishing Georgia Collection, emn112.

Both military and civilian leaders failed to grasp the seriousness of the outbreak until too late, and belated measures such as the use of cloth masks and the closing of public places proved ineffective. Patients spilled from hospitals to makeshift tent cities, and frightened citizens avoided contact with their neighbors. Vessels carrying troops to Europe became death ships. Within weeks, the disease had encircled the globe.

The virulent strain of influenza attacked the lungs and ultimately compromised the body's immune system, leaving its weakened victims susceptible to measles and especially pneumonia. As terrifying as the bubonic plague, it sometimes killed within 10 hours. The youngest and the healthiest were the most likely to die. By the time the pandemic had run its course in 1920, some 500,000 had perished in the United States and between 50 million and 100 million worldwide.

In rural areas and small towns, influenza trod more lightly. To be sure, the ban on public meetings in Swainsboro didn't totally prevent contagion, but the dispersion of the population through the county tended to slow the spread of the disease. Although some 30,000 Georgians died from the illness in 1918, Swainsboro suffered relatively little, according to the *Forest-Blade*:

> While there is quite a number of cases in and around
> the city, there have been no serious cases reported, and
> in fact there has not been a single white death in the city
> with this disease at all.

Whether the pandemic had claimed the lives of any African American residents, the newspaper didn't say.

COTTON

DUNCAN FIELDS, Joe Ehrlich, and every other farmer in Emanuel County relied heavily on cotton as the principal cash crop. The county ranked third in cotton production in all of Georgia. With high prices generating unheard-of profits, the farmers tried to ignore the impending arrival of the plant's implacable foe.

The boll weevil, a tiny beetle native to Mexico and Central America, used the cotton plant as a host for propagation. The adult bored into a cotton bud and laid eggs, and the resulting larvae fed on the fiber and quickly matured. A single planting season might see four or five generations of the insect. This pest, reminiscent of an Old Testament plague, invaded Texas from Mexico about 1892 and inexorably moved eastward, devastating the cotton economies of the South.

Growers in Georgia watched from afar with uneasy fascination, marking the steady progress of the boll weevil toward their own lands. They discussed possible remedies and hoped that some miracle would avert disaster.

The infestation eventually reached southwestern Georgia in late 1915. By November of the following year, the *Forest-Blade* reported, residents of neighboring Johnson County had spotted the insects. Over the next two years, Emanuel farmers would begin their long association with the pest.

With more than two decades to prepare for Armageddon, Georgia was as ready to meet the challenge as could have been expected, thanks largely to the federal government. In 1902, as several Southern states reeled from the onslaught of the Mexican beetle, a Department of Agriculture special agent had introduced the notion of the "demonstration farm." He persuaded a Texas grower to follow his instructions precisely and invited neighbors to see for themselves the advantages of scientific methods. The experiment worked, and the techniques quickly spread.

Georgia adopted the approach in 1907, hiring seven demonstration agents that year and increasing the number thereafter. The Smith-Lever Bill, co-sponsored by Senator Hoke Smith of Georgia, institutionalized the system nationally in 1914 by creating the Agricultural Extension Service. Federal, state, and county governments, in collaboration with land-grant colleges and private organizations, supported a growing army of agents who covered the countryside, not only to show farmers how to overcome the scourge of the cotton fields but also to introduce modern agricultural methods.

With them went home demonstration agents--women who instructed the farmers' wives and daughters in hygiene, canning, and other domestic skills. Both kinds of agents were teachers above all, and they organized boys' and girls' clubs to impart the new ways to the rising generation.

Fortified by this expertise, many Southerners believed cotton culture could be salvaged. Like a small boy whistling past the graveyard, the *Forest-Blade* asserted in 1919:

> Must we concede that cotton is a thing of the past and become pessimistic as some are inclined to do? Never! Cotton is our best cash crop for practically the entire state and will doubtless ... remain so for all time to come.

The newspaper passed on the suggestions of experts who proposed a variety of techniques for combating the boll weevil. Some methods attacked the insect directly by poisoning the bolls with calcium arsenate or, after the harvest, plowing under the bare cotton stalks to evict the weevils before they went into hibernation. Others emphasized limiting acreage or the growing season, soil-building through crop rotation and fertilizers, and developing new varieties.

Crop diversification became a kind of secular religion, its litanies invoked by the newspapers, extension agents, and guest lecturers from the colleges. Specialists enjoined farmers to rely less on cotton and place more emphasis on raising livestock and planting peanuts, soybeans, tobacco, and pecans.

These suggestions might have resonated more effectively except for one thing--the arrival of the boll weevil in Georgia coincided with an unprecedented cotton boom. Although the outbreak of the Great War in 1914 had disrupted the market and seemed to spell disaster for the South, the crisis soon passed. Indeed, massive purchases by Great Britain--and by the US government after it entered the war in 1917--for uniforms, explosives, and other war matériel encouraged farmers to increase their acreage and entrepreneurs to establish new textile factories in the South.

Exempted from price controls, cotton rode wartime inflation to dizzying heights. "A large number of automobiles are being sold in Emanuel County now, thanks to seventeen c[en]ts cotton," the *Forest-Blade* noted in 1916. More and more farmers drove Fords, Overlands, and Dodges as the value of cotton climbed past 21 cents per pound the following year and even beyond. Duncan Fields was one of them, and his Model T Ford became a familiar sight on Emanuel's dirt roads and Swainsboro's streets. Quite literally, the farmers were "living in high cotton," an expression connoting prosperity.

Eventually the fall came, and it was the worst in cotton history, from almost 41 cents in April 1920 to less than 14 in December. Throughout the South, the profit margins that had permitted farmers--and even sharecroppers--to splurge on autos, store-bought clothes, new furniture, and more land suddenly gave way to hard times. Growers couldn't recover the costs of their crop, and vain efforts to drive prices back up by withholding cotton from the market left them even more strapped for funds. Many lost their farms or jobs, and Georgia towns filled with African American men begging for work.

Swainsboro merchants slashed prices to try to move their inventories. Through the *Forest-Blade,* Joe Ehrlich offered to cash Victory and Liberty Bonds purchased during the flush days of the war and to accept "chickens, eggs, fat hogs or cows either in trade or on accounts" at his drygoods store. Although cotton prices began to recover the following year, the scars of 1920 and the boll weevil, then having its full impact, made farmers more receptive to the notion of crop diversification.

Joe Ehrlich's dry goods store on the courthouse square in Swainsboro, ca. 1930. Courtesy, Southern Historical Collection, Wilson Library, University of North Carolina.

Trying to escape from dependence on cotton, of course, proved difficult. Other crops suffered the same price fluctuations that periodically savaged cotton planters. In 1916, for example, Emanuel farmers filled more than 100 railroad cars with watermelons at $110 per car. The following year the growers planted enough melons to fill 200 cars but found the price had dropped to only $30-$40. Rather than sell at a loss, many farmers chose to feed the fruit to their hogs. Other crops required learning new skills that were not easily mastered. Such was the case of flue-cured tobacco.

In 1920, Joe Ehrlich, whose various farms totaled 700 acres, decided to abandon cotton altogether. He went to Douglas, an important center of tobacco cultivation in South Georgia, to find out everything he could about the crop. He hired a man named Newsome, who claimed to be an experienced hand from the Carolinas, to run the operation. Ehrlich forbade his tenants to plant cotton. Instead, he told them to plant a certain percentage of their lands in tobacco, which covered 110 acres in all, and the rest in peanuts, hay, and corn. The owner built 30 curing sheds scattered over his properties and purchased sprayers and other necessary equipment.

The *Forest-Blade* twice devoted front-page articles to the experiment, predicting that other farmers would follow Ehrlich's lead if the tobacco crop yielded $800 to $1,000 per acre as expected. Joe drove out from Swainsboro twice a day to observe the preparations. His 15-year-old daughter Frances insisted on taking a turn on the mule-drawn, sulky-like planter.

As overseer, Duncan Fields dutifully managed the planting, harvesting, and curing of tobacco on the Ehrlich lands under his care, while sticking to cotton on his own farm. Despite the intensive labor tobacco required--an average of 270 days a year versus 180 for cotton--and despite Newsome's heavy drinking, which frequently interfered with his instruction, the tenants made the crop. They tied the leaves in bunches at intervals along uniformly cut sticks, which they hung in the curing sheds where flues distributed the heat from wood fires. For the first time, the farmers and sharecroppers of the area caught the distinctively sweet smell of roasting tobacco as the green leaves dried and turned golden.

Ehrlich rented a boxcar to transport the cured tobacco to market in North Carolina, and Newsome went along for the sale. Unfortunately, the experiment took place in the very year of the economic collapse. Bright tobacco, which had brought 44 cents a pound the previous year, fell to 21 in 1920. Ehrlich lost $40,000, and his tenants earned nothing from their shares of the worthless crop. It was the last year that Duncan Fields served as overseer on Ehrlich properties.

The next year Joe returned to cotton while devoting substantial acreage to peanuts. In the aftermath of his failure, no other farmers rushed to plant tobacco, but interest in the crop eventually revived as the extension agents continued to push for diversification. By 1929, tobacco claimed some 4,000 acres in the county, and peanuts, soybeans, and corn also became increasingly important. Even so, after decades as king, cotton wouldn't disappear entirely from Emanuel County's fields.

RAILROAD MAN

BLACKLISTING, the railroad owners' practice of sharing the identities of strikers and union organizers, kept Emmit Stroud on the move following the unsuccessful 1919 strike in Fitzgerald. He would find a job as a shopman and work for a month or two until his new employer's inquiry turned up his name on the industry's list of troublemakers. Then he would move on to another repair facility, only to be fired again when his past resurfaced. In June 1920, he resided in Lineville, a railroad town in Clay County, Alabama, still—somehow—on the Atlanta, Birmingham & Atlantic (AB&A) payroll. Subsequently he held jobs with the Chicago, Rock Island & Pacific (CRI&P) and the Cincinnati, New Orleans & Texas Pacific (CNO&TP). By 1923, he would later tell his wife, he had worked in all but three of the 48 states.

Emmit probably participated in the strike of 1922, although his whereabouts and activities are unknown. In 1920, Congress, which had rejected the Plumb Plan the previous year, returned the rail lines to their owners and created the Railroad Labor Board to set policy. In June, the board approved pay increases for all workers; the shopmen's raise amounted to 13 cents an hour.

A depression that year sharply eroded company earnings, however, and in mid-1921 the board allowed the railroads to slash wages and suspend overtime rates for work on Sundays and legal holidays. The owners had already begun farming out repair work to nonunion contractors, leading to substantial layoffs among shopmen, and spurned the board's order in June 1922 to halt the practice. Moreover, some railroads seized the opportunity to promote docile, company-controlled unions in a bid to break the organized shop crafts. The board's decision to reduce wages by another 12 percent in mid-1922, on top of the other adverse developments, prompted the shopmen to vote overwhelmingly for a walkout, which took place on July 1.

The 400,000 strikers confronted formidable obstacles. The Railroad Labor Board declared the strike illegal and encouraged owners to form company unions. The "Big Four" unions didn't support the action. In September, the Attorney General obtained the most sweeping injunction ever directed against labor leaders in the United States.

The strike failed dismally, and the unions agreed to seek separate agreements with the different lines. Some 175,000 were forced into company unions. The membership of the boilermakers' union already had shrunk since 1919, and the failure of 1922 further weakened the organization.

The railroads themselves faced a troubled future. Rate restrictions by state commissions had limited revenues—and therefore investment—during the years before the Great War, and the cumulative effects had begun to show. Moreover, new competitors had emerged. Trucking companies, taking advantage of the rapidly expanding network of highways, appropriated a growing share of freight handling, the railroads' bread and butter. Passengers increasingly opted for interurban electric trains, buses, private automobiles, and eventually airplanes. The railroads that had played such a critical role in economic development and the opening of new territories now took a downward slope toward deterioration and receivership.

Nonetheless, Emmit had no call to regret his choice. In comparison with his kinfolk still eking out a precarious existence on Georgia farms, he enjoyed relative security and prosperity. A man with a trade, he could lay claim to a bright and imminent future.

Of all the communities he'd visited, Emmit preferred Somerset, Kentucky. The seat of Pulaski County, located among rolling hills in the south-central part of the state near the Cumberland River, Somerset was no more than a sleepy hamlet until 1877. That year, completion of a single-track rail line from Cincinnati to Chattanooga transformed it into a bustling town. The railroad stimulated the local coal and timber industries, and hotels, stores, and residences sprang up to satisfy the needs of Somerset's growing population. In 1920, Pulaski County claimed 34,000 residents, all of them native Whites with the exception of fewer than 1,000 African Americans and fewer than 70 foreigners.

Inside the Ferguson machine shops, 1916. Public domain.

The railroad to which Somerset owed its development became the CNO&TP, eventually absorbed by the Southern Railway. When Emmit returned to Somerset in early 1923, the blacklist no longer haunted him. As one of the first companies to reach an agreement with the unions after the 1922 strike, the Southern had accepted terms that preserved the shop craft structure.

Financier J.P. Morgan had organized the Southern Railway in 1894. Rapidly gobbling up smaller lines, it developed an extensive network and amply deserved the slogan it adopted in 1924: "The Southern Serves the South." One of the most famous railroad songs, "The Wreck of the Old Ninety-Seven," recounted the tale of the 1903 derailment of a Southern Railway locomotive near Danville, Virginia and the fate of its engineer. The well-known tune later turned up with new lyrics in the Kingston Trio's "MTA" and the Chad Mitchell Trio's "Super Skier."

Between 6:00 and 6:30 each morning, Emmit and dozens of other men poured into the streets and headed for the depot on the south edge of town by foot, bus, or streetcar. At the depot, they boarded the shop train for Ferguson, a small community two miles south of Somerset, home to the CNO&TP's repair barns. Emmit changed into his heavy overalls for another day of repairing boilers. After work, he swapped clothes again, taking the grimy, scorched overalls home to have them washed. He scrubbed his hands, never able to remove all the grease. He turned in early, ready to begin the cycle again in the morning.

Life went on like this until a young woman disrupted his routine.

ORPHANS

ABOUR 1913, JIM and Ella Stroud decided to try their luck farther south. With their remaining children--Jessie and Jewel had married and left home by this time--they moved to a tenant farm outside Douglas in Coffee County. When Jim visited Blun in mid-1914, he told a *Forest-Blade* correspondent that "Douglas is alright for those who have always lived there but there is no spot in the whole world like old Emanuel." Soon he'd have occasion to return.

In 1915, Ella took ill with typhoid fever. Although he lacked medical training, Jim had a good deal of practical experience as a nurse, often staying up all night with sick neighbors. Despite his ministrations, his wife, only 43 years old, died after a few days. Jim shipped Ella's body to Emanuel County for burial in Summertown. Her tombstone bore the following inscription:

> She's gone to worlds above
> Where saints and angels meet
> To realize our Savior's love
> And worship at His feet

By this time, Emmit and Denver had gone for the life of railroad men, and Jim moved back to Emanuel County with the four youngest children. The reduced family took up residence on a tenant farm north of Swainsboro, on the road between Blun and Dellwood, not far from the farm of Duncan and Jessie Fields.

Jim and Sudie Scott Stroud, ca. 1920.

In October 1918, Jim married a widow named Sudie Scott and moved with his children and hers to work a farm near Fitzgerald in Ben Hill County. Twelve-year-old Kermit Stroud drove a mule-drawn wagon with the family's personal belongings while the others traveled by train.

The trip took three days, and at nightfall each day Kermit would knock on the door of a farmhouse and ask for shelter. As was customary, strangers gave him food and a place to sleep, feeding his mules and harnessing them the next morning so he could continue his journey.

Jim died under suspicious circumstances in 1923. One evening he returned obstreperous from a day-long fishing expedition. Another member of the party, a physician, gave him an injection to calm him. Jim died during the night, and his neighbors gossiped that the doctor, who allegedly had designs on Sudie, had murdered him.

Jim's death left his three youngest children orphans. They accompanied his coffin on the train ride to Emanuel County, where he was buried beside Ella at Summertown Cemetery. Kermit, now 17, left to find his livelihood as Emmit and Denver had before him. Alice and Maude would need the protection of their older brothers and sisters for a few years more. Margie and Waitus Scott took Alice into their home in Swainsboro, with the understanding that Emmit would contribute to her upkeep. Maude went to live with Denver in Detroit, and Kermit would chip in to help cover her expenses.

Maude and Alice Stroud, 1923, when Alice went to live with Waitus and Margie in Swainsboro, and Maude with Denver in Detroit.

Miraculously, the two girls had escaped the dreary life of the farm. They would never return to it willingly.

Ron Seckinger

HARDSCRABBLE

LIKE MOST FARMERS, Duncan Fields lost heavily when cotton prices plummeted in 1920. In December 1922, he leased his farm to his friend Dennis Rich and relocated his family to a green-painted house just south of Blun.

Jessie's seventh child, Lucy, born at the old home place on the first day of December 1921, had just celebrated her first birthday. The Fields followed the custom of scalding the walls and floors of the house with hot water and potash to clean out any lice, dirt, or other detritus left behind by the previous occupants. They settled in before the wood had dried, and in the December cold, Lucy and seven-year-old Leila took ill and developed pneumonia.

The two children lay in separate beds in the sickroom while Jessie and other relatives kept watch around the clock. Leila came out of her delirium once and, before slipping back under, saw two of her aunts, Hannah Dyson and Margie Scott, crying at the foot of the beds. Only later did she understand that her baby sister had died.

Death, to be sure, was no stranger to the Fields household. At times, it seemed that they attended the funeral of a relative or neighbor every month. But the loss of an infant just taking her first steps hit the family hard. The older children had cuddled her and wiped her runny nose, extended their fingers for her tiny hands to grasp, and coaxed smiles from her innocent face. Seeing her lifeless form struck their hearts in a terrible way, far different from beholding the corpse of an aged, leather-faced relative.

Death photograph of Lucy Fields, January 12, 1923.

The next day the women laid out 13-month-old Lucy for burial, and a photographer captured her image for the first and only time. After services at Fields Chapel, the family and other mourners traveled the short distance to Hall's Cemetery and watched as the diminutive coffin was lowered into the earth and covered with soil.

They stayed on for a while at the green house, where Jessie gave birth to Rachael Wynelle in May 1923, just months after Lucy's death. At length the family returned to the farm Duncan had received from his father, and there Jessie bore her last child, Novis Kenneth, nicknamed "Knob," in December 1925. Of her nine children, physicians had delivered only the first and the last.

The unpainted, weathered farmhouse had a tin roof and rested on log pillars about four feet high. Wooden steps descended from the front porch and directly from the back door to the ground. They called one of the poorly furnished front rooms "the parlor," although it hardly merited the name. Jessie and Duncan, along with the smaller girls, slept in a room with three beds. Rosa, the eldest daughter, had a small bedroom to herself, and the boys spent the nights in a third room. The dining room, furnished with a long table and benches, was the largest in the house and adjoined the kitchen. The windows had wooden shutters and no glass. Chinks in the walls and floors--one could see chickens scratching underneath the house—made it a drafty residence in the winter. Fireplaces in the parlor and dining room, along with the woodstove in the kitchen, provided the only heat.

The Fields owned few furnishings other than iron bedsteads, a few chests of drawers, and plenty of rocking and straight-back chairs. Large photographs of Jessie's mother and sister Jewel, mounted in black oval frames in the parlor, constituted the only decoration. Clothing, hats, and pots hung from nails on the walls.

The yard was bare earth. A huge oak tree cast its shade in the front, and a chinaberry tree in the back. Beds of verbena, zinnia, thrift, and sweet William added dashes of color to the gray landscape. A wire fence surrounded the entire farm to keep the stock from straying. Near the house, morning glories and running roses blanketed the fence.

The well presided over the backyard and, at a distance, the two-seat outhouse with last year's Sears, Roebuck catalog, which served as toilet paper. When the catalog was gone, a basket of corn cobs took its place.

Plowing behind a mule and beside a cemetery, Emanuel County, date unknown. Courtesy, Georgia Archives, Vanishing Georgia Collection, emn79.

A large barn with a hayloft housed the mules at night and sheltered farm implements and Duncan's Model T. A smaller barn held cotton during the harvest. Other structures on the small uncultivated area of the farm included a smokehouse, a syrup house, a cane grinder, and a chicken coop. Except for woods along the edge, cultivated fields took up the remainder of Duncan's 50-acre property.

The Farmer's Almanac, which foretold the phases of the moon by which growers planned the planting and harvesting of different crops, determined the rhythms of their lives. In the spring the older boys hitched the mules to their plows and broke the soil. It took physical strength to control the mule and guide the plow in a straight furrow across the field. The youngest children came behind, dropping seeds by hand and covering them with the dry, sandy earth. Manure from the feedlot served as fertilizer, which the children distributed by hand from large aprons.

Any relatives living on the farm—at times including Jessie's siblings Kermit, Alice, and Maude, and Duncan's brothers Garry B. and Joe—helped out in the fields.

Although they planted corn, velvet beans, and peanuts, cotton remained the mainstay. Like other farmers, the family came to accept the boll weevil as merely another obstacle, like fluctuating prices and the caprice of nature, to be overcome by hard work and luck.

When the stalks broke through the soil in the late spring, Jessie and the children "chopped cotton," working their way along each row with long-handled hoes, thinning out the plants and destroying the weeds that threatened to choke the precious crop. As the bolls ripened, the boys would use a small mop to dab each one with molasses, to be followed by up to three dustings with calcium arsenate in the ongoing war against the weevil. When the bolls opened and the husks--or "squares"--fell off, the younger children would pick them up for burning, following a common belief that the measure would limit insect infestations the next year.

The Fields farm and surrounding area. The federal government took thousands of such photos to help monitor the crop allocation program. This one dates from September 16, 1937, six years after the Fields family had moved, but little had changed. Courtesy, National Archives and Records Administration.

August brought the hardest task of all—picking. From then until October, they worked all day, from can't-see till can't-see. A loudly ticking clock that chimed the hours woke them at 4:00. The children groggily dressed by the light of kerosene lamps. The girls emptied and rinsed the enamel chamber pots and made the beds while the boys let the stock out to forage in the woods and filled a large, galvanized tin washtub with water from the well. Jessie milked the cows, and Rosa fired up the woodstove and put on a pot of peas to simmer all morning.

They had a meager breakfast, often no more than milk and "flour bread," biscuit dough cooked in a skillet and served with cane syrup and fresh cream. Before cockcrow they trudged through the dark and the heavy ground fog to the fields, where they lay down on their cotton sacks to wait for dawn.

At first light they began. The rows of bushes bearing white fiber stretched before them, from the fence surrounding the house area to the very edge of the woods. They moved slowly along the rows, bent over, plucking cotton bolls until both hands were full and then transferring them to the sacks hung across their shoulders. Their hardened hands occasionally suffered scratches from the stalks.

Within an hour their backs ached. The smaller children complained but got no sympathy from Jessie. To ease their protesting muscles, they crawled along on their knees for a while, dragging the bulging sacks behind them. At the end of a row everyone dumped the cotton on large burlap sheets. They took a drink of water from a bucket and rested for a few minutes before starting back across the field with their empty sacks. The gnats and no-see-ums swarmed so thick that the pickers smeared kerosene around their eyes in a futile effort to keep the insects at bay.

The sun was not red but white. A colorless landscape swallowed them up—cotton bolls, bleached sackcloth dresses and shirts, dry and dusty soil, white-hot heat shimmering before their eyes. By 9:00 the sun had become unbearable, loosing rivulets of sweat through the layers of dust that irritated their skin. But bear it they did, as the growing mounds of cotton marked their progress toward surviving another year on the land.

Margie Scott, Kermit Stroud, and Jessie Fields in a well-picked cotton patch on the Fields farm, ca. 1927-1929.

Rosa returned to the house to prepare dinner when they heard the whistle of the Georgia & Florida train about 10:00. The pickers, who could see the smoke from the stove and catch kitchen smells on the rare breeze, listened to their stomachs growl until Rosa finally rang a bell mounted on a post in the backyard, summoning them from the fields.

They marched back, more eagerly than in the morning, and washed their faces and hands before sitting down to the long table. During the winter and early spring, they got only peas flavored with fatback, flat cakes of skillet-fried cornbread, and possibly some ham, but at this time of year the garden overflowed. Rosa would serve fresh tomatoes, corn, lima beans, turnips, collard greens, fried okra, beets, cucumbers, and sometimes rice or boiled potatoes. They had a wholesome diet compared to many Southern families and never suffered from pellagra, the scourge of the rural poor.

They ate in shifts, one group fanning the flies away while the other shoveled food into hungry mouths.

After lunch. Leila would wash the dishes while Romie Delle dried, and Rosa would cover the leftovers with a tablecloth to keep the flies off. The pickers sprawled on the porch for a short rest and then put on their straw hats and returned to the cotton plants waiting patiently in the afternoon sun.

At dusk, Jessie would call a halt. They pulled together the four corners of the burlap sheets filled with fiber and carried them to the cotton barn. After completing the other chores--penning up the stock for the night, gathering eggs, feeding the mules--they picked a bushel of peas from the garden and shelled them on the front porch for the next day's mid-day meal, while scratchy records played on the old wind-up Victrola.

Eventually, they took turns bathing in the washtub, its water warmed by the sun, and sat down to supper. Mostly they got leftovers, although Rosa might fry a couple of chickens. For dessert they usually had biscuits with syrup and fresh cream—Rosa often used two 24-pound bags of flour in a week—and sometimes blackberry or huckleberry pie, or "jelly cake," made with cane syrup instead of sugar and frosted with homemade jelly.

Exhausted, they went to bed early. On those suffocating Georgia nights when the weight of the air was palpable and a greasy patina covered their skin, they dragged the mattresses to the porch in the vain hope of catching a breeze. Battalions of mosquitoes feasted on them whether they slept inside or out.

The four chimes of the clock came, it seemed, as soon as they closed their eyes, and they got up to repeat the cycle. The beginning of the school year brought a respite to the younger children, who escaped the fields during school hours while the older ones labored with Jessie.

By late September or early October, the cotton plants at last stood bare. The older boys put the "gates" on the flatbed wagon, making a high-walled container into which they dumped the accumulated cotton. Each

Ron Seckinger

acre in Emanuel County yielded about 150 pounds of processed cotton on average, a paltry showing that the county agent attributed to the utilization of marginal lands that should have gone to other crops or to pasturage. Duncan drove the wagon to one of the gins—Warren Kea's in Modoc or Randolph Coleman's in Swainsboro, for example—and sold his crop for the prevailing price. The humming machinery of the gin separated seeds from the fiber and spat out bales wrapped in jute, each weighing roughly 500 pounds.

Farmers deliver wagon loads of cotton to a gin in Coweta County, date unknown. Courtesy, Georgia Archives, Vanishing Georgia Collection, cow143.

At 50 acres, Duncan's farm was slightly larger than the average of 33 acres for Georgia farms in 1920. Assuming the Fields planted 30 acres in cotton—using the remaining 20 for buildings, yard, pigpen, barnyard, corn patch, and vegetable garden—and obtained the average yield, they produced about nine bales each year. The cash, provided Duncan didn't get drunk and gamble it away, allowed the family to pay off its creditors and make a few purchases, such as a new pair of shoes for each child, livestock or implements for the farm, and possibly furniture or other store-bought goods.

Other work remained. After harvesting the corn, they "pulled fod-der," tying the husks in bundles for the cows to eat in winter. Jessie and the girls put away garden vegetables, sterilizing the Mason jars with boiling water before filling them with stewed tomatoes, lima beans, corn, okra, string beans, squash pickles, and field peas, sealing them with new lids from Ehrlich's store. They also made jams and jellies from plums, blackber-ries, and scuppernong grapes collected along the roads and from the pro-duce of their few peach, pear, and fig trees. For their part, the boys turned the hogs into the cornfield and chopped wood, not only for the kitchen stove but also for the fireplaces during the coming winter. They also dug up the sweet potatoes, which were placed in straw-lined "hills," and Irish potatoes they spread out under the house or in the barn.

Grinding cane on a farm in McDuffie County, 1940s. Courtesy, Georgia Archives, Vanishing Georgia Collection, mcd195.

Two farm chores in the late fall and winter called for festivities-- cane grinding and hog-killing. Most farmers cultivated a small plot of sugar cane to make syrup for their families' use. They fed stalks into a metal grinder mounted on posts and driven by a mule walking in endless cir-cles. They collected the olive-green juice and poured it into the large sugar

Ron Seckinger

kettle—mounted in cement with room for a wood fire underneath—in the syrup shed and cooked it for hours. The adults skimmed off impurities with a long-handled dipper, and as the water evaporated the juice slowly thickened and turned brown. They funneled the finished syrup into old liquor bottles and sealed them with new corks.

A cane grinding provided the excuse for a party, and neighbors came to dance, talk, and drink glasses of the incredibly sweet juice while their children played games. The last syrup in the pot was cooked down for candy and transferred to a pan to cool. When it could be handled, two young people would take a handful and pull, swapping ends, until it turned a whitish color. They stretched it out on a table, cut it into pieces, and—if their teeth were strong—chewed as much as they liked. Sometimes they mixed the candy with roasted peanuts or pecans to make brittle.

Hog-killings took place only in cold weather so the pork wouldn't spoil. On the preceding night, the boys filled the sugar kettle with 30 or 40 gallons of water from the well and laid wood for fires under it and a separate three-legged iron pot. In the morning, one of the men dispatched a hog with a bullet in the head and then slit its throat. They scalded the animal's hide in the boiling water of the kettle, scraped away the hair with sharp knives, rinsed the carcass, suspended it by the hind legs, and quickly gutted it.

The farmers used every part of the pig but the squeal. They ate the small intestines as chitterlings or used them as sausage casings. For the latter purpose, Jessie and Rosa emptied the intestines, flushed them with water, turned them wrong side out, and scraped them till they became transparent. The women ground some of the pork in a hand mill and heavily seasoned it with red pepper and sage. They cooked a little of the sausage meat in a skillet so the adults could test the seasoning. If deemed satisfactory, the meat was pressed through a tubular instrument into the casings.

The large intestine went for liver pudding and the stomach for tripe. They pickled the head and feet—the flesh from the head eventually winding up in Brunswick stew—and cooked the brains with scrambled eggs. They cured some of the fat to use as flavoring for vegetables and boiled down the rest in the three-legged pot to make lard, used as cooking grease. Farm families ate "cracklins," the hardened, cooked skin left when the lard had rendered, as a snack or crushed and mixed with cornmeal to make "cracklin' bread."

The Fields children, 1924-1925. Front row, from left: Leila, Wynelle, J.D., Romie Delle. Back row: Ralph, Rosa, John A. Note the identical shirts and dresses made by their mother, Jessie Stroud Fields. The last child, Novis or "Knob," was born in 1925.

Pork anchored their diet. They packed the hams, shoulders, and fatty sides in barrels with salt or sugar for curing. Later, the meats would hang over a slow fire in the smokehouse. They remained there after the smoking, and Rosa would cut off a slab at mealtime. The family seldom ate beef, save when a neighbor butchered a cow and came around in his wagon to sell extra cuts.

Poultry was more common, though still second to pork. Sunday dinner invariably called for fried chicken, and sometimes they ate boiled chicken and dumplings, squares of dough that stretched a meal. Guinea hens—odd, gray-colored, tufted fowl—often went into the pot with dumplings, because their flesh was entirely dark meat. Rosa killed a chicken or guinea by wringing its neck until the head came off in her hand. The headless carcass would run around the yard on reflexes until its heart stopped beating. Game and fish provided the only other break from ham and fatback.

Other chores kept the family busy. They made soap by heating animal grease and potash in the syrup boiler. On Mondays, Rosa boiled dirty clothes in the syrup kettle with pieces of homemade soap, rubbed them on a tin washboard, and rinsed them in three tubs of water. With 10 members of the family plus assorted relatives in the house, the clothesline couldn't handle all the garments, and Rosa spread the extra ones on the fence to dry.

Jessie made most of the clothing, except the overalls, on a pedal-driven Singer sewing machine. She saved buttons in a cigar box and made pin cushions of cloth stuffed with beans or rice. Since she rarely had money for store-bought fabric, Jessie used "gunny" sacks—which originally held guano, or fertilizer—and flour bags. She boiled them until the lettering faded, dyed them, and fashioned them into frocks or shirts. As each child outgrew a piece of clothing, he or she passed it down to the next in line. By the firelight, Jessie also embroidered doilies for the mantelpieces, chests of drawers, and chair arms.

The work never ended. Even late in her life, when she had no need to labor from dawn till beyond dusk, Jessie never lost her drive to do something useful. Like many Southern women, she proved stronger than any man.

NOOSE

SOON AFTER ALICE Stroud moved into Waitus and Margie Scott's home in Swainsboro, she attended one of the occasional rituals of small-town America—a hanging. It was the first execution in Emanuel County in more than 12 years.

The condemned man was a young African American named Seaborn ("Seab") Johnson. Born in 1900, he was convicted of forgery in 1916 and sentenced to six months on the Emanuel County chain gang. In January 1919, he married Ethel Cowart, and in late December 1920, he arranged to work as a sharecropper and turpentine runner for Frank Ware, a White man who owned lands near Lexsy, about five miles south of Swainsboro on the road to Stillmore.

About two months later, Ethel Cowart Johnson left her husband and moved to the home of her sister and brother-in-law, Linda and Jack Phillips, on the neighboring plot of land. Seab accused her of consorting with her cousin, James Chance, a single man who also lived at the Phillips place, and had words with him on several occasions.

On the fifth Sunday in May 1921, Johnson shot and killed his wife and her niece, Mattie Phillips, and wounded his sister-in-law, Daisy Cowart. Ware, who heard the shots from his home, apprehended the suspect and turned him over to Sheriff Otis Coleman in Swainsboro. The authorities held Johnson for the fall session of Superior Court. On October 10, a grand jury of 23 White men returned a true bill of particulars against Johnson for two counts of murder and one count of assault with intent to murder.

The trial began on October 20. Judge R.N. Hardeman, who had figured in Swainsboro's celebrated case concerning the rights of children to attend movies on school nights, presided. He had sentenced Johnson to the chain gang five years previously.

According to witnesses for the prosecution, Seab Johnson had appeared at the Phillips residence at about 9:00 in the morning, brandishing a pistol and insisting that Ethel return home with him. Otis Cowart testified that Seab said he intended to kill his wife and burn the house. Emma Cowart, Ethel's widowed mother, arrived at the Johnson place about two hours later, accompanied by her daughter Daisy and her granddaughter Mattie, both teenagers.

As they argued, Seab suddenly began firing his .38-caliber revolver. Two bullets struck Mattie, sitting in the doorway. Daisy, inside the house, took one round and probably escaped death when a second bullet misfired. Ethel ran for the fence, but Seab caught up with her and forced her back to the house, where he emptied his pistol into her body, reloaded, and began firing again.

"I thought he was shooting at them to scare them," Emma testified, "until, I didn't believe it until he went and shot his wife down, and went and stood over her like that, like he was shooting a snake."

Taking the stand in his own defense, Johnson claimed the Cowart women had assaulted him in his home. Mattie had a "cutter," he said. Emma threw a Coca-Cola bottle at him and waved a screwdriver, and Daisy struck him with a half-gallon fruit jar.

> I had the pistol in my pocket and it looked like they was
> going to mob me and they had done beat me up two or
> three times, one of them, my wife, had a piece of stick, a
> piece of shovel handle, about that long and she had hold

Ron Seckinger

of that and hit me, she hauled off and hit me and that blinded me and staggered me and I went to shooting.

He also charged that the Cowart family had long sought to separate him from his wife and had frequently picked fights with him.

The Emanuel County courthouse, built in 1920 and burned in 1938, where Seab Johnson stood trial for murder. Courtesy, courthousehistory.com.

Most of the witnesses corroborated key points of the accusations against Johnson, and the multiple wounds to Ethel undercut his claim of self-defense. On October 21, a jury of 12 White men found him guilty of one count of first-degree murder–of his wife–without recommendation of mercy. Judge Hardeman pronounced sentence:

> Whereupon, it is the judgment of the Court that you, Seab Johnson, be taken hence from the court house to the common jail of said county, where you shall be kept in close confinement until Friday December 2nd 1921, and that on said date, between the hours of ten o'clock A.M. and two o'clock P.M. at the common jail of said county, or such other place as may be provided by the County Commissioners of said County in the presence

of such of your relatives and friends as you may desire and designate to be present, and in the presence of such minister or ministers of the gospel as you may desire to minister to your spiritual needs, in the presence of such guard as the Sheriff may deem sufficient to have present, and the physicians hereinafter named, otherwise in private, that you be hung by the neck until you are dead. And may the Lord have mercy on your soul.

Johnson's court-appointed attorney, Ivy W. Rountree, filed a motion for a new trial the same day, and Governor Thomas W. Hardwick soon granted a stay of execution. Seab remained in the county jail while his case snaked through the judicial system.

The jail sat in the "boneyard," across Green Street from the southwestern corner of the courthouse square. Either dusty or muddy depending on the weather, this sunken lot had wooden stairs that led to the sidewalk and street on higher ground. The farmers who flocked to Swainsboro on Saturdays parked their wagons there and watered their horses in a large, communal trough. Practically deserted during the week, the boneyard served as merely another playground for the children of town families.

Jerry Rich and Russell Coleman, both about six years old when Seab Johnson took up residence in the jail, lived a few houses apart on Green Street and often prowled the neighborhood. As the sheriff's son, Russell had access to the building, and the two became friends with many of the prisoners.

When Johnson heard their voices outside, he would call out, "Jerry, you and Russell go down there and buy me a 10-cent cake," or chewing gum, or an apple or banana. From his cell window he would lower a tobacco can with a few coins inside. The boys emptied the can and ran to one of the nearby stores—Cadle's or Middens and Hinsen's—to make the purchase. Then they trooped into the jail, where Russell plucked the key ring from a hook and unlocked the door to the cell area. Through the bars, the boys delivered their goods to Johnson or whatever prisoner had entrusted them with the errand. They often stayed to chat with the men, and Seab was one of their favorites.

On May 3, 1922, defense attorney Rountree filed an amended motion for a new trial, citing two technicalities in the original one. First, the Solicitor General had urged the jury to find Johnson guilty without a recommendation for mercy. This request, Rountree argued, infringed on the jury's exclusive right to determine the punishment. Second, Johnson sat in a cell adjoining and open to the courtroom during the jury's deliberations. When the jury returned, the judge asked whether the defendant waived a poll of each member, and the attorney had answered for him without Johnson's presence in the courtroom proper.

Judge Hardeman, however, found no merit in the petition and ruled against the condemned man:

> In view of the seriousness of the case and ... the fact that the death penalty had been imposed, I have reviewed and scanned the record with the greatest care and the most mature consideration. If I could be convinced that there was the slightest error or injustice done the defendant, or if the evidence was even weak, or to any considerable extent conflicting, I would grant the motion, but upon review of the case it appears no error of law was committed, the defendant was ably defended, and the evidence not only warrants, but in my judgment demanded the verdict returned by the jury. Therefore, without nullifying the law, I can find no reason to disturb the verdict. The motion, therefore, is overruled and a new trial refused.

Johnson's attorney next petitioned Governor Hardwick for executive clemency. By this time, many of the prominent White citizens of Emanuel County had taken up the defendant's cause.

Convicted murderer Seab Johnson, ca. 1921. His brother is on the left and Deputy Sheriff Thomas E. Brown on the right. Courtesy, Georgia Archives, Vanishing Georgia Collection, emn041.

Ron Seckinger

Those in the Lexsy area provided depositions in his favor, arguing that the unsavory Cowart family had repeatedly mistreated Johnson. Frank Ware, for example, declared that "the reputation of the Cowarts is entirely bad, that they are a bunch of negroes who live mainly by moonshine and gambling, and the women are all immoral characters." Ware and Sheriff Coleman said Johnson had been intoxicated on the morning of the killing and therefore not responsible for his actions. Others swore that Emma and Daisy Cowart had confessed to having perjured themselves during the trial.

In Swainsboro, dozens signed a petition asking Seab's sentence be commuted to life imprisonment. Separate petitions from 13 county officials—including City Judge George Kirkland, Sheriff Coleman, and Deputy Sheriff Thomas E. Brown—and 12 attorneys echoed the request. The county Board of Commissioners and the Ladies' Missionary Society of Swainsboro Methodist Church sent telegrams to the Prison commission, and Ida Belle Williams, a prominent teacher, dispatched one to the governor. The editors of the *Forest-Blade*, while admitting that Seab was "rather a mean negro," took up his cause: "This hanging business is a serious matter, when you come to think of it, and it also looks a little barbarous."

Most surprising of all, 11 of the jurors signed an affidavit saying that, had they heard testimony from those who now took Seab's side, they "would never have consented to a verdict carrying with it the death penalty." Like the rest of the condemned man's champions, they asked the governor to change his sentence to life imprisonment.

The Prison Commission, unimpressed, unanimously declined to approve a reduced sentence. Governor Hardwick nonetheless issued a two-week stay of execution on February 9, for the consideration of new evidence. He subsequently postponed the sentence until May 4 and then until July 27, ordering the Emanuel Superior Court to reexamine the case.

With the inauguration of Clifford M. Walker as Hardwick's successor, Seab Johnson's luck ran out. Walker had lost the gubernatorial election to Hardwick in 1920 but, with the support of the Ku Klux Klan, defeated the incumbent two years later. Although the new governor issued another two-week stay of execution on July 27, he refused to intercede a second time.

The condemned man apparently had come to terms with his impending death. Two days before the scheduled execution, a visitor from the *Forest-Blade* found him shining his shoes and smoking a cigar.

> When asked if he was ready to 'go', he answered that no one was ever ready to die, but that he was as near ready now as he ever was. He said, "I am not going to cry a bit, I'm a man."
>
> Johnson didn't seem to want to talk about himself very much, and would change the subject when he was mentioned. He would laugh and joke with the few that were in the jail.
>
> Seab said he wanted to thank everybody that has been so good to him and the ones that have tried so hard to save his life.

On Friday, August 10, 1923, after more than 27 months in the Swainsboro jail, Seab Johnson walked out for his date with the hangman's noose at 2:00 in the afternoon.

Jerry Rich's mother, aware of her son's strong attachment to Johnson, had taken the boy into the country to visit his aunt. But several hundred others, including Alice Stroud and Margie and Waitus Scott, gathered outside the jail.

The condemned man addressed the crowd from the steps of the jailhouse. According to the *Forest-Blade*, he advised all, especially the young boys, to be careful of whiskey and bad companions. He said that whiskey, bad women, and pistols were the cause of his trouble. He talked for about 30 minutes and then asked for a Coca-Cola, which Deputy Tom Brown sent for. When he had finished the soft drink, he stated that he was ready to go.

Johnson walked to enclosed gallows behind the jail in the boneyard. Jerry and Russell had played in the structure in recent days without comprehending its purpose. At the top of the steps, Seab sat down to remove his footwear, saying he didn't want to die wearing shoes. Inside the enclosure that hid the gallows from view, a Black preacher offered what solace he could. Johnson prayed briefly before taking his assigned space.

Sheriff Coleman sprung the trapdoor, and Johnson fell several feet before the rope tightened and broke his neck. Two court-appointed physicians pronounced him dead, and his relatives claimed his body for burial in Stillmore.

Their morbid curiosity satisfied, the citizens of Swainsboro returned to their homes. Unbeknownst to all, they had witnessed the last execution in Emanuel County.

CHICAGO

AFTER BURYING his wife Jewel in 1920, Fred Hooks left his four daughters with his parents at Hooks Crossing and set out once more to make his fortune. In Bamberg, South Carolina, a town of some 2,200 inhabitants located northwest of Charleston, he managed to buy a seven-chair barbershop of his own.

On entering George Ducker's grocery store one day, Fred met the owner's daughter, a petite young woman with light brown eyes and reddish-brown, almost auburn hair. He began courting Annie Lee Ducker, just shy of her 25th birthday. They attended church or went to the movies or sat on the porch of her father's house. On January 1, 1921, eight months after Jewel's death, Fred took Annie Lee as his bride in a ceremony held in the parlor of George and Missouri Ducker's home.

The newlyweds rented a house of their own, and a month later, Fred returned to Emanuel County to reclaim his family. Honoring Jewel's wishes and Lillian Hooks's preferences, he left the infant Freddie in his mother's care.

On February 8, Mae's 11th birthday, Fred arrived in Bamberg with his three oldest daughters, who met their stepmother for the first time. Annie Lee bought yards and yards of cloth and took the three girls to a seamstress. She soon had them dressed to a T and, deciding her stepchildren lacked manners, started coaching them in the social graces. Before

Ron Seckinger

yearend, she had transformed Mae, Thelma, and Melema into proper town girls. In February 1922, the family grew with the birth of Gloria Vivian, Annie Lee's first child and Fred's fifth.

Melema, Thelma, and Mae Hooks, Bamburg, South Carolina, ca. 1922.

In their home Annie Lee displayed a double picture frame with photos of herself and Jewel. Occasionally a friend expressed surprise that she kept a likeness of her husband's first wife, but she'd say, "I'm not jealous of her. She's dead." On one of their periodic trips to Emanuel County, Fred, Annie Lee, and Lillian Hooks spent hours at Moore's Cemetery, weeding Jewel's gravesite and decorating it with flowers.

Fred continued to accompany his wife to the Methodist Church in Bamberg, and they associated with other young couples active in church circles. Fred had always accepted religion as an integral part of his life. His grandfather and uncle had served as circuit riders, and his mother enjoyed nothing more than playing hymns on her treasured piano.

One morning, Fred told Annie Lee that a voice had spoken to him the previous evening as he sat on the porch after she had gone to bed. He'd heard a call to enter the ministry.

"I'm going," he said. "We can sell what we got and let's go. If you're willing."

"Of course, I'm willing," she replied, echoing Ruth of the Old Testament. "Whatever you want."

Moody Bible Institute in Chicago in the 1920s. Courtesy, Moody Bible Institute.

And so they made plans to begin a new life. Since he had no college degree, Fred took the Ministerial Course of Study of the Methodist Church, offered at Emory University in Atlanta, by correspondence. Completing the program in 1924, he sold his barbershop. Some Bamberg residents donated money to help them get started. Annie Lee and Gloria moved in with the Duckers, and Fred took the older girls to Hooks Crossing. Alone, he set out for Chicago, where he matriculated at the Moody Bible Institute in September 1924.

Dwight L. Moody. Public domain.

The famous evangelist Dwight L. Moody had established the Institute more than three decades earlier. Arriving in Chicago in 1856 as a 19-year-old, the Massachusetts-born Moody quickly succeeded in business, and in 1860, he decided to devote his life to religious work. After heading the city's Young Men's Christian Association, he started a mission in "Little Hell," a notorious slum district on the North Side, and founded a church there in 1864.

For several years Moody and singer Ira D. Sankey staged immensely successful revivals throughout Great Britain, and in 1875-77 they did the same in the major cities of the United States. Only the famous Billy Sunday rivaled Moody's prominence in the evangelical movement in the late 19th century.

The Bible Institute for Home and Foreign Missions, organized by Moody's Christian Evangelization Society in 1889, proved the revivalist's principal legacy. School officials bestowed his name on the Institute in 1900, the year after his death, when it already had become a Mecca for Protestant fundamentalists. Its physical plant at the corner of Lasalle Street and Chicago Avenue—"Little Hell" stretched out to the west, and Lake Michigan lay a dozen miles to the east—grew along with the Institute's success. Through its doors passed generations of ministers, missionaries, church musicians, and Christian educational leaders to spread Moody's conservative theology across the globe.

As soon as Fred located an apartment, he sent for his family. Annie Lee and the four girls rode the train to Chicago, where Fred and some of his fellow students met them at the station. "Spartan" best described their lodgings, on the second floor of a tall building not far from the Institute. They crowded into two bedrooms, a combined living-dining room, and a kitchen.

To pay the bills, Fred worked in the Institute's barbershop. Between work and studies, he had little time for his family, but he was happy.

Preparing for the ministry provided the focus he'd always lacked, and Annie Lee was content to help him attain his goal.

The bustling streets of Chicago contrasted sharply with the Hooks family's small-town background. Courtesy, chuckmanchicagonostalgia.wordpress.com.

After the small-town tranquility of Bamberg, the Hooks family found Chicago both exhilarating and frightening. It was a dirty, sprawling, energetic city with a diversity unknown in the South. Its streets swarmed with Catholics and Jews, Germans, Swedes, Ukrainians, Lithuanians, Italians,

Ron Seckinger

Poles, Irish, Chinese, and growing numbers of Southerners, both White and Black.

In the first of his *Chicago Poems* (1916), Carl Sandburg characterized his hometown as "a tall bold slugger set vivid against the little soft cities." He continued:

> Laughing the stormy, husky, brawling laughter of Youth, half-naked, sweating, proud to be Hog Butcher, Tool Maker, Stacker of Wheat, Player with Railroads and Freight Handler to the Nation.

Chicagoans took less pride in their city's well-deserved reputation as America's crime capital. Extortion, prostitution, and municipal corruption had flourished since the 19th century, and the advent of Prohibition sealed the triumph of lawlessness.

In the reformist atmosphere that followed the Great War, the long-standing efforts of temperance advocates to secure a national ban on the manufacture and sale of liquor resulted in the 18th Amendment and its enforcement vehicle, the Volstead Act, in 1920. The law had little impact on the demand for alcohol while transferring supply from the hands of legitimate businessmen to those of criminals. The proximity of Canada facilitated smuggling, and the existence of a thoroughly corrupt city administration—including the police and the judiciary—made Chicago a heaven for bootleggers, who also contested control of other vices.

The Hooks family arrived at the beginning of the gangland wars subsequently popularized in dozens of Hollywood movies.

Fred personally knew one of the most notorious gangsters, Dion O'Banion, who regularly visited the Institute's barbershop for a shave and haircut. With his father, O'Banion had moved from a suburb to "Little Hell" at the age of 12. He completed elementary school at nearby Holy Name Cathedral, where he served as acolyte for years. Short and stocky, with broad shoulders, he walked with a limp—the result of falling from a streetcar while working as a paperboy.

A brawler and petty thief, before the age of 20 O'Banion had spent two three-month stretches in Bridewell Prison. With other Irish toughs, he worked as a "slugger" or strong-arm, first for 42nd Ward politicians and then for the *Daily Tribune* during a series of bloody newspaper circulation disputes.

Taking up with a gang of safecrackers, he subsequently branched into hijacking, gambling, and the beer and liquor trade. He soon controlled all the breweries on the North Side. After his death, the police judged that his take from alcohol alone surpassed $1 million a year. He carried three pistols in specially made pockets. Estimates of the number of men he killed ranged from 25 to 62.

In 1922, O'Banion bought a half-interest in a florist shop on North State Street, across from Holy Name Cathedral. His shop's trucks provided cover for deliveries of booze, and the gangster tradition of sending elaborate floral wreaths to the funerals of both friends and enemies ensured a lot of legitimate business. But the shop was more than just another money-making venture. O'Banion loved flowers and had a knack for making artful arrangements. The idiosyncrasy made him seem less irredeemably evil, and ironically this shallow streak of humanity played a part in his death.

Dion O'Banion, ca. 1922.

Ron Seckinger

Each time O'Banion sat in the barber's chair over two to three months, Fred Hooks talked about religion and the virtues of living right, gently trying to turn his customer away from the world of crime. They made a strange pair, the gangly Protestant preacher-in-training from Georgia and the beefy Irish Catholic hoodlum from "Little Hell." The former acolyte tolerated his barber's proselytizing as the scissors clicked and the razor glided smoothly across his face. Afterwards, the gangster paid for his shave and haircut and walked out, unaffected by Fred's entreaties, to resume his career as vice lord.

Although the different gangs often managed to agree on the territorial limits of their empires, the competition for control of the rackets sometimes turned ugly. O'Banion hated his Italian rivals Johnny Torrio, the Genna Brothers, and Al Capone. Whenever a colleague advised him to make peace, he merely exclaimed, "Oh, to hell with them Sicilians."

Mike Merlo, head of the Unione Siciliana, a confederation of the Italian crime families, opposed murder and restrained his associates from retaliating against the Irishman. On November 8, 1924, however, Merlo died of cancer. His successor, Angelo Genna, didn't share his scruples.

Torrio, Capone, and one of the Genna brothers placed orders for floral arrangements with O'Banion. When three of Genna's men entered the shop at noon on November 10, O'Banion asked, "Hello, boys, you want Merlo's flowers?" He advanced toward them with shears in his left hand and his right hand outstretched. As soon as one man took the proffered hand, another pulled a pistol and fired six shots into the Irishman, who fell among his beloved flowers.

O'Banion's murder marked the opening battle in an underworld war. His gang killed two of the Genna brothers within months, and the culmination of the bloodletting would come with the St. Valentine's Day Massacre in 1929, when Capone's hoods would gun down seven associates of "Bugs" Moran, heir to O'Banion's organization.

Annie Lee wanted to attend O'Banion's funeral, but Fred would have none of it. Cutting a gangster's hair was one thing. At least the barber had the opportunity of trying to show him the light. But paying respects to the dead man was quite another.

Some 40,000 curiosity-seekers visited the Sbarboro funeral chapel on North Wells Street to view the body, laid out in a $10,000, silver-toned, bronze casket shipped specially from Philadelphia. About 10,000 persons, as well as 24 cars heaped with flowers, participated in the procession to Mount Carmel Cemetery, where another 10,000 waited to witness the burial.

Although O'Banion's plot lay in unconsecrated ground and the Cardinal had forbidden a Catholic service, a priest and long-time friend of the deceased said a few prayers for the dead. All in all, it was a spectacular send-off for a man the police chief called "Chicago's archcriminal."

O'Banion's death came not long after the arrival of Fred Hooks' wife and daughters. Annie Lee learned how to get around on the trolley lines and purchased heavy winter clothing for the first time in her life. She and the girls marveled at the bustling streets and stopped to listen to sidewalk evangelists.

As a properly raised woman from a small Southern town, Annie Lee smiled and nodded to passers-by as she walked with the children through "Little Hell" to Montgomery Ward's on Chicago Avenue, several blocks west of the Institute. They transited Orleans Street, where Italian immigrants came out of the tenements to stare at the procession, oblivious to Annie Lee's polite nods. On one excursion, Annie Lee heard pistol shots around the corner and hurriedly retraced her steps. That same day, one of the Moody students spotted her and the girls and reported this information to Fred, who sternly warned her that Catholics and other dangerous types inhabited those streets. Afterwards, she avoided the area.

The Institute served as the center of their life. Fred and Annie socialized mostly with the other students, several of whom came to Sunday dinner practically every week. As the students progressed through the curriculum, they received preaching or teaching responsibilities.

Several Sundays each month, Fred and Annie Lee boarded a trolley, often taking Gloria along, and traveled south for 20 blocks or so to Chinatown, where Fred taught Bible studies to young boys and girls. Little Gloria fascinated the Chinese youngsters, who would have preferred to play with her all afternoon. Fred insisted that they learn the stories of Cain and Abel, Joseph and his coat of many colors, Jonah and the whale, and Jesus.

When he could get away from studies and work, Fred liked to accompany Annie Lee on her frequent visits to city parks, where she would sit on a bench and watch the children play. He had little time or money for other pastimes. Unable to keep up the payments on a small insurance policy, he let it lapse. Then he worried about how his family would cope if he died. During his three years in Chicago, he never attended a baseball game—not even when his old acquaintance Ty Cobb, manager of the Detroit Tigers from 1920 to 1926, brought his team to play the White Sox.

After hours in classroom and barbershop each day, Fred pored over his texts, sometimes returning to the apartment after midnight. A robust man when he arrived in Chicago, he gradually became gaunt, and at times his spirits fell.

*Fred Hooks at the time of his graduation from Moody
in 1927. Courtesy, Moody Bible Institute.*

"I can't stand this much longer," he told Annie Lee on several occasions. "I don't think I can take it. I'm too tired.

"Now, honey," she'd encourage him, "the Lord wouldn't have called you if he'd wanted you to quit. I'm with you. I don't care where you go, I'm with you. We'll make it."

And they did. On April 21, 1927, Fred Hooks walked across the stage at Moody to receive his diploma, one of 68 members of the spring graduating class. Fred fairly burst with pride, the hard work and long hours forgotten, as he hugged his wife and daughters.

Afterwards, they packed to return home to Georgia. Their Chinese friends threw a farewell banquet and insisted that Gloria stand on a table and sing a song. At the Institute, Fred and Annie Lee said goodbye to the others—those who, like Fred, were leaving to begin their ministries, and those who remained to complete their studies. At last, they drove off in an old Model T, with Chicago and the exhilaration and pain of the last three years behind them, and the future to the fore.

KLAN

FRUGALITY AND lack of interest made Waitus Scott a stay-at-home type. Outside the barbershop, the home, and visits to relatives, he had little interaction with the world. He did participate in the activities of his lodge, the Woodmen of the World, a fraternal life insurance society that established a chapter in Swainsboro in 1923. And, according to his sister-in-law, he belonged to the Ku Klux Klan.

The original Klan began as a social club that six young college graduates founded for former Confederate officers in Pulaski, Tennessee in December 1865. Appropriating *kuklos*, the Greek word for "circle," as their motif, the men invested their creation with the mystical trappings common to fraternal orders. Riding through the night in masks and white sheets apparently began as horseplay but soon took on sinister purposes.

By 1867, the Klan had transformed itself into a regional terrorist organization of disenfranchised ex-Confederates determined to overthrow the Reconstruction governments imposed by Congressional Republicans on all the Southern states save, ironically, Tennessee. A conclave in Nashville named General Nathan Bedford Forrest, the notorious leader of Confederate irregulars, Grand Wizard of the order and created a hierarchy of Grand Dragons, Titans, Giants, and Cyclops.

Throughout the South, the Klan's nightriders terrorized Black freedmen as well as Whites who collaborated with the Reconstruction governments, burning homes and beating or murdering opponents. Forrest, unable to control the local chapters, disbanded the organization in 1869 and burned its records. Its more prominent members withdrew out of disgust with the unchecked violence, and the federal authorities acted to suppress the order. By 1872, it had disappeared.

In 1915, an Alabamian named William J. Simmons brought the Klan back to life. Formerly a Methodist preacher and traveling sales-man, Simmons found his niche as a fraternal organizer. He joined several Masonic orders, the Knights Templar, the Congregational and Missionary Baptist Churches, the Spanish American War Veterans, and the Woodmen of the World. Having thrilled to his father's tales of riding with the original Klan, Simmons longed to resuscitate the organization. Eventually, his opportunity came after a North Carolinian and a Kentuckian had prepared the way.

The North Carolinian, Thomas Dixon, Jr., published a novel called *The Clansman* in 1905. It depicted a proud and noble civilization brought low by military defeat, debased by the rule of the occupying forces' puppet governments, and redeemed only by the timely intervention of the gallant knights of the Ku Klux Klan.

At a time when Confederate veterans met in annual rallies, the United Daughters of the Confederacy claimed some 100,000 members, and the events of the 1860s and 1870s remained within living memory, Dixon's dramatic rendering of Southern mythology resonated with his country-men. The book, ratifying common White beliefs about Southern valor, Northern perfidy, and Black brutishness, proved enormously successful throughout the region and reached an even larger audience through a stage version performed by touring companies. Retailers tried to cash in on the popularity of Dixon's story. In Swainsboro, Proctor's store offered "a good, honest, man's shoe called 'The Clansman'" for $2.50 a pair.

If Dixon's book and play reached thousands, it fell to Hollywood filmmaker D.W. Griffith to carry the message to millions. A native of

Kentucky, Griffith, like Simmons, had learned of the Klan at his father's knee, and he shared Dixon's romantic vision of a heroic people resisting Yankee domination.

Griffith utilized Civil War themes in several of his early films, and in 1914 he set out to portray his own understanding of Southern history, based in part on *The Clansman*. Nearly three hours long, "The Birth of a Nation" featured spectacular battlefield scenes patterned on Matthew Brady's wartime photographs and followed the intertwined stories of two families, the Southern Camerons and the Northern Stonemans.

In a key scene from D. W. Griffith's "Birth of a Nation," Klansmen seize a freedman allegedly out to rape a White woman. Public domain.

Central to the plot were the perceived threat that ex-slaves posed to the social order in the war's aftermath and the darkest fears of Southern Whites—the rape of White women by sex-crazed Black men. One heroine leapt from a cliff to escape such a fate, and in the climactic scene, hooded and robed Klansmen rode to rescue actress Lillian Gish from the Black militia, the leader of which met the nightriders' vigilante justice.

The film opened in New York City in March 1915 and subsequently in all corners of the nation. Enthusiastic Whites flocked to theaters in the

South. Since Swainsboro still lacked a movie house, several dozen citizens traveled by train and auto to Augusta to see the movie, returning with rave reviews for their neighbors. Authorities in Northern and Western cities unsuccessfully tried to censor the film.

To stifle negative reactions, Dixon arranged a special screening for his former college classmate at Johns Hopkins, the Virginian who currently occupied the White House. Moved by the film, Woodrow Wilson reportedly declared, "It is like writing history with lightning." The endorsement of Edward White, Chief Justice of the Supreme Court and a former Klansman, also helped to deflect criticism.

Some patrons returned again and again. Within a few years the movie grossed $18 million. Some 3,000 persons, paying an unprecedented 50 cents to $1.50 each, attended the first showings in Swainsboro in May 1917, and many of them would see the film again when it returned in 1918, 1921, and 1927.

Not all citizens in Swainsboro enjoyed the movie. In 1917, when the court case dealing with children's right to patronize the local theater on school nights began, Judge R.N. Hardeman "severely excoriated some of the picture productions," according to the *Forest-Blade*. "He declared that the celebrated 'Birth of a Nation' was both pernicious and degrading and ought not to be shown anywhere."

The impending opening of the film in Atlanta, scheduled for early December 1914, provided William Simmons with his opportunity. On a night in late November, he founded the Invisible Empire of the Ku Klux Klan before a flaming cross on the summit of Stone Mountain, an enormous granite promontory north of Atlanta.

The middle-class White men who constituted its membership apparently considered the Klan no more than another fraternal organization, albeit one with a penchant for secrecy and an explicit ideology of "100 percent Americanism" and White supremacy. When the United States entered the European conflict in 1917, the Klan's various chapters appointed themselves guardians of the war effort, rooting out draft dodgers and countering the putatively nefarious deeds of aliens and labor agitators. By 1919, several thousand men had enlisted in the order.

The Klan's fortunes improved the following year, when Simmons struck a deal with two publicists who ensured newspaper coverage and embarked on a nationwide recruitment campaign. Dividing the country into regional sales districts, the publicists dispatched a horde of recruiters, their zeal sharpened by a pyramidal arrangement for distributing the resulting monies.

This ad for the first showing of "Birth of a Nation" in Swainsboro appeared in the Forest-Blade, May 4, 1917. Courtesy, Forest-Blade Publishing Co.

The response surpassed all expectations. For a one-time $10 initiation fee, plus an equal sum for costume and assorted symbols, a White Protestant male could join the ranks of a self-designated patriotic organization imbued with an aura of mystery and purportedly dedicated to the protection of American values. By 1923, more than 3 million belonged to

Klan chapters from Maine to California, from Detroit and Long Island to Tulsa and Miami.

The new recruits included many men who, like Waitus Scott, had migrated from the countryside to cities and towns, where they tried to bolster their uncertain status through membership in civic organizations. In the unsettled days following the economic collapse of 1920, many farmers scraped together enough cash for the initiation fee, finding solace by attributing their troubles to evil forces. For the most part, they were neither the wealthiest nor the poorest, but the men in the middle.

Wartime patriotism, a reaction to the massive immigration that had taken place before 1914, and fear of radicalism--culminating in the "Red Scare" of 1919 in the wake of the Bolshevik Revolution--set the stage for a nativist backlash. Aliens and alien ways were by definition un-American and therefore suspect.

In its self-arrogated role as protector of the American way of life, the Klan identified three enemy categories. Catholics topped the list. Protestant churches, especially the Methodist, the Baptist, and the Disciples of Christ, provided many of the recruits, and their ministers often conferred legitimacy by serving as Klan officers. These men equated Protestant precepts with "Americanism" and lent credence to wildly improbable tales of Papist conspiracies to subvert American civilization.

While strongest in the North, where most of the recent southern Mediterranean immigrants had settled, the Klan's anti-Catholicism also struck a chord in the South. In Georgia, former Populist leader Tom Watson's diatribes against the Vatican contributed to the impulse, which found expression in such incidents as the Klan's attempts to have all Catholic teachers dismissed from public schools in Atlanta.

Jews ranked second on the order's list of enemies. Blamed for the death of Christ and envied for their commercial success, Jews had long been held responsible for a variety of social ills. Many Americans still believed medieval fantasies of occult Jewish ceremonies involving the sacrifice of Christian children. Nonetheless, Jewish communities had existed in Savannah since the 18th century and in Atlanta since the 19th, and small numbers resided in rural communities where "Jewish store" was a synonym for a dry-goods emporium. Anti-Semitism had been rare as long as American Jews were few in number and eager to assimilate. The flood of Russian-Polish Jews in the late 19th century had ignited prejudice in Georgia and throughout the country.

Fueled by Tom Watson's vitriolic ravings, anti-Semitism reached its peak in 1913 during the trial of Leo Frank, the manager of a pencil factory in Atlanta, for the murder of one of his employees, 13-year-old Mary Phagan. As a Jew, a Northerner, and a representative of the disrupting impact of industrialization, Frank was an outsider—so much so that he was convicted on the testimony of a Black man, an unprecedented event in Georgia.

Leo Frank, victim of anti-Semitism, ca. 1913.

Governor John M. Slaton, persuaded of Frank's innocence after reviewing the evidence, commuted the death sentence to life imprisonment. Angry citizens demonstrated outside the governor's mansion, and Slaton left the state after surrendering his office. Two months later, a mob abducted Frank from the state prison farm in Milledgeville and hanged him from a tree outside Marietta. His murderers never stood trial. The Klan tapped the rich vein of anti-Semitism laid bare by the Frank case.

"Inferior" and "mongrel" races represented the order's third enemy. Local chapters abused Asians in California and Mexicans in Texas, and in Georgia the Klan ordered all Lebanese and Syrians to leave Marietta. In both the old slave sections of the South and the Northern cities to which Southern Blacks fled during the 1920s, the Klan's principal concern lay in keeping Blacks "in their place."

Yet for all its overt hostility toward Catholics, Jews, African Americans, and other "inferior" peoples, the order most often visited its displeasure on fellow Whites. Concealed beneath their pointed hoods, members used their anonymity to settle old scores or to enforce their own perverted form of Puritanism. Accused adulterers, wife-beaters, initiators of divorce actions, prostitutes, moonshiners, critics of the Klan, and anyone who committed the most trivial offense to local mores suffered flogging, tarring and feathering, or worse.

In Emanuel County, the editors of the *Forest-Blade* showed sympathy for the secret organization. In September 1921, when an exposé in the New York *World* touched off a national controversy by accusing Klan leaders of corruption and immorality, the Swainsboro newspaper rushed to the order's defense.

> The three "K's" are still coming in for a considerable share of notoriety. They are being attacked from fore and aft, but we are here to bet that nothing comes of the investigation, only a lot of free advertising, just exactly what the Clan is after getting. We know that man Simmons, and we know that he is not licked every day.

In 1923, when floggings reached epidemic proportions in Macon, the *Forest-Blade* publicized the $1,500 reward offered by senior Klan leader M.O. Dunning for the arrest and conviction of the guilty parties. The newspaper continued:

Ron Seckinger

He also states that the Klan is never guilty of any law-lessness and that he is determined to bring to justice all perpetrators of crime who are hiding behind the Klan, and that if a member of the Klan so far forgets himself, as to be guilty of such conduct he will be dealt with as he should be.

Another Klan official, Judge Thomas L. Hill of Atlanta, took the same line in an interview granted to the *Forest-Blade* during a tour of the state in November 1923. The idea that the Klan stands for flogging, he said, "is the vilest slander ever uttered against any organization on earth." Hill said that the Klan wasn't fighting against Catholics, Jews, and "colored people," but rather merely wanted to keep them separate from Whites. He claimed that Georgia had some 50,000 members in more than 200 chapters.

Emanuel County was home to one of those chapters. Some weeks after Hill's visit, the Emanuel County Ku Klux Klan donated $25 to a committee responsible for erecting a community Christmas tree in honor of Christ, "the Klansman's only criterion of character."

By 1924, the order had become a formidable political force throughout the country. It had helped to elect governors in Georgia, Alabama, California, and Oregon in 1922, and Texas had sent one of its members to the US Senate. Seventy-five Congressmen reputedly had the Klan's backing, and rumors prompted the Attorney General to deny that he and President Warren G. Harding belonged to the Klan. Hiram Evans, the dentist who had wrested control of the national organization from Simmons in 1922, moved his national headquarters to Washington, DC the following year. In Indiana, Grand Dragon D.C. Stephenson, whose independent Klan dominated state politics, dreamed of snaring the Republican nomination for President in 1928.

The Klan figured prominently in the 1924 Presidential contest. Oscar Underwood, an Alabamian who hoped to head the Democratic ticket, repeatedly denounced the order and made it an issue in the campaign. The

Forest-Blade called Underwood's position "one of the broadest blunders ever made by a politician." The newspaper continued: "We believe, as hundreds of thousands of others believe, that there is no purer, cleaner, nor an organization with higher ideals than the Ku Klux Klan." The editors chortled when Underwood's chief rival, William G. McAdoo—a Georgia-born politician from California who maintained a prudent silence on the subject of secret organizations—carried Emanuel County in the Democratic primary.

Underwood took the issue to the Democratic National Convention in New York City, where a bitter platform fight over whether to denounce the Klan by name badly split the party. The popular Republican standard-bearer, Calvin Coolidge, who like McAdoo said nothing about the Klan, scored an easy victory in November with 54 percent of the vote.

In early October 1924, the Emanuel County chapter petitioned the city council for permission to hold a public parade in Swainsboro on the night of November 11. The council members quickly voted to grant the petition, saying "that they didn't desire to be understood as opposing this request even in the remotest degree." The *Forest-Blade*, which urged one and all to attend the event, described the Klan's goal:

> It stands for the American home; for the protection of womanhood, and for the everlasting preservation of American ideas and institutions. It stands four square for Protestant Christianity regardless of denomination, and will fight to the last those influences that would undermine the foundations of our government, and destroy our civil and religious liberties.
>
> As the original Klan dissipated the cruel storm of the American reconstruction, the Klan of today, imbued with the same spirit, will drive back the wild eyed hordes that would wreck and ruin the greatest government ever conceived by mortal mind. As long as the nation is in

danger from these forces that would destroy, the Klan will live, and work, and fight.

On Tuesday evening, November 11, the festivities began at 6:30 with a parade from the fairgrounds up South Main Street, lined with hundreds of onlookers, to the courthouse square. At the front came two riders, clad in the peaked hoods and white robes familiar to those who had seen "Birth of a Nation," mounted on horses similarly draped in white. Behind came a Klan band, and then the marchers, each carrying a red flare. At the courthouse, the Klansmen solemnly mustered at the right of the speakers' platform as the Reverend R.M. Miller of the First Christian Church of Athens told the crowd that the order supported four principles–"Patriotism, White Supremacy, Protection of the Home and Womanhood, and the Protestant Christian Religion."

The Emanuel Klan, Chapter No. 184 in the Realm of Georgia, considered the event a smashing success and decided to make it an annual affair. In the fall of 1925 and 1926 the Klansmen of the surrounding counties gathered again in Swainsboro to parade and share a barbecue dinner.

The *Forest-Blade* reported no Klan-inspired violence in Emanuel. No Catholics resided in the county, and African Americans tended to rebel against violence and discrimination by fleeing to the North. Joe Ehrlich's daughter Frances recalled encountering no overt anti-Semitism. As in many small Southern towns, the few Jews in Swainsboro were seen as pillars of the community. The Ehrliches, Rosenbergs, and Subotnics, who owned department stores on the square and traveled to Savannah to worship, took care to stay on good terms with their Protestant neighbors. Men from these families attended services at all four Protestant churches and contributed to their offering plates. Although some Klansmen no doubt held them in contempt, no one in Swainsboro appears to have considered the Jewish families a threat to the established order.

Hoods and passwords didn't protect the identities of Klan members from their neighbors. Waitus Scott never spoke of his association, but his sister-in-law Alice Stroud noted that he disappeared whenever the Klansmen turned out in their finery. During one parade, Jessie Fields recognized a ring on the hand of a marcher and realized that his costume concealed the face of her husband Duncan. Many of the most prominent men in town belonged to the order. Will McMillan, Jr., about nine years old at the time, recognized the voices of a judge and several other community leaders as the parade passed.

Klansmen stage a massive parade down Pennsylvania Avenue in Washington, D.C., 1925. Courtesy, Library of Congress.

Having won substantial prestige in the 1924 elections, the order staged an impressive parade in Washington the following year. Thousands of robed Klansmen--mostly from Pennsylvania, Ohio, New York, and New England, but including delegations from the South and West--marched through the streets and later gathered to hear speeches at the outdoor Sylvan Theater on the Mall near the Washington Monument.

Yet the Klan's star waned quickly. Postwar fears of radicalism, Catholicism, alien conspiracies, and Black militancy faded. Unseemly squabbles among Klan leaders over power and money received wide publicity, and a court case between the national organization and a group of secessionist chapters in western Pennsylvania exposed a sordid record of chicanery, malfeasance, and unrestrained violence. Many of the solid citizens who had joined when the Klan appeared to be a status-conferring fraternal order now turned away in disgust.

In Emanuel County, violence cost the Klan the support of the *Forest-Blade* and much of the populace. On a Friday night in February 1927, four hooded men intercepted Horace M. Flanders, editor of the Soperton *News* in neighboring Treutlen County, as he returned from a business trip to Swainsboro. The men beat him into unconsciousness.

Flanders had worked for the *Forest-Blade* until his purchase of the *News* in 1918, and his friends and fellow editors at the Swainsboro newspaper termed the incident "a heinous, infamous and diabolical crime" and "One of the most damnable and brutish outrages ever perpetuated in any supposedly civilized country." They attributed the attack to retaliation for a recent *News* editorial in which Flanders had denounced lawlessness in general and bootleggers and vigilantes in particular:

> Right at our doors it has been a custom for several
> months for bands of hooded outlaws to go out, and with
> no regard for life or limb, whip, beat and sometimes kill
> men and women for the sake of vengeance. Who is safe
> with this ever-increasing practice within our bounds?
> And just why are these things happening? It is because
> the law abiding people have let a set of hell-born villains
> parade the country under the cover of darkness and
> with their faces hidden behind masks, and do as they
> please, when they please. This is a practice that should
> be curbed or we are doomed to worse things. In the end
> it will cause a revolution if not stopped.

Flanders had gone on to criticize jurors for refusing to convict such rabble and judges for suspending sentences.

Neither Flanders nor the *Forest-Blade* openly blamed the Ku Klux Klan for the affair. But only the most obtuse reader could have missed the barely veiled references in Flanders's subsequent account of his flogging at the hands of the "hooded gang": "Little did these brutes who assailed me, assaulted me and left me insensible, realize that their folly would hasten the end of the reign of their clan and kind."

The Emanuel County sheriff soon arrested five men, including the sheriff of Truetlen County, for the crime. When the first to stand trial received a sentence of five years in the state prison, the *Forest-Blade* asserted its pride in the citizens of Treutlen.

By June, the editors of the Swainsboro newspaper had had their fill of the seemingly uncontrollable practice of flogging. Admitting their previous denials of the order's responsibility for such behavior, they now acknowledged evidence that the men who recently had participated in a wave of beatings in Toccoa, Georgia had worn Klan regalia. As a result, the *Forest-Blade* for the first time distanced itself from the secret order, now so mercenary that "almost any man able to pay the fees can become a member."

Two months later, the *Forest-Blade* celebrated the conviction of floggers in Alabama and again spoke out against the Klan:

> Members of the Ku Klux have no more right to admin-
> ister floggings to parties for crimes, either real or fan-
> cied, than does any other citizen; neither does belonging
> to the Klan excuse them of the fact that they are lower
> down than the very lowest scum of the earth. Hell
> itself is too good for parties who will commit crimes of
> this kind.

The Emanuel chapter held no parade in 1927 or in the years there-after. Attitudes toward the organization had changed so markedly that the

Ron Seckinger

Forest-Blade in January 1928 published a satirical column suggesting form letters for use by ill-educated members of the Georgia and Alabama Klans:

> Dear Bill,
>
> Yore actions ain't a suiting u. So, turn frome your wiked ways and bewore! Leather strops are plentiful and we don't mean mebbe.
>
> Sincerely,
> Cross Bones

> Mrs. Susie Ann,
>
> You have not went to church for 2 months. We have our eyes on you. We don't need folks in this here community that don't serve the Lord, so get right, and tell your daughter, Jenny, to do likewise, or take the consequences.
>
> Respectively yours,
> Vigi Lantees

By 1928, the Klan's national membership had fallen from its peak of 3 million to a few hundred thousand. The *Forest-Blade* noted approvingly that no lynchings had taken place in Georgia during 1927 and only 16 in the entire country. Those Klaverns that survived during the Great Depression functioned more as social organizations than vigilante gangs.

The order would reemerge in 1946—again at Stone Mountain—in response to growing African American demands for equality and an end to racial discrimination.

COURTSHIP

AFTER A DAY of hammering at metal plates in the belly of a locomotive, Emmit Stroud trudged home to a room in Nellie Stringer's boarding house in Somerset. He wasn't a handsome man. About five feet six, he had brown hair and blue eyes, a round face, and a slight build. He dressed neatly but with no pretensions, and he never went outdoors without a wool cap or felt hat.

As he looked down from the window of his second-floor room one day, the 29-year-old boilermaker spotted a young woman--a girl, really-- in the neighboring yard. Each day he watched as she played with her fox terrier. Although he knew she helped out in the kitchen of the boarding house, he had no way to make her acquaintance until one Sunday when he returned home after the evening meal. Mrs. Stringer told the girl to serve Emmit a plate of leftovers, and the two came face to face for the first time. Afterwards, Emmit took care to say hello and chat at every opportunity.

The object of his scrutiny was Frances Winwood Bell, a 15-year-old with long brown hair and glasses who lived next door with her mother and grandmother. Frances's grandparents had settled in Somerset about 1880. George Winwood Harrison, a former coal miner from Ohio turned bookkeeper and surveyor, laid out the route of the original Cincinnati-to-Chattanooga railroad and subsequently operated one of the line's coal chutes. Along the way, he acquired a wife, Bertha Frances Harrison, a

German immigrant who'd arrived in the United States in 1854, at the age of seven. The family lived in Illinois and Tennessee during the 1870s before moving to Kentucky.

Bertha Harrison in front of her house on South Main Street in Somerset, Kentucky, ca. 1910.

The youngest of their six children, named Bertha after her mother, married another Ohioan named George Sherman Bell after the turn of the century and moved to Ohio with him. Frances, an only child, was born in Minerva, just south of Cleveland, in June 1907.

Ten years later, Bertha Bell left her husband and, with Frances, returned to Somerset to live with her mother, now widowed and occupying a large house on South Main Street. Frances saw her father only once more. He came to visit, but she sided with her mother and made him feel unwelcome. He died in late 1923, the same year Frances met Emmit Stroud.

A few weeks after their first conversation, Emmit asked Frances to the movies on a Saturday night. Bertha Bell consented, provided someone else went along. Frances persuaded Marie Stringer, the landlady's daughter, to accompany them to the Virginia Theater as chaperone, and Emmit brought Ray Chadwick, another shopman who boarded with the Stringers.

The following afternoon, a beautiful Sunday in April not long after Easter, the four set out on an excursion to Crystal Park. It lay in a hollow about half a mile west of the town square. A spring issued from a limestone cave, and the locals came to picnic on the grass or to sit on the rocks and talk. Emmit and Frances chatted for hours and posed for a photograph, the respectable working man in his cloth cap and the sheltered teenager in her new hat.

Frances Bell and Emmit Stroud at Crystal Park in Somerset, April 1923.

Despite the 14-year difference in their ages, Frances took to Emmit, whom she found interesting and kind. By the summer they had become sweethearts. Because her mother allowed no outings during the week and church claimed Sunday evenings, their dates were confined to Friday and Saturday nights. Usually, they took in a movie and then went to Tony Benelli's ice cream parlor.

On Sundays, Emmit called on Frances's grandmother, who frowned on the romance because of the difference in ages. His deference, sobriety, and gentleness won him points with Frances's mother as well as her uncle and aunt, Clarence and Artie Harrison.

The imposing matriarch, however, proved a tough adversary. Strong-willed and rigid, Bertha Harrison thoroughly dominated her daughter and did her best to control everyone in her circle. Although Frances became the ward of her Uncle Clarence after her mother's death in January 1924, she remained in her grandmother's home. Emmit would have to win over the old lady if he was to marry his sweetheart.

Bertha Harrison set strict limits on the courtship. When Emmit bought an old Model T Ford in 1924, the matriarch forbade Frances to ride in the vehicle. Indeed, she insisted that Emmit park it in an empty field beside her home so she could see from the dining room--her favorite spot in the house, where she sewed, read, or just held court--that her grand-daughter was not gallivanting around in that infernal machine. Emmit and Frances knew better than to challenge her directly, so they put up with the restrictions and walked everywhere, even when they visited Clarence and Artie on the south side of town near the depot.

Only once, with Clarence's encouragement, did they defy Bertha's edict. Preparing to take several neighborhood children to hunt for hickory nuts, Frances's uncle told the two sweethearts to go in Emmit's Ford. When Bertha came out to get into Clarence's vehicle, she spied the Ford passing and said, "That looked like Stroud and Frances in that car!"

Clarence kept his peace and allowed his mother to grouse for the entire trip without pointing out that Emmit and Frances followed behind them. As Bertha descended from the auto on reaching their destination, she was startled to see granddaughter and suitor stroll past.

Hearing her sputtering complaint, Frances muttered, "Uh oh!"

Emmit laughed. "Yeah, we're getting the devil now!"

Frances had absorbed many of her grandmother's Victorian ideas. Modest to the point of prudishness, Frances didn't approve of women in trousers or with exposed arms. She once wore a new bathing suit--a black outfit that covered her arms to the elbow and legs to the knees, with flounces at the hips--on a Sunday school picnic to Burnside on the Cumberland River. Embarrassed, she never wore another swimsuit. Her preferred clothing ran to long-sleeved and -hemmed dresses with black stockings and high-buttoned shoes, and her sense of rectitude extended to all areas of life. She expected conformity with established principles of behavior and held in contempt those who failed to meet her exacting standards.

Emmit occasionally broached the subject of marriage but always with the proviso that he first had to finish paying for the farm his father had worked in Fitzgerald. In the fall of 1924, Emmit arrived at the boarding house on a Friday night with a big grin. "Guess what?" he said to Frances. "I paid off the farm today!"

Actually, it was more complicated than that. In October 1923, Emmit had loaned $600 to his father's widow, Sudie Scott Stroud, so she could purchase the farm, which covered 140 acres. She had agreed to retire the note, at 8 percent interest, in one year and also assumed liability for a $1,500 lien on the property incurred by the seller. Apparently, Emmit took the lien himself, and it probably was the final payment on this obligation that he celebrated in the fall of 1924. Sudie Stroud proved unable to repay the $600 within one year, and Emmit, acting as her attorney in fact, would put the farm up for auction in February 1926. He and his brothers Denver and Kermit offered the top bid of $200, payable to their father's widow, and the deed passed to their hands for a total outlay of $2,300.

Emmit now felt free to take on the responsibility of a wife. That same Friday night in October 1924, he and Frances celebrated with double-dip ice creams at Benelli's and began making plans for a wedding the following summer. Suddenly impatient, Emmit persuaded Frances to drop out of high school and marry him immediately. They set the date for late November.

A few weeks before the wedding, the ban on their sharing an auto was lifted. As the two prepared to leave Bertha's one night in search of an apartment for rent, Frances appealed to her Uncle Clarence: "Can we take his car? It's cold out there."

"What do you mean, can you take his car?" replied Clarence, feigning ignorance of Bertha's rule. "You mean you've been walking everywhere?"

They rode together that night, and Bertha never said another word about Emmit's Ford. For years afterward they joked about her grandmother's obsession. Every time they left home, one asked the other, "Well, can we take the car, or are we going to have to walk?"

After 18 months of courtship, Emmit finally won his bride, with Bertha Harrison's grudging blessing. On Saturday afternoon, November 22, Frances's parson married them in his home in the presence of a few friends and relatives.

During the shopmen's annual two-week Christmas vacation--without pay--Emmit took Frances to Florida, using his railroad passes. They visited Jacksonville and St. Augustine, strolling along the beaches and seeing the sights. Emmit bought his wife a souvenir wooden box lined with velvet and covered with shells, with four tiny shells as feet. Frances treasured the memento of her honeymoon and felt terrible when someone stole it years later.

The newlyweds returned to their small, second-floor apartment on Hawkins Avenue on the north side of Somerset. It came fully furnished. Emmit believed, as he would for most of his life, that renting other people's furniture made more sense than spending money on his own.

Frances wasn't going to work outside the home, of course. As a railroad man, Emmit made good money. He expected his wife to keep house and take care of any children who came along. How else should God-fearing people live?

MOTOR CITY

LADIES' MAN, his sisters called him. Handsome and dynamic, Denver Stroud had a way with women. They stirred in his wake, responding to his smile, flashing brown eyes, and dark brown hair slicked back with pomade. With broad shoulders and a muscular build, he stood just under five feet six inches and weighed 135 pounds when he returned from the war in his sailor's uniform.

The girl who won his heart was 15-year-old Bernice Register, whom he married in September 1922 in Fitzgerald. The couple lived for a few months in Somerset, Kentucky, where Denver's older brother Emmit visited their apartment.

After Jim Stroud's death in 1923, Denver took his wife and younger sister Maude to Detroit, lured by the prospect of a job in auto manufacturing. Like the Hooks family in Chicago, the Strouds found the crowded tenements and streets as strange as a foreign country. Nine-year-old Maude wrote her sisters Margie and Alice with some astonishment that Black and White children attended school together.

In heading north Denver participated in a great exodus. Between 1910 and 1960 some 9 million Southerners, almost evenly divided between Whites and African Americans, abandoned their homelands for new opportunities in other regions. The outbreak of the Great War severed the flow of European immigrants, and Northern industrialists looked to domestic laborers to take up the slack.

Bernice Register and Denver Stroud, 1922.

As Southern families lost their farms or were evicted from tenant lands, a process hastened by crises such as the collapse of 1920 and the Great Depression, many seized the opportunity for factory work--if not in Atlanta, Birmingham, or Richmond, then in Pennsylvania, New York, Ohio, Illinois, or Michigan.

In Southern cities, these newcomers displaced Black artisans and factory hands, who had little choice but to head north. Escaping the oppressive racial regime of the South added to their incentive, and recruiting agents facilitated the process. Northern employers often provided railroad passes for prospective workers. Some 400,000 Blacks fled the South during 1916-1918 alone, and by 1920 the number had surpassed 1 million.

Detroit, one of the principal destinations, lay on the Detroit River between Lake Erie and Lake St. Clair. It had grown during the last three quarters of the 19th century from a fur-trading outpost to a major manufacturing center as entrepreneurs exploited the local fishing grounds, timber stands, and iron and copper deposits. Thanks to the talent of local automobile designers and builders, the city by 1910 had become the center of auto production, leaving behind rival manufacturers in cities such as Springfield, Massachusetts; Indianapolis, Indiana; and Rochester, New York.

Henry Ford, 1919. Courtesy, Library of Congress.

By the 1920s, Detroit ranked third, behind New York and Chicago, among American cities in generating wealth and had become one of the most important destinations for Southerners in search of a better life.

In January 1924, the *Forest-Blade* noted the departure of three young Swainsboro men for Detroit with the expectation of working for Henry Ford, a pilgrimage common throughout the South.

Ford, arguably the person who had the greatest impact on American society in the 20th century, played a key role in transforming Detroit into Motor City. A Michigan farm boy turned mechanic, he participated in the feverish tinkering that changed the horseless carriage from a novelty into a practical means of transportation. His technical savvy won him financial backing, and with the founding of the Ford Motor Company in 1902 the brash 37-year-old embarked on a success story seldom equaled. His Model A, introduced the following year, sold as fast as units rolled out the factory door. By September 1907 the company had marketed more than 8.000 cars and was earning an annual profit of $1 million.

Denver, Bernice, and Lillian Stroud, Detroit, ca. 1924.

But Ford's drive to improve his product left little time for self-satisfaction. While most automakers concentrated on luxury models for the well-heeled, he set out to design and produce an inexpensive auto for the masses. Ford personally took part in most of the engineering decisions--advances such as the introduction of vanadium steel, the one-piece cylinder block, and the insulated magneto, as well as the reversion to the planetary transmission--that made possible the realization of his vision. The public responded immediately and overwhelmingly to the Model T, first marketed in 1908, despite its hefty price of $825.

Other innovations soon brought Henry Ford's machine within the reach of even larger numbers. The company's use of standardized, inter-changeable parts lowered production and service costs, and a fundamental change in production methods trimmed expenses further while revolution-izing manufacturing. Although all of the elements of the moving assembly line predated the automobile industry, the Ford Motor Company first put them together in a coherent, efficient manner.

Introduced in 1913, the "line" brought chassis past the workers, each of whom repeated certain standardized tasks. As engineers improved and speeded up the process, the time required to assemble a chassis fell from 12 and a half hours to just 93 minutes, allowing the company to increase production while saving substantially on labor costs. Ford's Highland Park plant, which turned out 160,000 Model Ts during the 1912-1913 produc-tion year, almost doubled its output the following year while reducing the labor force by 10 percent.

In 1916, the Model T cost only $345, making it truly a vehicle for the multitudes, as Henry Ford had intended. In 1925, the price of a run-about, the cheapest version, had fallen to $260, F.O.B. Detroit. As of 1918 the Model T accounted for almost half of the cars in the entire world. By the time changing public attitudes forced the company to introduce new models 10 years later, Ford had produced 15 million Model Ts.

Simple, sturdy, and reliable, the car was a godsend for rural America. Although farmers in the 1890s had resisted the intrusion of the automo-bile--which frightened horses, damaged roads, and symbolized the more comfortable lifestyle of the well-to-do--its advantages eventually became apparent. Moreover, the relatively low price of the Model T, fondly known as a "flivver" or "Tin Lizzie," further eroded hostility.

Duncan Fields and farmers throughout the country recognized a good deal when they saw one. A man could jack up his Model T, attach a belt to the rear axle, and obtain power to operate a small sawmill or other farm machine. He also could use the vehicle to haul produce to town and supplies back to his home, for the Tin Lizzie proved a match for pitted, marshy country roads. By making some chores easier and sharply reducing transportation time, it allowed farm families more leisure for social occasions in town, church, or neighbors' homes.

A Model T pulls a thresher, ca. 1910-1920. Courtesy, Henry Ford Museum.

At the turn of the century, traveling photographers usually posed subjects in front of their houses, but by the 1920s people preferred to use their most prized possession, the family car, for background.

Although Denver Stroud apparently never worked for the Ford Motor Company—and indeed, which manufacturer employed him is unknown—Henry Ford had much to do with the conditions of life in Detroit. The efficiencies of production that made the automobile accessible to all came at a significant cost to the workers. Ford's perfection of the moving assembly line, copied by other car makers, radically altered the nature of industrial labor. Work became routine and required less skill. As a result, the worker lost his artisan status and became a cog in a giant machine. Moreover, the emphasis on cutting unit costs prompted management to speed up the line, forcing laborers to operate at an increasingly rapid pace. Thus emerged the key problems of modern industrial production--loss of job satisfaction, shoddy workmanship, and high rates of absenteeism and worker turnover.

Ford appeared the champion of the working man when he announced the Five-Dollar Day early in January 1914. The new scale, aimed at securing a more stable labor force, doubled standard wages, and it came with an eight- rather than nine-hour day. The announcement warranted banner headlines in newspapers across the country, and the reaction was electric. Overlooking the fine print—a profit-sharing bonus for which workers became eligible after six months constituted half of the new wage scale— thousands of laborers flocked to the gates of Ford's Highland Park factory.

Within days the company had selected enough applicants for all three shifts and ceased hiring. On January 10, some 10,000 frustrated jobseekers waiting in nine-degree weather became unruly. Plant guards sprayed them with a high-pressure water hose. Covered with ice, the unfortunates scattered, no longer encumbered with illusions about Henry Ford's concern for the common man.

Even those who obtained the cherished workers' badges found employment for the Ford Motor Company far from idyllic. They were subjected to humiliating physical examinations and a paternalistic regime. Handbooks instructed employees to devote the profit-sharing portion of their wages to investment and to improving their lifestyles. Inspectors from the company's Sociological Department intruded in the personal lives of the workers to ensure their fealty to Henry Ford's idiosyncratic vision of appropriate behavior. Employees who failed to maintain acceptable standards of lodging and hygiene, and those who sought solace in the embrace of a saloon or a public woman, might find themselves jobless.

The other auto companies had less interest in their laborers' activities outside the workplace, but otherwise their approach to labor differed little from Ford's. In addition to speed-ups on the assembly line, they used piecework pay scales for the manufacture of parts to exact maximum production at minimum expense. Other techniques for trimming labor costs included hiring women for lower pay--despite Michigan law forbidding gender discrimination in wage scales--and replacing senior workers with young men. The companies did little to check the abuses of foremen, who often extorted favors or kickbacks.

Notwithstanding a long list of grievances, labor organization made scant progress in Detroit. The older craft unions lost their power with the introduction of the assembly line and the consequent move to unskilled workers. "Open-shop" laws hampered unionization, as did the employers' use of blacklists and strikebreakers. Thousands of farmers, European immigrants, and Southerners considered themselves lucky to win a place with one of the auto companies and hesitated to risk their jobs. Strikes were infrequent and rarely succeeded. The formation of the United Auto Workers didn't come until the late 1930s.

The Strouds had ample opportunities for amusement when work schedules and weather permitted. Detroit boasted a number of fine parks, including Belle Isle, an island playground designed by Frederick Law Olmsted, the creator of New York City's Central Park. During the winter, they could try out the skating pond in Highland Park, next to the Ford plant. From spring until fall, Denver could take in games at Navin Field, where Ty Cobb managed the Tigers until leaving to join the Philadelphia Athletics in 1927. The city's movie palaces beckoned as well, especially to Maude, who found Hollywood fantasies more entrancing than school and daily life.

Like many others in Detroit, they suffered from a critical housing shortage. The population had exploded from some 285,000 in 1900 to nearly 1 million in 1920 and would exceed 1.5 million by 1930. In 1919, the city government estimated the shortage in dwellings at more than 30,000, and a construction boom during the 1920s didn't keep pace with the swelling population. Between 1924 and 1930, the Stroud family—including daughter Lillian, born in Detroit in May 1924—lived in at least seven different residences. They moved from Fourth Avenue to Trumbull to Twelfth to Hobart to Holden to Trumbull again to Lee Place. Their homes almost certainly were old, decaying buildings or squalid, overcrowded tenements in filthy working-class neighborhoods.

With the onset of the Great Depression, jobs became scarce and life more precarious. Denver would have little choice but to search for employment in another locale.

BARBERSHOP

A FRUGAL HOMEBODY, Waitus Scott squirreled away his money. In December 1924, he had enough to purchase the barbershop where he worked on the courthouse square in Swainsboro. Now an independent merchant rather than an employee, he renamed the establishment Scott's Barber Shop. He ceded the first chair to one of the younger men who had no regular clientele and took the last chair for himself.

Usually dressed in black pants and a white shirt with a black bow tie, Waitus opened the shop at 8:00 six days a week and worked until the last customer departed. On Saturdays, when Swainsboro overflowed with farmers, he often didn't lock up before 11:00 at night.

The shop was narrow, 10 feet wide and 50 feet deep, with ceiling fans and bare light bulbs suspended from above. Four barber's chairs lined the right wall. Waiting clients could use the few extra seats in the rear.

Except for Saturdays, the pace was slow. The barbers usually had plenty of time to sit in their chairs and gossip with friends who dropped in to pass the time and periodically launch mouthfuls of tobacco juice in the direction of a spittoon. Waitus managed to read the Savannah *Morning News* each day in the intervals between customers. Sometimes he hired an African American handyman to sweep up the piles of hair, obtain a Mason jar of hooch for the back room, and run other errands.

Waitus Scott stands at the first chair in Kimberly's Barber Shop, ca. 1923. He bought the shop in 1924 and moved to the rear chair.

When a customer requested a 25-cent haircut, Waitus put a paper neck strip around the man's Adam's apple, popped the white apron that protected the client's clothing, and fastened it in place. Electric clippers hummed and scissors clicked quietly as swaths of hair wafted to the floor. Done, the barber chose one of the various bottles adorning the shelf behind his chair—Slikum Hair Dressing, Mahdeen Tonic, Newbo's Herpicide, or Wildroot Quinine Bouquet—splashed some onto his hands and worked it into the customer's hair. If he couldn't persuade the client to try a cooling head massage with Osage Rub, he finished with a careful combing.

If someone wanted a 15-cent shave, Waitus pumped the man's chair to a horizontal position and covered his face with a steamed towel. The client could hear the rasp of steel against whetstone and then the *wisk! wisk! wisk!* of straight razor against leather strop. Using a fine-haired brush to whip up lather in a ceramic cup, the barber removed the towel, applied a generous portion to the client's face, and scraped away the tough beard,

Ron Seckinger

wiping the foam on a shaving paper balanced on his arm. At the same time, he carried on an animated conversation with the client. Afterwards he anointed the smooth-shaven face with bay rum, Tiber Rub, Lilac or rose water, or perhaps Budda Oriental Odor Face Powder.

As Waitus performed this ritual one day, an oscillating fan blew the shaving paper into the air. Lunging for it with his left hand, he struck the razor in his right hand and sliced his thumb to the bone. A doctor closed the wound with eight stitches, and the barber soon returned to work.

Waitus walked home for lunch each day and, if business permitted, took a nap afterwards. In the evenings, he returned home straightaway, bringing candy for Ellie and his sisters-in-law. Alice had joined the household in 1923 and Maude in 1926, having abandoned Detroit because she fell out with Denver's wife Bernice.

Waitus socialized with men through the daylight hours and had no inclination to spend the nights at card tables or other masculine pursuits. He smoked Camels and liked a nip of liquor as well as the next man, but he was no drunk. At home, he puttered in the yard and tended his vegetable garden and beehives. As extra pounds accumulated on his large frame, he came to resemble a great bear. Almost always in a good mood, he loved to tease his family and anyone else who came near.

Storms terrified Waitus. If a big one began to blow up at night, he'd bundle the entire household into his car and drive to the barbershop, where he felt safer. Wrapping Ellie in a blanket to sleep in the floor, the adults would sit in the barber's chairs and talk, frequently dozing off as the thunder and lightning subsided. At first light, they'd hurry home through deserted streets, and Waitus would return to the shop at the usual opening hour.

From late April to late August, Waitus and other Swainsboro merchants closed their stores at midday each Thursday and took the afternoon off. Waitus would buy a mess of mullet and load the family into his car for the five-mile ride to Duncan Fields' farm near Blun. Ellie played with his cousins while the grown-ups chatted on the porch and Rosa fried the fish. Margie took old copies of the *Saturday Evening Post* to Jessie and helped out at hog-killings and harvest time, picking cotton with the rest of them.

Waitus and Ellie Scott, probably at McKinney's Pond, ca. 1930.

On Sundays, Waitus often took Margie and Ellie for a ride in his Ford, raising clouds of dust that settled behind them on trees and fence posts as they sped along the country roads. In the spring and early summer, blossoms greeted them everywhere. Dogwood, redbud, honeysuckle, and flowering plums, peaches, and crabapples grew wild, and the yards in front of farmhouses boasted phlox, thrift, verbena, flowering quince, weeping forsythia, and morning glories.

Doting on his only child, Waitus took Ellie on excursions to McKinney's Pond and Coleman Lake. Even before the boy reached legal age, Waitus let him drive the Ford on dusty back roads. Proud of his son, Waitus smiled as the boy hunched forward to see over the dashboard and sped through a benevolent universe.

OKEECHOBEE

LIKE HIS OLDER brother Fred, Delma Hooks flirted with a career in baseball. He started playing for one of the Swainsboro teams as a sixth grader. He continued through high school and at the Citizens' Military Training Camp at Camp McClellan, Alabama, in the summer of 1924.

Although he stood five-feet-five and weighed just over 100 pounds, his speed, fielding skills, and ability to get on base caught the attention of a scout for the Atlanta Crackers, a Triple-A team. Returning from Camp McClellan by train, Delma and J.D. McLeod were called off the coach in Atlanta and offered contracts, but neither would sign without consulting his father. John Hooks wouldn't countenance baseball on Sundays, and Delma, a dutiful son, passed up the opportunity. He continued playing on amateur and semi-professional teams, over the years taking the field on diamonds throughout Georgia, Alabama, the Carolinas, Florida, and Cuba.

Nearing his 19th birthday in 1925, Delma decided to chase his fortune farther south. A cousin who worked for a roofing company in Florida turned up in Hooks Crossing, and Delma proposed to return with him. His mother reluctantly agreed but insisted Delma's brother Mendel go along. Other locals threw in, and on July 1, seven young men, wearing ties and their only suits, set out in an old Chevrolet with no top. Before they had traveled three miles beyond Swainsboro, a passing Buick hit a puddle and sprayed them with muddy rainwater. They found a vacant house where they stripped and washed their sodden clothes before continuing the journey.

Henry Flagler's Florida East Coast Railway extended to Key West in 1912. Courtesy, State Archives of Florida.

Henry Flagler, who with John D. Rockefeller founded Standard Oil, made Florida a destination. When Flagler first visited the state during the winter of 1876-1877, it had only 250,000 inhabitants and was the most backward of the 38 states then in the union. In the mid-1880s, the multi-millionaire decided to invest some of his considerable fortune in developing the region. He built two luxury resort hotels in St. Augustine and then turned his attention to railroads. By 1896, his Florida East Coast Railway had snaked down the Atlantic coast to Miami, hardly more than a village, and in 1912 it reached Key West. Flagler's railroad made possible the settling of the area and the large-scale production of citrus fruits and winter vegetables for Northern markets.

Other entrepreneurs followed. The construction of a bridge from the mainland to Miami Beach in 1913 and the erection of resort hotels there established the Biscayne Bay area—along with Palm Beach, which Flagler developed—as the playground of the nation's well-to-do. Paradise also

Ron Seckinger

attracted the middle and lower classes, thousands of them pouring from railroad coaches and cheap autos in search of the proverbial pot of gold.

In 1906, Governor Napoleon Bonaparte Broward, far right on second row, led a drainage tour of the Everglades. Courtesy, State Archives of Florida.

Many of them sought it by speculating in urban and suburban lots in the early 1920s. The City of Coral Gables, built by George Merrick on 10,000 acres to the southeast of Miami Beach, was the most famous of the new developments, using Spanish architecture and street names to capitalize on the exotic setting. At the Venetian Pool, William Jennings Bryan earned a $50,000 annual salary by singing the praises of southern Florida. Irving Berlin and George S. Kaufman exploited this fevered ambience for their play, "The Cocoanuts," which featured the Marx Brothers and opened on Broadway in 1925, just as the South Florida bubble had reached the point of bursting. The movie followed four years later.

Another kind of land boom occurred to the north and east of Florida's Gold Coast. After his election in 1904, Governor Napoleon Bonaparte Broward—former steamboat captain, county sheriff, and gunrunner to Cuban rebels, a man as flamboyant as his name—proposed digging a series of canals from the Atlantic to Lake Okeechobee, already linked to the Gulf of Mexico by the Caloosahatchee River and Canal. The project, Broward claimed, would not only provide a passage linking the Atlantic with the Gulf of Mexico but also, by draining the Everglades, open the swampy lands of South Central Florida to settlement and cultivation.

Approved by the state legislature, Broward's scheme spawned a host of swindles. Investors frequently arrived to find their property under water, giving rise to the expression "buying land by the gallon rather than by the acre." The canals, along with the extension of the Florida East Coast Railway in 1915 to the town of Okeechobee on the north shore of the lake, facilitated the arrival of settlers and furnished an outlet for local products.

Lake Okeechobee, the Seminole word for "big water," dominated the region. Covering 730 square miles, in the United States it's second only to Lake Michigan in size. Since the 1880s, paddle-steamers had plied its surface, delivering mail and moving passengers and goods. Fishermen each day ventured from camps along the shore to gather prodigious catches with seines. In the decade following 1915, catfish alone earned an estimated $1 million annually.

Lightly touching the lake on its eastern and western shores, the Everglades extended southward like a long, flowing beard. The soil of these swampy lowlands, barely above sea level, consisted of wet, black muck that, like peat, burned for days if ignited by fire or lightning. Tall, sharp-bladed sawgrass gave the impression of a gently undulating sea of grass. Tangled hummocks and occasional stands of pine, cypress, and palmetto stood out like islands.

The 'Glades teemed with wildlife. The locals generally left the wild-cats and panthers alone and killed deer, bears, and turkeys only for food. Animals of commercial value--otters, raccoons, alligators, and American crocodiles--fell prey to professional hunters. Most prized were the egrets that furnished plumage for fashionable women's hats. By indiscriminately killing off the flamingos, great white herons, and roseate spoonbills, the hunters eventually deprived themselves of a livelihood, and many turned to fishing.

Settlers from the South and Midwest began farming both the saw-grass muck revealed by the draining of the upper Everglades and the rich soil formerly covered by custard apple trees to the east of the lake. To the north and west lay sandy plains dotted with palmettos and pines where cat-tlemen tended their herds, as well as hardwood forests exploited by loggers. By the 1920s sugar cane and winter vegetables claimed substantial acreage. Migrant labor camps mushroomed on the edges of the fields, inhabited by Blacks from the Bahamas and, particularly during the winter, by Georgia and Alabama sharecroppers who welcomed the off-season work.

The seven Emanuel County youths arrived in Ft. Lauderdale on Sunday, July 4, in the heat of noon. Delma struck up a conversation with a man who promptly offered to hire all of them to help build the first high school in the city. The next day he handed out shovels and asked them to move a huge pile of rocks. By the end of the week Mendel and four others had quit, calculating that $4 a day undervalued heavy labor under the Florida sun. After another week, the sixth of the recent émigrés from Georgia followed suit, leaving only Delma, the puniest of the lot.

The labor foreman, an Irishman named Billy Baker, said, "Well, I thought you'd be the first one to leave here, you're so small."

"No," replied Delma, "I didn't come here to quit."

Within months, Baker had put him in charge of assembling and dis-mantling scaffolding around the buildings, and his salary had risen to $1 an hour. But another opportunity beckoned.

In November, his brother Audie persuaded Delma to work with him at a restaurant in Canal Point, a small settlement in Palm Beach County on the southeastern shore of Lake Okeechobee. Delma set out at night in his old Dort auto and, passing Twelve Mile Bend, the halfway point on the Palm Beach Canal, innocently drove under a wooden arch onto a well-graded road. Within minutes, a motorcycle policeman pulled him over for entering the Conners Highway without paying the required toll.

The builder of the private toll road, W.J. Conners, was a self-made millionaire from Buffalo, a former stevedore who'd earned a fortune in shipping on the Great Lakes. Newspaper readers unknowingly laughed at him each week as they perused a comic strip called "Bringing Up Father." Its creator, George McManus, had courted the millionaire's daughter in Buffalo, but Conners's socially conscious wife had squelched the romance. McManus got his revenge by portraying his ex-sweetheart's mother as the ill-tempered Maggie, and Conners as the hen-pecked dandy, Jiggs.

Having no access to the 12,000 acres he owned along the eastern and northern shores of the lake, Conners won the state legislature's blessing for the construction of a toll road from Twenty Mile Bend through Canal Point to the town of Okeechobee on the north shore of the lake. Some 2,000 cars made the journey from Palm Beach to Canal Point for the official opening-day festivities on July 4, 1924, when a crowd of some 15,000 heard a succession of orators liken Conners to Henry Flagler and make outrageous predictions that Okeechobee would become the "Chicago of the South."

After the completion in November of the last stretch, which linked Tampa to the east coast, boosters estimated that 400 automobiles would pass through Canal Point each day. The complex toll schedule charged four cents per mile for an auto seating two or more persons, plus one cent per mile for each additional passenger; four cents per mile per ton for a rubber-tired power truck with driver; one cent per mile for a pedestrian, bicyclist, or one-horse vehicle; and two cents per mile for each domestic animal.

The Conners Highway literally put Canal Point on the map. In November 1924, the *Everglades News* reported that Rand McNally and Company of Chicago, the country's leading map publisher, planned to show both the town and the toll road on its latest issue.

After paying up, Delma continued his journey to Canal Point. He arrived at 4:00 in the morning and at 5:00 started work at Brigham's Restaurant on the south side of the canal. Only later in the day did he have the opportunity to take a look at the environs.

The Everglades presented an exotic world for a young man from the piney woods of Georgia. Palm Beach County had burgeoned from some 5,600 souls in 1910 to about 18,600 in 1920, with a diverse population unlike that of Emanuel. Foreign-born Whites accounted for 9 percent. Canadians, English, Irish, Swedes, and West Indians had the largest numbers, but Austrians, Danes, Dutch, French, Greeks, Hungarians, Italians, Norwegians, Poles, Russians, Scots, Spanish, and Syrians also sought their fortunes in southern Florida. In the lake region Belgians, Chinese, and other foreigners farmed, and a Japanese couple operated the Watanabe Hotel in Clewiston.

Seminoles lived in their own villages in the Everglades but traded with merchants in West Palm Beach and other towns. Courtesy, Library of Congress.

Several hundred surviving Seminoles lived in settlements around the lake. Clad in long, colorful garments, they came to Canal Point to sell blueberries harvested in the swamps or poled their boats down the North New River Canal to sell handmade goods in Ft. Lauderdale.

Blacks, who numbered 5,500 or 30 percent of the county population, included Bahamian migrant laborers with their lilting speech and share-croppers from other Southern states.

Even though the *Everglades News* condemned an effort to organize a local chapter of the Ku Klux Klan in mid-1924, Blacks in the 'Glades suffered the same discrimination and vigilante law prevalent in other parts of the South. In July 1925, a posse lynched a Black man named Roy Palmer after he allegedly attacked a White woman on Kraemer Island. "An informal coroner's jury," reported the *News*, "found that the negro came to his death at the hands of persons unknown."

Agriculture, life's blood of the region, rested on the rich muck, which extended to a depth of eight to 16 feet. Farmers often planted tomatoes and beans in alternating rows and, after harvest, sowed a summer crop such as corn or peanuts on the same land. Other crops included sugar cane, celery, peppers, asparagus, cabbages, potatoes, onions, pineapples, mangoes, and even bananas.

Growing cabbages in the 'Glades, ca. 1926. Courtesy,
Historical Society of Palm Beach.

Ron Seckinger

The sawgrass farmers wore high boots or leggings for protection against cottonmouth moccasins and the muck. They shod their mules with "muck shoes"—wide, iron implements that kept the animals from sinking into the wet earth—and eventually introduced tractors with broad metal wheels. Newcomers, attracted by the ads of such enterprises as Florida Muck Farms, Inc., continued to arrive every week.

The farmers sold their vegetables to the packing plants and their sugar cane to one of the mills that increasingly dominated the economy of the lake region. An attempt to grow cane and produce sugar on the north shore in the 1890s had proven unprofitable, but other entrepreneurs came forward to try the crop in the lands to the south and east of the lake.

In 1915, the Southern Land and Timber Company began cultivating cane and built syrup mills at Canal Point and on the St. Lucie Canal. By 1922, the Moore Haven Company was turning out 200 tons of low-grade sugar annually, and the Florida Sugar and Food Products company inaugurated a 400-ton capacity refinery at Canal Point the following year. Moreover, the US Department of Agriculture opened a cane experimental station at Canal Point in 1920 and soon cultivated 400 varieties for testing, providing further impetus to the industry. Acreage devoted to cane rose from a mere five in 1914 to 1,500 in 1922.

Farm machinery sported wide metal wheels to protect against sinking into the Everglades muck. Courtesy, State Archives of Florida.

In 1925, Bror G. Dahlberg, a Swedish immigrant who had risen from elevator operator to president of the Celotex Company of Chicago, came on the scene. His Southern Sugar Company planted fields of cane from Clewiston to Canal Point to produce not only sugar but also cellex, an inexpensive building material made from bagasse, the fibers of crushed cane stalks. He bought the Florida Sugar and Pennsylvania Sugar mills and moved them to Clewiston as the basis for a 1,500-ton operation. By 1930, the Southern Sugar Company had 25,000 acres planted in cane, half the total acreage in the 'Glades, and had expanded the mills' capacity to 5,000 tons.

The sugar industry contributed to the growth of the lakeshore towns that serviced the needs of farmers, loggers, and fishermen. Packing houses and canneries sprouted like mushrooms and provided employment to hundreds. Sometimes the smoke from muck fires became so thick that storeowners had to light their lamps in mid-afternoon. The inhabitants of the towns wore wide-brimmed hats, rolled their pants to the knees, and carried machetes. Mosquitoes flourished in such numbers that, the locals said, you could swing a pint cup and gather a quart.

Roads linking the towns were sandy and treacherous. Any automobile that strayed from the ruts was likely to get stuck; the 40-mile trip from Canal Point to Belle Glade could take as long as 12 hours.

Delma Hooks's arrival in Canal Point, located at the lake end of the Palm Beach Canal and the terminus of the railway line from Okeechobee, occurred during a period of rapid growth. R.G. Dun and Company had listed a single mercantile establishment in the town in its *Reference Book* in January 1920, but by September 1923 it found Brigham's Restaurant, the Canal Point Garage, the Florida Sugar and Food Products Company, the Glades Hotel, the publisher of the *Everglades News*, a wholesale produce plant, and eight general stores worthy of inclusion.

Despite the booming economy, the inhabitants remained generally poor, as reflected in the shabby housing available. Canal Point claimed few solidly constructed buildings, such as the Custard Apple Inn and a frame house occupied by the operators of the collection booth on the toll road. Other businesses had to settle for ramshackle wooden structures. Most people lived in tents, lean-tos, or shacks. Delma's original residence was an open platform covered with a sheet of tin behind Brigham's Restaurant. He and the cook climbed up a homemade ladder through a hole in the platform, where they slept on cots.

Delma Hooks and Nell Horn, ca. 1924.

Residents bathed in the canal or the lake or from buckets. In January 1926, the *Everglades News* reported that an unnamed resident of Canal Point had obtained an unusual household item: "Bath tubs are so rare in the Everglades that the addition to the small list must be recorded as a matter of news even if the paper loses a subscriber by it."

Delma's first job in Canal Point didn't last long. When Brigham fired his brother and sister-in-law, Mendel and Ava Lou Hooks, Delma quit in solidarity and walked two doors down to work for a rival establishment, the Lakeview Lunch. Between the two restaurants sat the Glades Hotel, where Boe's Restaurant occupied the first floor. All of these businesses were located in the town's principal strip along the south bank of the canal. The shore of Lake Okeechobee lay barely a hundred yards to the west, and endless sugar cane fields stretched away to the east.

Soon after his arrival, Delma heard other young men talking of a pretty 16-year-old named Nell Horn. He met her one night when he took Vera Todd to a movie house—in reality, a tin shack—in Pahokie. Nell and her date, Willis Smith, sat down in front of the couple, and Nell turned to chat with Vera.

Delma thought the petite, vivacious redhead was the prettiest thing he'd ever seen. Following up on the chance meeting, he initiated a whirlwind courtship. A native of Early County, Georgia, Nell had joined her father, who operated one of the tollbooths on the Conners Highway, in March 1925. Delma soon won her over. After their marriage in May 1926, they shared a room in the two-story house occupied by her parents.

By the time of the wedding, Delma had begun working with Audie in Boe's Restaurant. Soon afterwards, the brothers bought the establishment, and their wives, Nell and Iva, worked with them.

But in June 1927, a man named Bass offered to sell his grocery business. Delma explained that he had no money—just 25 hens, a rooster, a single-barreled shotgun, and a bean patch ready for harvest. Bass told him,

"Gimme the chickens, the shotgun, and that bean patch, and the store is yours."

And so Delma became a grocer. He had to borrow $5 so he could make change the first day, and he cut meat with a carpenter's saw and a dull knife on top of a homemade wooden box with a block of ice inside. But he now had a business that belonged to him alone. He never looked back.

CAVE MAN

BY FEBRUARY 1925, Frances Stroud had begun a difficult and dangerous pregnancy in Somerset. She lay in bed for six weeks, on her right side, unable to move or to keep much food down. The doctor gave her little chance to survive.

A friend, Mrs. Johnson, came every day to give Frances a sponge bath and comb out her waist-length hair. It was Mrs. Johnson who, in early February, brought her the news--Floyd Collins was trapped in a cave.

Below the green farmlands of central Kentucky lies a vast limestone formation, porous and easily dissolved by water. Over millions of years, rivers and the runoff from rain and snow gradually ate away parts of the limestone, forming crevices, tunnels, and vast caverns. The most spectacular of these, Mammoth Cave, had become a profitable tourist attraction by the end of the 19th century, and dozens of Kentuckians began crawling beneath the earth's crust in search of commercial opportunities. The discovery of Great Onyx Cave and other profitable underground formations spurred the efforts of caving entrepreneurs.

Among them was Floyd Collins, a native of the cave country who found and opened Crystal Cave to visitors in 1918. Lacking easy access to the main roads, Crystal stole few of Mammoth's customers, and Collins kept searching for a more conveniently located attraction. Eventually he concentrated on a narrow fissure, later called Sand Cave, that he hoped would lead to cathedral-like chambers that would rival Mammoth's and make his fortune.

On Friday morning, January 30, 1925, he slithered along a chute so confining that in most places only one person could pass. As he returned to daylight about noon, he wriggled through a small opening and was working his way up a 45-degree slope when he dislodged a stone that fell across his left ankle and pinned him in a space with no more room than a coffin. Alone, in the dark, 55 feet below the surface, Floyd Collins waited for help.

Neighbors located the trapped man the following morning. By evening, Homer Collins had reached his brother and begun the task of freeing him. The confined space, however, restricted his movement. After eight hours, Homer had removed the mud and gravel from his brother's upper torso, but Floyd's leg remained imprisoned. Exhausted, Homer withdrew, leaving Floyd, cheered by his discovery and bolstered by food and drink, in his solitary tomb.

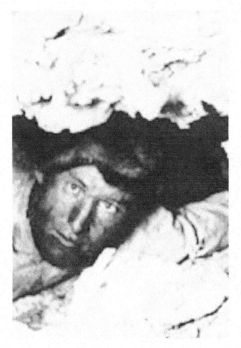

Floyd Collins trapped in Sand Cave, February 1925. Public domain.

By Sunday evening, more than 100 persons had gathered at the opening to Sand Cave. As Homer and other would-be rescuers returned periodically to their task, the mob grew ever more unruly. A local magistrate unsuccessfully tried to prohibit the consumption of alcohol. While Floyd—his body chilled in the damp, 54-degree atmosphere of the cave— began hallucinating, the number of curiosity-seekers above him continued to swell. Workers on the Louisville & Nashville Railroad carried the news across the state, and the press quickly assessed the story as a potential blockbuster.

William "Skeets" Miller of the Louisville *Courier-Journal* arrived on Monday morning. Brusquely told by Homer Collins to go down in the cave if he wanted information, Miller accepted the challenge. Only five feet five, the diminutive reporter managed to squeeze through a narrow hole that had kept larger men from descending into the lower cave. There he had his first, hurried conversation with the trapped man before succumbing to his terror and scrambling to daylight.

Volunteers use picks and shovels to dig a shaft to reach Floyd Collins. Public domain.

Ron Seckinger

Miller's dispatches from Sand Cave brought Floyd Collins's plight to the world's attention and helped transform a personal tragedy into the country's first great media event. Picked up by the Associated Press and distributed internationally, Miller's reports conveyed a human-interest story that met every editor's dream. As of Tuesday, February 3, the unfortunate caver's predicament became a staple of front pages not only in the cities and towns of Kentucky and the surrounding states but also in Chicago, New York, Washington, Atlanta, Philadelphia, and Los Angeles.

But radio made this story different. Although the entire country had only 29 stations at the beginning of 1922, within two years the number had grown to 1,400. By the time Floyd Collins's dilemma came to light, the new medium was reaching an increasingly large audience. Those who couldn't afford receivers of their own clustered around sets in shops or visited more fortunate acquaintances.

Crowds of curiosity seekers come to Sand Cave to take part in the Floyd Collins drama. Public domain.

Radio would change popular culture dramatically over the next three decades, bringing a wide range of music, drama, and comedy to the masses, hitherto dependent on local performers or traveling shows. Even more profound was the impact of radio on the news business, because it had an immediacy no newspaper could match. Radio informed its listeners of events at the very moment they unfolded—a radical change in communications.

Stations around the country had begun leading their news broadcasts with updates on the rescue operation in Kentucky by February 4, the fifth day of Collins's mishap. Radio announcers, newsreel cameramen, and more press reporters descended on the cave country as public interest soared. Frances Stroud followed the story from her sickbed in Somerset, 75 miles east of Sand Cave, and eventually the drama captured the imagination of the entire globe. Newspapers and radio stations in London, Paris, and other world capitals discovered that the affair held fascination for their audiences as well.

Meanwhile, the rescuers squabbled over methods. A Louisville fireman vociferously advocated strapping Floyd into a harness and winching him out, at whatever cost to his body. Miners from a nearby town proposed sinking a shaft to the narrow chamber where Collins lay helpless. A man with an oxyacetylene torch claimed he could burn away the limestone over Floyd's head. None of these schemes found backers, and Skeets Miller and another man continued the agonizingly slow work of digging the rubble from Floyd's legs.

By Tuesday night, the solution was at hand. Using an automobile jack, Miller, lying across Collins's body and extending his hands downward, tried to raise the stone from Floyd's ankle. The jack was too short, however, and the wooden blocks Miller placed under it kept slipping out. After several hours of frustrating labor, the newspaperman once again abandoned Collins. He emerged from the cave about 1:00 Wednesday morning and returned to his hotel to rest up for one final descent with a jack of appropriate length. Floyd Collins would at last escape his limestone tomb.

Afterwards, Miller would blame himself for not thinking of binding the wooden blocks together to form a solid platform for the jack. He never got another opportunity. About 4:00 that morning, part of the chute that provided access to the trapped man collapsed, leaving Floyd Collins totally alone.

On Thursday, February 5, a National Guard contingent took control of the rescue effort, bringing some order to the milling crowd of 250 on-lookers at the cave entrance. Judging that the tunnel couldn't be cleared, the rescuers turned to the option of a shaft some 20 feet from the mouth of the cave.

A power shovel could send fumes into the cave, and dynamite or pneumatic drills could cause a collapse of the cave roof. So, with nothing but picks and shovels, the volunteers, working in shifts around the clock, began excavating a shaft six feet square. The original estimates of 36 to 72 hours to reach the caver proved optimistic. Shoring up the sides of the shaft and removing large boulders by hand made the work painfully slow, and intermittent rain further hindered the operation.

Even while the locals despaired of seeing the doomed man alive, newspapermen and radio announcers kept feeding the story, embellishing every development and inventing others. Around the country congregations prayed for the deliverance of Floyd Collins. At breakfast tables, in barbershops, on streetcars and farms, the man in Sand Cave remained the principal topic of conversation. Theater performances were interrupted so patrons could hear the latest bulletin. By February 12, the Chicago *Tribune* was receiving 4,000 daily phone inquiries.

On Wednesday the 13th, Mrs. Johnson brought Frances Stroud the Somerset *Journal* with its terse account:

LATE NEWS FROM CAVE

Sand Cave, Ky.–Feb. 12 (Special to the Journal).–At twelve o'clock today the rescue work is going forward with all rapidity possible. It is thought Collins will be reached by midnight tonight. The shaft has been drilled to about ten feet of the tunnel in which Floyd Collins is trapped. "We have now reached a point where most anything may happen," said H.T. Carmichael, who is in charge.

What happened was further delay. Not until Saturday, February 16, did the volunteers reach a depth of 55 feet and begin to excavate a lateral tunnel to the point where Collins lay, and not until the early afternoon of Monday the 18th did the quest finally end. Former miner Albert Marshall broke into the chute and found Floyd dead, never to know that his ordeal had inspired the morbid fascination of millions of strangers.

With the drama over, nothing remained but tying up the loose ends. A coroner's inquest certified Floyd's death, which according to physicians who examined the body had come at least three days before the arrival of his erstwhile saviors. The authorities opted to leave Collins in his limestone tomb. Funeral services at the shaft opening on Tuesday included the hymns "Nearer My God to Thee" and "We'll Understand It Better, By-and-by."

Tourists gather at the glass-covered coffin containing Floyd Collins's body, ca. 1927. Public domain.

Ron Seckinger

On the following day, February 20, workers filled in the gaping hole intended for Floyd Collins's salvation. The rescue operation had cost $200,000, of which the state government had provided $75,000.

Around the world, those who had hoped against hope that Collins would emerge alive now mourned the death of their icon. The New York *Times* carried the unpleasant news on the front page beneath a three-column headline, but within a few days the nation's reporters were chasing other stories. Even Skeets Miller, who would win a Pulitzer Prize for his dispatches from Sand Cave, had to worry about tomorrow's edition.

Others saw commercial gain in keeping the story alive. Several of those involved in the rescue attempt, including Floyd's father, took their experiences to the vaudeville circuit. Albert Marshall, first to reach the dead man, chilled Midwestern audiences with his first-hand account of the Sand Cave adventure, complete with movies of the digging and the throngs of hangers-on. He brought his show to the Kentucky Theater in Somerset on March 22, but neither Emmit nor Frances, only recently arisen from her sickbed, attended.

Those who exploited Floyd's memory were outdone by those who exploited his very flesh. Homer Collins had the shaft cleared and brought the famous caver to the surface in April 1925 after three months below ground.

Homer embalmed the cadaver, partially eaten by cave crickets, and buried it in the family cemetery. Two years later, Floyd's father sold Crystal Cave, along with the rights to move the body there.

Thus Floyd Collins, whose name had served as a synonym for courage, became a tourist attraction. Visitors to "Floyd Collins Crystal Cave" could view the body in a bronze coffin with a glass cover.

A final indignity followed. In 1929, thieves stole the cadaver, which lost a leg before its recovery later the same day.

The legend endured. A blind Atlanta evangelist named Andrew B. Jenkins penned a mournful ballad, "The Death of Floyd Collins," in the spring of 1925. Vernon Dalhart's recording of the song in two years sold more than 3 million copies. Decades later, the musical "Floyd Collins" opened in New York in 1994 and went on to other venues. Floyd lives.

FARM KIDS

HIGH POINTS in the hardscrabble lives of Jessie and Duncan Fields's children came on the weekends and at special times during the year. On Sundays, Jessie took them to nearby Fields Chapel. A circuit-riding minister preached only once a month, but Sunday school classes met each week in the afternoon. Duncan himself rarely attended, much to the children's relief, since he'd once embarrassed them by showing up drunk at a Christmas event.

The simple, unpainted church building had no steeple. In hot weather the worshippers left open the doors on the sides to admit the occasional breeze, while the women inside churned the air with paper fans bearing a Biblical scene with a mortuary's advertisement. Jessie and her brood occupied the last pew, reserved for the Fields family because Duncan's father had deeded the half-acre lot to the congregation. Brother Fowler, an Advent Christian pastor known as "the fighting preacher" because he smote the air while shouting his message, delivered interminable sermons on the horrors that awaited sinners in the afterlife. The children would grow fidgety, easily distracted by each other or the sight of gout-swollen flesh ballooning over an old lady's high-buttoned shoes. Jessie would still them with a slap or a piercing glare that promised corporal punishment at home.

Members of Oak Grove Primitive Baptist Church north of Stillmore, Emanuel County, 1904. Fields Chapel was a wooden structure perhaps similar to this one. Courtesy, Georgia Archives, Vanishing Georgia Collection, emn147.

After the final hymn the faithful stayed to gossip, and the children had the opportunity to play with friends. Sometimes a baptism in South Prong Creek or dinner on the grounds followed the service. The children's classes always presented a dramatization of *A Christmas Carol*, and once Romie Delle played the role of Tiny Tim. Jessie often invited the preacher and others to the noon meal—known as "dinner"—at her home, where Rosa would fill the table with fried chicken, fresh vegetables, cornbread, and hot biscuits. The children, who ate after the adults, sometimes made do with skinned chicken feet.

About once a month, families who had plots at Hall's Cemetery would gather on a Saturday with hoes and rakes to pull up the weeds and burn any trash. The Fields tended baby Lucy's grave, as well as those of Duncan's parents and brother Joe. They looked down on families who neglected their own portions of the cemetery.

When the crops were laid by in mid-summer, Fields Chapel, like most of the other churches, hosted a protracted meeting or revival. For a

Ron Seckinger

week, the congregation gathered every night to sing and renew vows, usually with a guest pastor sharing the pulpit with Brother Fowler.

The children enjoyed the occasion, more joyous than the preacher's usual apocalyptic sermons, and looked forward to the hymns. Leila particularly loved "The Old Rugged Cross."

Jessie made a pallet of quilts where the younger children could fall asleep. After the service, she bundled them into the back of the wagon, where they continued sleeping during the ride home.

The Fields and many of their neighbors also attended autumn rivals at the Holiness Church in Pine Grove, more for entertainment than worship. During the 19th century, reaction against established churches' accommodation to secular ways had sparked a series of efforts to recover purer, more authentic forms of worship. Methodism, itself an 18th century offshoot of Anglicanism, spawned the Holiness Movement in the years immediately following the Civil War. This attempt to recreate the sanctity of the early Christians took a new form at the turn of the century, when congregations in Kansas, Oklahoma, and Texas began "speaking in tongues." Adherents claimed that conversing in unknown languages signaled a crucial, essential religious experience. Pentecostalism spread quickly across the South, and its practitioners ignored the contemptuous label of "holly rollers" as they sought spiritual perfection.

The members of the Holiness congregation at Piney Grove shouted, fell on their knees, spoke in tongues, and threw themselves to the floor in apparent seizures. The services drew curiosity-seekers from miles around, until the church filled and latecomers had to watch through open windows.

The Fields children took in the strange scenes, which served as the raw material for one of their favorite games—"playing preacher." On Saturdays when the farm work was lighter, they slipped away, along with visiting friends or relatives and the children of African American sharecroppers like the Pheanious family, to the tobacco barn on the Ehrlich place to mimic the worshippers at Holiness Church.

As the oldest of the younger kids, Leila insisted on playing the role of preacher, and the others had to pull her around in a red wagon. Their cousin Nell Dyson used a stump as a pretend piano while Leila stood on another, loudly broadcasting a confusing litany of sin and salvation. Romie Delle, Jean Dyson, Wynelle, little Knob, and the other children took the part of the audience. They threw their arms in the air, "testifying" with shrieks and made-up words, rolling on the ground as though possessed.

They played other games as well. When the weather permitted, the gang roamed far and wide. They walked to the railroad tracks to watch the train pass, waving to the engineer and—by tugging an imaginary cord—coaxing him to blow the steam whistle.

They often played in the woods by the creek, using vines as jump ropes, fashioning clothing and hats from leaves and thorns, balancing on the trunks of bent-over trees, or picking wild violets for their mother. They took turns riding the mule or keeping a metal hoop rolling with a stick. Sometimes J.D. or John A. took the whole bunch for a ride in the ox cart, or they filled the two-horse wagon with hay and wrestled as one of the older boys drove up and down the country roads.

Unidentified boy wades in the McKinney's Pond millrace, ca. 1910. Courtesy, Georgia Archives, Vanishing Georgia Collection, emn104.

In the summer, they piled into the wagon and went to the creek at Steven's Crossing, where—having no swimsuits—they wore their clothing into the water. Occasionally Jessie sent them to the grist mill at McKinney's Pond to have a bag of corn ground into meal or grits, and they swam in the cool water of the millrace, keeping an eye out for water moccasins. They also went fishing, hunted for rabbits, played marbles in the yard, or pelted each other with chinaberries. From spring until fall, they ran barefoot, the soles of their feet thickly calloused but still sensitive to sticks, rocks, and sandspurs.

Jessie's children anxiously awaited Christmas. For months, they examined the "wish book," as they called the Sears, Roebuck catalog, choosing toys and clothing that they almost never received. Their parents sometimes invited relatives and neighbors to a Christmas Eve party featuring pound cake and hot chocolate, a rare treat. One year, Jessie made 14 cakes, and not a single slice remained on Christmas morning.

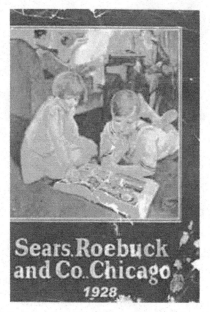

The cover of the 1928 "wish book." Courtesy, Sears Roebuck & Co.

Anticipation always outstripped reality. One of the children might say, "I wish I had that doll from the catalog." Jessie, whose girlish wonder had long since yielded a no-nonsense acceptance of hard work and deprivation, would reply, "Wish in one hand and spit in the other, and see which one fills up first."

Although some years she managed to squirrel away enough money to buy each child an inexpensive gift of some kind, Christmas at the Fields household usually consisted of a few apples, oranges, tangerines, and raisins on the vine, placed under a pine tree decorated with paper chains, popcorn or macaroni strings, and small candles.

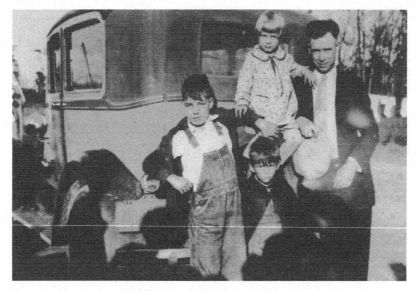

Ellie Scott, Knob Fields, Hilma Stroud (on tire), and Emmit
Stroud during a visit to the Fields farm, ca. 1930.

Indeed, the children might have had no Christmas to speak of but for their Uncle Emmit and Aunt Frances. They often came from Kentucky to Emanuel County in December, traveling for free on Emmit's railroad passes. They brought gifts—dolls for the girls and guns for the boys—as well as a two-gallon, galvanized tin can with four or five kinds of candy. When unable to come for Christmas, Emmit and Frances sent the gifts and candy by mail. One year, they sent multicolored tam-o'-shanters to Leila and Romie Delle, and Leila was heartbroken when a fellow student took hers.

Ron Seckinger

After the holidays, life returned to its everyday, black-and-white quality. Jessie's kids would talk about the gifts and candies for months afterwards, with little but the next Christmas to occupy their fantasies for the coming year.

DESPERADOS

AS DELMA HOOKS discovered on arrival in Canal Point, the residents of the rapidly growing towns on Lake Okeechobee were a rough bunch. Delma had to take care of a boisterous, 240-pound drunk in the restaurant by leaping into the air and cracking a ketchup bottle over his head. The toughs who lounged in the shade or haunted the pool hall in Canal Point taunted newcomers. One of Delma's nephews, an 18-year-old from Georgia, earned their respect by thrashing two or three of his tormentors, who left him alone thereafter.

Many of the original fishermen on the lake had fled justice in other jurisdictions, and their successors proved equally indifferent to civilized ways. On the weekends, Okeechobee, Canal Point, and the other towns filled with fishermen, cattlemen, loggers, farmers, and field hands eager for hard drink and ready for a brawl. A sign in the Clewiston Inn warned patrons, "Saturday nights dancing from 9 to 11, fights from 11 to 2."

Bootleggers made their own 'shine in the swamps or bought whiskey from offshore smugglers and resold it to illegal establishments spawned by Prohibition. Luther Levins, who'd come to the lake area in 1916 as a teenager, turned to bootlegging after trying his hand at farming, running a mailboat, and trapping raccoons. He dealt with Black islanders, known as "conchs," who brought liquor from the Bahamas to Riviera Beach.

For every 12-quart case of Gordon's Gin, Levins would pay $3.50 up front, plus another $5 in freight charges on delivery. Loading 25 to 30 cases of gin or Canadian Club or scotch into his Studebaker, he would drive through the night to Orlando, where the Runymeade Club or one of the other "blind tigers" would pay him $65 per case. In a single night, he could clear more than $1,500, much of which he then squandered on entertaining companionable women.

Postcard view of Canal Point in 1930, taken from the railroad lift bridge on the edge of Lake Okeechobee and looking south-southeast along the Palm Beach Canal and the Connors Highway. Courtesy, Lawrence E. Will Museum, City of Belle Glade, Florida.

Slot machines made their appearance in the Everglades during the '20s. Nickel, dime, and quarter machines purchased for $75 each in Ft. Lauderdale quickly repaid the investment. An entrepreneur delivered the devices to practically every restaurant, hotel, or grocery store in the lake region. A proprietor kept 40 percent of the take and paid the distributor an equal share. The remaining 20 percent typically went to pay off the sheriff, the judge, and the prosecuting attorney.

No one lacked for a place to drink and carouse. At the Southern Chili Parlor and Barbecue in Canal Point, customers could order sandwiches and play pool on the ground floor, gamble at the poker tables and slots upstairs, and imbibe illegal liquor on either level. A.L. Deroo recalled encountering "Pistol Pete" Harrison of Pahokee one evening as Harrison rushed from the building. "Don't tell anybody I was here tonight," he pleaded before vanishing. On investigating, Deroo found a drunk who terrorized his fellow card players with a .45-caliber handgun.

More serious were the activities of the Ashley gang. John Ashley, the eldest of five brothers born and raised in the 'Glades near Fort Myers, belonged to a rough clan. He and his father had worked as wood cutters during the construction of the Florida East Coast Railway. All of the Ashleys were crack shots and knew how to handle themselves in the swamps.

John first ran afoul of the law at the age of 23. In December 1911, he murdered a Seminole hunting companion named DeSoto Tiger and stole 85 otter hides and $400 in cash. Other Seminoles reported Ashley as the likely suspect, but the news lagged behind him. The killer sold the hides for $1,020 in Miami. In West Palm Beach, the city marshal detained him for drunkenness and discharging a weapon but, unaware of the murder charges, released him on $25 bail. Two sheriff's deputies looked for the gang in the 'Glades, but John and his brother Bob got the drop on them. John fled to New Orleans and then worked as a logger near Seattle.

In 1914, Ashley returned to Palm Beach County and surrendered, apparently believing no jury in the 'Glades would convict him. But when the prosecutor requested a change of venue to Miami, Ashley scaled a 10-foot chicken-wire fence and escaped. With his brother Bob, a Chicago gunman named Kid Lowe, and others, he embarked on a crime spree. The gang robbed a passenger train on the Florida East Coast Railway and in February 1915 held up a bank in Stuart. During the bank job, Lowe accidentally shot John Ashley in the jaw, costing him the sight in his left eye. The outlaw had no choice but surrender for medical treatment.

The prosecutor having obtained a change of venue, the authorities moved John to the Miami jail to stand trial for the murder of DeSoto Tiger.

On June 2, Bob Ashley attempted to free his brother, killing a jailer and a policeman before falling mortally wounded. John remained in the Miami lockup until the prosecutor dropped the murder charges. In November 1916, he pled guilty in his trial for the bank robbery in Stuart, receiving a sentence of 17 years and six months.

Transferred to the state penitentiary at Raiford, he escaped from a road camp in mid-1918. His gang focused on making moonshine and running rum from the Bahamas until he was apprehended and returned to Raiford in June 1921. Two of his brothers drowned or were killed by hijackers while ferrying a load of liquor from Bimini a few months later. Ashley escaped again in September 1923 and reassembled his gang.

Laura Upthegrove and John Ashley, ca. 1924. From Hix C. Stuart, The Notorious Ashley Gang (1928).

John Ashley was as colorful as any Hollywood gangster. Slender, he stood five feet ten, weighed 145 pounds, and had black hair and grey eyes, one of them—after the incident in Stuart—artificial. He bore a scar on the left side of his mouth and, on his arms, tattoos of a cross, a sword, an American flag, and a sailor's head.

Said to distribute his loot among the poor in Robin Hood style, Ashley and his mistress, Laura Upthegrove, shared a reputation not unlike that later enjoyed by Clyde Barrow and Bonnie Parker, the romanticized Midwestern desperados of the 1930s. Laura, twice divorced and mother of four children, earned the sobriquet "Queen of the Everglades" and carried a .38-caliber revolver strapped to her waist. She directed the unloading of contraband liquor and on several occasions warned the gang of the approach of sheriff's posses. During one raid on Ashley's camp deep in the 'Glades, lawmen shot his father dead and wounded Laura with nine buckshot in her hip.

Eventually, the gang leader's luck ran out. Receiving a tip that Ashley and his buddies were traveling to Jacksonville, law officers from three counties intercepted them at the Sebastian Bridge in St. Lucie County, north of Canal Point, on the night of November 1, 1924. According to the official report, Ashley and three others got out of their car at gunpoint but suddenly reached for revolvers while standing in the road. In the ensuing shootout, all four died, while no law officer received a wound.

A friend told Luther Levins that, returning from the northern part of the state, he arrived at Sebastian Bridge just after the shooting and saw that all four corpses wore handcuffs. At the inquest Ashley's mother and other relatives charged that the lawmen had murdered the suspects in cold blood, but a coroner's jury ruled the killings justifiable and refused to reopen the case.

Thus, in death as in his crimes, Ashley foreshadowed Clyde Barrow. A large crowd of friends, relatives, and curiosity-seekers attended the burial of Ashley and two of the other men at Fruita, in the northern part of the county.

Laura Upthegrove mourned her man for several years before remarrying in 1927. A few weeks after the wedding, she got into an argument with a man over a pint of corn liquor. Knocked down in the struggle, in a rage she drank poison and died before a doctor could pump her stomach. The man who punched her hid out at the Glades Hotel in Canal Point for three days, ordering his meals from Delma Hooks, terrified that the remnants of the Ashley gang would come to avenge the Queen of the Everglades.

But the gang no longer existed. Delma Hooks recalled decades later that two deputies brought Joe Tracey, the last of Ashley's sidekicks, to Canal Point to look for the gang's money. According to Delma, Tracey either escaped from the lawmen or they killed him. No records of Tracey or these events have been located, and the story likely is apocryphal.

HIGHWAYS

BY MAKING the automobile available to vast numbers of ordinary citizens, Henry Ford dramatically increased the constituency for good roads. By the time the Great War began in Europe, entrepreneurs throughout the United States were pressing for interstate highways that would make auto travel convenient.

One of the early schemes called for a major artery linking Chicago and Miami, the Dixie Highway. Launched in 1915, the project involved 50 county and 10 state governments as well as private investors and required some 15 years to complete.

The road-building frenzy continued through the 1920s. In Missouri, war veteran Harry Truman, having lost his haberdashery as well as the first election in a political career that ultimately would take him to the White House, supported his family in 1925 by selling more than 1,000 memberships in the Kansas City Automobile Club.

Emanuel County owned five Caterpillar tractors for grading roads in 1924, and by 1926 its share of revenues from state gasoline taxes amounted to some $30,000 annually. In 1928, Georgia embarked on a massive road-building and improvement program. The following year, it ranked sixth among the 48 states in completed roads. Although the Georgia state highway department was notoriously corrupt and the road network expanded haphazardly, more in response to political concerns than reason, travel gradually became easier.

Building one of the earliest stretches of the Dixie Highway near Trenton, Georgia, ca. 1920. Courtesy, Chattanooga (Tenn.) Public Library.

For its part, Washington committed to building a national road network after the passage of the Federal Highways Act of 1916 and deserves credit for much of the growth. US Route One, stretching along the east coast from the Maine-Canadian border to Key West at the southern tip of Florida, was the first major artery projected by the federal government in collaboration with the states traversed by the road. The route bisected Swainsboro and Emanuel County, where paving began in July 1927. January 1933 saw the completion of the entire 2,432-mile highway, greatly facilitating seasonal traffic to Florida.

Despite the frenetic construction, cross-country travel remained a precarious venture. In June 1925, the Southern Railway laid off Emmit Stroud, who worked for a few months in Princeton, Indiana before a better job materialized. A telegram arrived from a man named Johnson, an old friend from the Atlanta, Birmingham & Atlantic shops in Fitzgerald, offering a job in the shipyards in Jacksonville, Florida.

Many Georgia "highways" were little more than mud-choked trenches, like this one pictured in 1910. Courtesy, Georgia State University.

Even though Frances's pregnancy had entered its final month, and she had been confined to bed for much of the time, the two set out in a Model T. The roads were unpaved, for the most part, and roadside accommodations were scarce. They managed to find a nice room in a tourist court the first night, but on the second clouds of mosquitoes drove them from their lodgings. They motored until 2:00 in the morning and parked in a farm driveway where the insects were tolerable. Frances slept inside the Ford, and Emmit, on a tarpaulin spread on the ground.

The trip took four days. They reached the outskirts of Jacksonville and slept in the open again because Emmit knew how to reach his friend's home only from the train depot. On Saturday, October 3, they located Johnson's house and rented a room for themselves with a family named White.

Ron Seckinger

Georgia tourist cabins, ca. 1936. Courtesy, Library of Congress.

They'd arrived just in time. On Monday, October 5, Frances gave birth in a hospital in Jacksonville. She'd carried the baby so lightly that she'd never switched to maternity clothes, and no one except Emmit had known of the pregnancy.

"We've got a new little girl at our house," Emmit proudly announced to the astonished Whites, who had just met Frances two days previously. The proud parents named the baby Hilma Frances.

As paved highways linked scattered towns, asphalt covered city streets as well. Swainsboro's citizens turned out for a street dance in October 1927 to celebrate the opening of the new, hard-surfaced roads that were replacing muddy thoroughfares in their community. Almost immediately, they confronted an unexpected and ominous institution: the parking ticket. In December, a new ordinance required motorists to park their vehicles within the spaces being painted on the pavement surrounding the courthouse square.

Communities at first welcomed poor motorists who crossed the country in search of work, but soon town fathers longed for a better class of travelers.

Along Route One and the other highways, auto camps sprang up to cater to the thousands who crisscrossed the country in search of jobs, adventure, or a new start. Communities built camps because their citizens wanted to encourage travelers to tarry long enough to patronize local businesses and at the same time to halt their littering and despoiling of farm properties. By the early 1920s, the country claimed between 3,000 and 6,000 camps. Emanuel County in 1922 established a free campground for transients en route to Florida. Similarly, two years later the Florida Sugar & Food Products Company offered to open a free camp for "tin-can tourists" in Canal Point, partly in anticipation that some would take temporary jobs in the cane fields.

Hilma and Frances Stroud, Somerset, Kentucky, ca. 1927.

These accommodating attitudes proved as transitory as the tourists. "Gypsying," or wandering by auto, originally had been the province of the middle class. But the Model T's accessibility allowed the near-destitute to travel as well, and the appearance of battered vehicles bearing a

Ron Seckinger

shabby human cargo gave a disreputable cast to the new mobility. In 1925, for example, the *Forest-Blade* expressed its disapproval of "gasoline gypsies"–"folks in desperate circumstances, who drift about the country in cheap automobiles, without settled homes or occupations," denying their children the opportunity for a good education.

Local jurisdictions began to charge fees as a means of excluding undesirables and, eventually, to close the camps. Entrepreneurs filled the void by establishing tourist cabins, the forerunners of the motel. Swainsboro's first opened in 1928.

Automobiles and highways led to other changes. Purveyors of goods and services at crossroads settlements fell on hard times as their formerly captive clientele ranged farther afield in search of bargains, quality, and recreation.

Even county seats were vulnerable. In Emanuel County in 1934, local merchants organized a "Buy-It-in-Swainsboro" campaign in an effort "to keep money at home." The *Forest-Blade* backed the businessmen: "Now-a-days, it's so easy to get into an automobile, journey to a distant city, make your purchases and get back before dark." One might consider such a trip mere "recreation," but the newspaper warned that commercial dealings in other towns drained the life blood from one's own community.

Expecting citizens to shop locally, like calls for a better class of traveler, represented a desire to have all the conveniences of the automobile without any of the negatives. But the effects of the Motor Age, both good and bad, were all of a piece. When Henry Ford and the other automakers unleashed the forces of change, no one had the power to control their impact. America would never be the same again.

REUNION

THINGS WENT BADLY for Denver Stroud in Detroit. He'd had to send his sister Maude back to Swainsboro because she'd argued with his wife Bernice. Worse, he and Bernice had problems of their own, and she decamped with the baby.

Alone, with Christmas coming, in December 1926, Denver decided to return home to Georgia, visiting Emmit in Kentucky on the way. He appeared without notice at Emmit's home at 9:00 on a Tuesday night. Emmit had returned to Somerset in January when his job with Southern Railway had come open again, ignoring the pleas of his friend Johnson to stay on with the shipyard in Jacksonville. A mistake, since Johnson soon became foreman and layoffs were rare, but at the time Emmit thought keeping his seniority with Southern mattered most.

Denver's surprise appearance delighted Emmit. After excited greetings and Denver's getting a peek at his 15-month-old niece Hilma, they sat down to talk. What were Emmit and Frances doing for Christmas? Well, Emmit needed an operation to have his tonsils removed, so they planned to spend the holidays in Somerset.

The next morning, they agreed that Emmit would stay with the baby while Frances accompanied Denver to pick up his luggage at the train station. As the two departed, Emmit casually said to Frances, "Go over to the freight office and see if my passes have come in."

The Strouds meet in Swainsboro, December 1926. Front row from left: Alice, Margie, Maude, Jessie. Back row: Denver, Emmit, Kermit.

Frances knew what that meant, and she didn't like it. She had a small child and the weekly laundry to do, she pointed out with some heat. She had no intention of traveling to Georgia, and that was that. Sure enough, the annual rail passes had arrived, and the row continued when Frances returned to the apartment. Eventually she capitulated, muttering under her breath as she washed the clothes and hung them outdoors in the cold to dry.

One afternoon that week, Frances finished cleaning up the kitchen after lunch and walked back into the living room, expecting to find Denver sitting there. Instead, he was standing beside the iron baby bed where Hilma took her nap. He said Hilma looked like Lillian, whom he hadn't seen in some time. His sadness caught Frances's attention, because the Stroud men rarely showed their emotions.

Denver left for Swainsboro on Friday. The others followed on Saturday, Frances fussing over the baby and still fuming at the disruption of her Christmas plans.

The seven surviving Stroud siblings gathered at Waitus and Margie's home in Swainsboro, the first reunion since their father's funeral in 1923. The house overflowed with children, raising a racket that neighbors down the block could hear. The men went out back for a snort of the moonshine that Waitus kept in the garage, and eventually they all sat down to feast on turkey and ham, canned vegetables from Jessie's garden, fried cornbread, and fresh biscuits with honey from Waitus's hives.

They caught up with each other's lives and talked about their current jobs and homes, and how much they missed Jewel, dead now for more than six years. But mostly they reminisced about their childhood, swapping tales about neighbors, games and pranks, about how Margie never forgave their father for butchering a goat she considered a pet, about parties and swimming holes and fishing. All of them save Jessie had escaped the hard life of their early years, and their memories could focus on warm and amusing moments rather than hardships.

When time came to part, they traded hugs and handshakes and promises to hold another gathering next year or the year after. It was the last time they would all be together.

TOWN KIDS

BY THE TIME of the reunion in 1926, Alice and Maude had left farm life behind three years earlier. At first, Maude lived with Denver in Detroit, but she moved to Swainsboro in 1926 and joined Alice at Waitus and Margie's home. They attended the school for White children, a large building with grades one through 11, located a half dozen blocks from the Scott home on Lee Street.

Alice did passable work in her classes, although she didn't consider herself bright and didn't enjoy her studies. Painfully shy, she somehow made friends. At every gathering, she joined the girls' caucus that identified the cutest boys. She sort of liked one of the Henry boys and one of the Waldens, but she had little use for men and never went on dates, even after entering high school in 1925.

Maude, in contrast, had a more outgoing personality. As a seventh grader she participated in a formal debate on the issue, "Resolved: That English is more important than Arithmetic"—her side lost—and, at graduation exercises in May 1928, read a poem before her classmates and their parents. The following fall, Maude entered Swainsboro High School, which would have 95 students in 1929 and 138 a year later.

"The Three Musketeers": Gladys Waller, Nesbit Rogers, and Maude Stroud.

"Everybody liked Maude Stroud," classmate Charles Harmon recalled decades later. "She wasn't a blabbermouth, but when you talked to her, she made sense." Before classes began in the mornings, she visited with Charles or Jerry Rich or other friends, talking about this and that until a bell summoned them to their seats.

Her closest chums were Nesbit Rogers, a tall blonde two years younger than she, and red-headed Gladys Waller, Nesbit's junior by a year. They spent so much time together that their classmates called them "The Three Musketeers."

Outside the classroom, school activities revolved around two literary societies: the O. Henry, named for the noted short story writer, and the Ernest Neal, after Georgia's poet laureate (1927-1943). The school authorities assigned students arbitrarily to the rival clubs. Each assumed responsibility once a week for chapel services, involving scripture readings, hymns, and inspirational messages. At other school assemblies, the societies competed in yells, cheers, debates, dramatic readings, and musical performances, accumulating points toward an annual award.

The rivalry peaked toward the end of the school year at a special Friday-night program attended by practically the entire White population of the town. The Ernest Neal Society decorated its side of the auditorium in black and gold streamers. The members of the O. Henry, the colors of which were purple and black, used wisteria blossoms, and the sweet smell of the flowers permeated the room.

In 1929, Ernest Neal himself attended the competition, only to see his protégés lose to their rivals despite a victory in the debate. The O. Henry's George Smith argued against the resolution that the state should provide free textbooks, citing the risk of spreading disease from one student to the next. But in the rebuttal, Charles Harmon skewered his opponent in a withering display of wit. "I delivered the Atlanta *Journal* for George Smith," Charles remembered saying, "and when I gave him the money he'd kiss it and put it in his pocket, and I knew he wasn't scared of that disease."

Charles won the debate again the next year, but once more the O. Henry Society triumphed, with a score of 45 to 35.

The Ernest Neal Literary Society at Swainsboro High School, 1931-1932.

Alice and Maude played big sister to their nephew Ellie. Margie had a second pregnancy in 1927, but the baby girl she carried was stillborn, and Ellie would never have a sibling. He basked in the attention of his parents, who doted on him, and his teenaged aunts.

Like the other boys, Ellie had the run of the town. With only 1,200 inhabitants in 1925, Swainsboro was no bustling metropolis. Yet the boys never lacked for excitement. Sometimes tourists passed through, like the four young men from New York who filled their tank at a service station in September 1929 and tried to leave without paying. Hauled before a judge, they received a sentence of six months on the chain gang. Soon afterwards appeared a bicyclist—"a Spaniard or some other nationality, not very well up on English," according to the *Forest-Blade*—who claimed to have ped-aled all the way from Buenos Aires and soon departed for Augusta. The periodic display of confiscated moonshine stills by a proud sheriff attracted dozens of boys, as did any other event of note.

Revenue agents with a confiscated still, Emanuel County, 1920s.
Courtesy, Georgia Archives, Vanishing Georgia Collection, emn053.

The town kids anxiously awaited the arrival of traveling shows, especially the annual visit of the Hefner-Vinson Stock Company, a vaudeville troupe that performed in a huge tent pitched on an empty lot south of the courthouse square. They begged their parents for permission and cash to attend the Christy Brothers Circus or other tent shows. Minstrel troupes, including famous ones like Silas Green's Minstrels of New Orleans, weren't to be missed.

Saturday matinees at the City Theater featured westerns starring Tom Mix, Ken Maynard, Bob Steele, and Buck Jones, as well as serials that lured children back each week to witness their heroes' latest escapes from peril. Ellie's pal Lynwood Screws frequently operated the hand-cranked projector so he could see the film for free. Whenever he became engrossed in the plot and slowed down, the manager would lean over and whisper, "Speed up, boy, speed up!" The movies became an even greater treat after the theater obtained equipment for talkies in 1929.

Ellie and his friends prowled the streets, known to all the merchants and passersby, and they often rifled the open trashcans in the alleys behind the stores in search of cast-off items they could use in their games and make-believe adventures. They made pistols and rifles of wood and used pieces of inner tubes, stretched over the wooden frames, as projectiles. They rode bicycles and raced on roller skates. The pavement of Green Street served as an impromptu hockey rink where boys on skates used tree limbs to propel a tin can toward a goal. Spills on the asphalt left their clothes in tatters, and they often faced their mothers' wrath. "Gonna make you wear those pants till they fall off!" a wayward son would hear as his mother pinched his arm or twisted his ear. "Brand new pants and you got a hole in the knee!"

They liked the summer best, of course. With no school and few chores, they ran barefoot from breakfast to bedtime. Their soles toughened quickly, but occasionally one of the boys would sit down and carefully pluck a sandspur from the hard pad on the ball of his foot, experiencing a slight, almost sensual pain. In the woods. the boys picked rabbit tobacco, wrapped it in brown paper, and lit up to ape their cigarette-smoking elders. When the heavens poured and rain danced on the streets like a cow pissing on a flat rock, they played board games inside or listened to their favorite radio serials.

Ellie and "Rock" Hall, who lived on Lucky Street, used scraps of lumber to build tree houses in the woods. They also played in the Scotts' back yard, shooting marbles or digging caves or running with Ellie's feist, "Snookums." A cable suspended from a tall tree gave them a zip-line ride to the ground. Miraculously, no one ever got hurt. Their mothers periodically reminded them not to yell, because night policeman Willie Fields slept all day in his house a few doors down the street.

Every afternoon Margie called Ellie to the back door, where she handed over a nickel and said, "Go get me a Co'-Cola." Ellie and Rock headed off across the city cemetery—taking time to play among the tombstones—to a refreshment stand operated by an African American woman at Yam Grandy Creek, returning eventually with Margie's soft drink.

All the town kids cheered the announcement in mid-1926 that W.E. and R.H. Vann intended to build a "Veritable Coney Island," with "swimming pools, dancing pavilions, parks, skating rinks, filling stations, club houses and all things for enjoyment and convenience," on a two-and-a-half-acre lot between West Main and Church Streets. While falling far short of New York's fabled amusement park, the new community center at least provided a place for weekly square dances, and the pool was a welcome addition for boys and girls who normally swam in creeks.

Ellie Scott and "Snookums," 1931.

After an early supper the children roamed the neighborhood. They gathered in a pack—Ellie, Rock, Lynwood, M.L. Anderson, Lamar and J.P. Curl, one of the Pritchard boys—under the streetlight on Lucky Street to play hare-and-hounds and other games, while their parents visited on front porches and swatted at mosquitoes in the sultry air.

If the boys ranged into the downtown area, Willie Fields likely would come on them as he made his rounds and send them home. At 8:00 or 9:00, they reluctantly obeyed their mothers' summons and washed up before crawling into bed.

Alice and Maude had their own pastimes. On Saturday nights, Waitus's sisters, Robbie, Ruth, and Lucille, along wth Nesbit Rogers and another classmate or two, joined the Stroud girls at Margie's home to play checkers, Rook, or setback. They laughed and gossiped as they shuffled the cards, sipping Waitus's homemade blackberry wine and listening distractedly to the "Grand Ole Opry" broadcast on the radio.

When Waitus arrived from his barbershop after 11:00, they'd beg him to dance. His specialty was the "buck dance," a mixture of African slave and early pioneer dances that became a staple of the minstrel shows. Even though he'd spent the past 15 hours on his feet, shaving and trimming the hair of dozens of farmers and townsmen, Waitus would give in with good humor and put on a brief performance. The delighted girls would squeal and applaud, importuning him to do another. But the exhausted barber eventually would lumber off to bed with Margie, leaving the young girls to play awhile longer before disbanding for the night.

On Sundays, they attended one of Swainsboro's four churches for Whites. The Methodist, Baptist, Presbyterian, and Advent Christian congregations held services once a month, rotating among themselves so that every Sunday furnished an opportunity for worship. After dinner, Alice and Maude often went to special afternoon programs for young people at a church or met the Scott girls and other friends at the home of Waitus's parents. They sang popular songs while Robbie, an accomplished pianist, provided the music. One of their favorites was "Indian Love Call," from Sigmund Romberg's operetta "Rose Marie," long before Nelson Eddy and Jeannette McDonald immortalized the tune in their 1936 film.

Young people held parties and proms at the school, went on excursions to McKinney's Pond or Coleman's Lake, and in the afternoons met friends at one of the drugstores. Alice, Maude, and their friends occasionally had the opportunity to study with dancing instructors who came from

Savannah to offer lessons over several weeks. In the summer, Georgians celebrated not only Independence Day on July 4 but also the birthday of Confederate President Jefferson Davis on July 3, then a legal holiday.

Alice and Maude spent the summers on Jessie's farm near Blun, helping with the chores. They made unwilling field hands, reluctant to accept the hard labor and boredom of farm life after the relative comforts of Swainsboro. As they picked cotton under the broiling sun, they couldn't help but think of their friends in town, lolling on front porches or meeting classmates at the movies, soaking in bathtubs instead of rinsing themselves in galvanized tubs. Their redemption eventually came in September, when school reopened and they could return to the house on Lee Street and the excitement of town life.

But the end of high school would arrive within a few years. What then?

STORM

IN JULY 1926, Nell and Delma Hooks, as well as most of the settlers around Lake Okeechobee, experienced their first hurricane. Little rain had fallen between 1910 and 1920, while Napoleon Bonaparte Broward's plans to drain the upper portion of the Everglades proceeded, and the return of precipitation levels to normal caused flooding of towns and croplands, surprising newcomers. Floodwaters inundated Moore Haven, on the southwestern shore, in 1922 and 1923. The following year, most of the farmlands remained underwater during the entire winter. Between 1923 and 1925, the state government built an earthen dike, five to eight feet high, along the southern shore to control rising waters, but it would prove of little use in a major storm.

The hurricane that struck in July 1926 caused some flooding but little significant damage in the lake area. In Canal Point, the Hooks family easily rode out the storm, and afterwards Delma waded across the highway in waist-deep water to reach the restaurant and clean up. Soon thereafter he got into a bitter argument with his sister-in-law and decided to take Nell to Emanuel County, where they remained for six months.

Safe in Georgia, they missed a more severe hurricane in September that killed about 150 persons in the lake area—mostly in Moore Haven, where the survivors buried dozens in a long trench beside the railroad tracks. More than 200 others perished in Miami and Ft. Lauderdale, and property damages in Miami alone amounted to $27 million, delivering a final blow to the Florida land boom.

In the Everglades, opportunities remained widespread. During the 1927-1928 growing season, Palm Beach County produced 3,000 railroad carloads of vegetables. The Southern Sugar Company planned to build a larger mill at Canal Point to handle the fruit of the expanding cane fields.

Laborers—particularly Blacks, both American and Caribbean—streamed into the lake area with their families. They remained even after the harvest, because local farmers allowed them to plant food crops on unused land. With a few chickens and the plentiful fish of the lake and canals, they could get by till the next harvest brought regular employment. Blacks inhabited shacks and makeshift shelters or slept in the open beside the canals or irrigation ditches.

In July 1928, the sugar company announced plans to build wooden buildings for its Black employees—three bunk houses, each with room for 250 persons, 100 houses for one or two families, a 750-seat mess hall, and a community laundry. Railroad problems delayed the delivery of the lumber, however, and little construction had been completed by September 1928.

Heavy rains put the locals on edge, and anxiety about flooding overshadowed the decision of Canal Point voters in early September to incorporate the town and choose a mayor. The *Everglades News* did its best to scuttle fears of another disaster like that of 1926. In mid-August, the newspaper reported that a Canal Point man, unable to sleep, had opened his Bible at random and came upon the story of Noah's Ark. By comparison, the *News* commented, "the flood stories in the Palm Beach Post the next morning read sort of tame." On September 7, the editors pointed out that the lake level was two feet lower than in 1926 and pooh-poohed the possibility of another big storm:

> Some more fool reports of a hurricane were in circula-
> tion early in the week, based on the big publicity given

by West Palm Beach daily papers to a hurricane in the Yucatan channel, a few thousand miles distant from the Everglades.

An African American turpentine runner slashes a pine in Thomas County. Later he'd return to collect the sap. The multiple cuts indicate this tree had been tapped for many years. Courtesy, Georgia Archives, Vanishing Georgia Collection, tho147.

In the midst of this uncertainty, Delma's mother summoned him back to Georgia. Earlier in the year, John and Lillian Hooks, unable to meet payments on a $2,500 loan contracted in 1920, had lost their farm in Emanuel County. They remained on the land, where John continued to farm on shares and, as he had done for years, to bleed pine trees as a turpentine runner.

Ron Seckinger

Collecting pine sap for the manufacture of turpentine was an unpleasant job. One man might have responsibility for 10,000 pines on different properties. From March to November, collectors moved endlessly from tree to tree, using a hatchet to make a six-inch gash in each mature pine and attaching a tin trough under each cut. Periodically he returned to dip the gum from the containers and transfer it to a wooden barrel on a mule-drawn sledge. No matter how careful the worker, traces of the thick, sticky sap invariably stuck to his hands and clothing, which then picked up dirt and bits of pine bark. Not until the end of the day could he clean himself with kerosene. After filling a 500-pound barrel, which could take three weeks, the runner would seal and deliver it to a turpentine still for processing.

In September 1928, a full barrel rolled over John Hooks. Those who found him unconscious thought he'd suffered a stroke, and Lillian Hooks so wrote Delma, who decided to move his parents to Florida. On Sunday, September 16, he and Nell set out for Georgia in their Model T in the rain. Two inches had fallen on Saturday, and before the day ended the skies dumped another nine inches on the lake region. At the St. Lucie Canal, the Hooks stopped to chat with Nell's father, Hayward Horn, who now collected tolls at another point on the Conners Highway.

"I think y'all better drive up to the house," Hayward told his daughter and son-in-law. "Somebody said something about a hurricane coming."

Located three miles farther north, the two-story, 12-room building housed the families of both tollbooth operators. Divided by a two-foot-thick interior wall with no connecting door, the house had separate entrances to each half from a porch on one side. When Delma and Nell arrived, they found that some two dozen neighbors who lived in tents and shacks had taken shelter there.

Warned by telephone from West Palm Beach, several local men had sounded the alarm. Around the lake. some residents piled into cars and headed north for safety. Those on the southern shore had no easy route of escape. Others had no automobile or, preoccupied with preparations for harvesting the fall crop, simply planned on riding out the storm, as they had done two years earlier.

This photo, taken along the southeastern shore of Lake Okeechobee as the eye of the hurricane passed, shows two waterspouts and a lightning strike, September 1928. Courtesy, Lawrence E. Will Museum, City of Belle Glade, Florida.

The hurricane had originated on September 10 among the Cape Verde Islands off the northwestern coast of Africa. Two days later, it ravaged the Caribbean islands of Guadeloupe, St. Kitts, and Montserrat. Laying waste to Puerto Rico on the 13th, the storm continued along a northwesterly path and struck the Florida coast at West Palm Beach about 6:00 in the evening on September 16 and moved inland. The waters of Lake Okeechobee, which had risen by 13 to 16 feet during the past 30 days, almost immediately began pressing on the dike, repaired since the 1926 storm.

The people huddled in the Horns' home listened to the winds from the south and to the creaking boards of the house. When the gale subsided near midnight, they considered themselves fortunate that, once again, the winds had spared the lake's northern shore.

Ron Seckinger

Delma decided to drive to Canal Point to see whether his home and store had suffered damage, and Nell's brother Sam offered to go along. They were forced to halt at St. Lucie Canal, where the storm had blown open the bridge. As Delma sat in the car and Sam surveyed the damage, they heard a rushing noise.

"You better get in this car quick!" Delma yelled. "There's something coming back again!"

As the eye of the hurricane passed, the gale returned, pushing them with such force that Delma turned off the ignition and let the car roll on the cusp of the wind. Pulling into the yard at the Horns', they ran for cover. Sam entered the northern side of the house, where all the men had gathered during the lull, and Delma, the southern side, which sheltered mostly women and children.

The winds roared all night, attaining 160 miles per hour, with gusts at higher velocity. The gale blew out every window on the southern side of the house, driving stinging rain into the building. Delma nailed a dining table and doors from interior rooms over the gaping window frames in a futile effort to keep out the water. Praying and cowering in the corners and behind furniture, the occupants feared for their lives. Children screamed as objects collided with the house, which threatened to collapse.

The brunt of the second phase of the storm, much more severe than the first, fell on the southeastern shore. The lake waters, like milk in a saucer, sloshed to one side and then, when the wind shifted, rushed back to the other side and over the edge. On the small islands to the southeast corner of the lake, practically every building came loose from its foundation, and dozens who'd refused to evacuate their homes never saw daylight.

Some 200 persons, half the population of South Bay, took refuge on a quarter boat secured to pilings at the canal lock by 16 steel cables. Ivan Van Horne bolted a bilge pump to the open deck and smeared grease on the spark plug and other ignition parts to keep the water from shorting it out. Hugging the pump to avoid getting washed overboard, he nursed it through the night while others manned a bucket brigade to help empty the hold. They somehow managed to keep the vessel afloat.

Most of them probably would have perished otherwise, for that was where the dike gave way. A wave 26 feet high destroyed South Bay and still measured 12 feet when it hit Belle Glade, a mile and a half to the southeast. At Sebring Farm, the water smashed into a house where 63 people had taken shelter, and only six survived. Half of the 22 souls cowering in a packed house at Chosen lost their lives when the flood waters turned custard apple trees into battering rams.

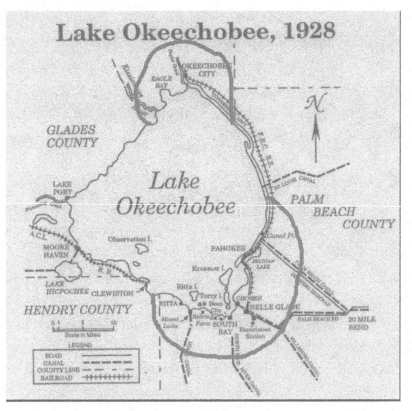

The hand-drawn lines indicate the areas of extensive flooding during the night of September 16-17, 1928. Courtesy, Lawrence E. Will Museum, City of Belle Glade, Florida. Original map by National Oceanographic and Atmospheric Administration.

It was a night of terror. Some climbed sturdy trees to escape the rising waters, but the force of the gale bent the trees back and submerged the upper branches with their human cargo. As the wind fluctuated, the trees stood partially erect again before plunging the refugees anew into the flood, each time threatening a final baptism. Those thrown from house, boat, or tree into the raging current swam blindly in the utter blackness, but the tangle of custard apple trees and wrecked buildings hooked many and dragged them under until, in a last, desperate gasp for air, their lungs filled with water. Others eventually found solid footing on hummocks in the Everglades but, weak and disoriented, died before they could find their way back to civilization.

The hurricane passed during the night, spawning violent storms as far north as Emanuel County. Eventually a cold, grey dawn came to Lake Okeechobee, with steely clouds obscuring the sky as rain continued to fall. Here and there the survivors emerged, crawling from smashed structures or cast up on a bank, too stunned to celebrate their escape. To the south of the lake, water stood hip-deep for as far as one could see.

Devastation along the south shore of Lake Okeechobee, September 1928.
Courtesy, Lawrence E. Will Museum, City of Belle Glade, Florida.

Hayward Horn's sturdy house came through the storm. Delma, Nell, and the others found themselves soaked but unhurt. The wind had carried a chicken coop from one side of the house to the other. Chickens, alive and dead, lay scattered everywhere.

Delma soon set out again, walking across the railroad bridge at the St. Lucie Canal and catching a ride on the other side. Canal Point had suffered extensive damage. The roof, walls, and stock of his grocery store had blown away, leaving nothing but the floor. The Hooks' personal possessions had survived because the floodwaters hadn't reached the second floor of the two-story house in which they resided. Only two citizens of Canal Point had perished—a woman crushed by a falling water tower and a man decapitated by a piece of tin riding the wind.

All along the southern shore of the lake, the storm had distributed death and destruction. Dead fish, cows, horses, poultry, dogs, snakes, alligators, birds and other animals floated on the floodwaters or remained caught, along with unfortunate humans, among the tangle of trees and buildings. Within 48 hours, the stench from flesh rotting in the Florida heat would become overpowering.

Cleaning up in Belle Glade, September 1928. The Black girl in the right foreground lost the other seven members of her family. Courtesy, Lawrence E. Will Museum, City of Belle Glade, Florida.

At first light on Monday, those who had escaped the storm began searching for loved ones and neighbors. They dug in the mud when they found a protruding foot or hand and chopped through snarled tree limbs to find the bodies, washing away the mud in puddles of water and leaving them by the roads for pickup. Two rescuers found an elderly woman alive but pinned in a tree. After freeing her, they brought one corpse after another until she had identified every member of her family.

Retrieving bodies near Belle Glade, September-October 1928. Courtesy, Lawrence E. Will Museum, City of Belle Glade, Florida.

Contingents from the Red Cross, the Salvation Army, the American Legion, the National Guard, and the Coast Guard soon arrived. The first doctors and nurses to reach Belle Glade had to wade through water and flotsam for the last two miles of the journey.

The government placed Belle Glade, South Bay, and other communities under martial law, and volunteers went to work clearing the roads to facilitate the arrival of supplies and the evacuation of the dead and homeless. The authorities sent surviving women and children to shelters in West Palm Beach, Ft. Lauderdale, and Miami, while their menfolk helped with the clean-up. The Red Cross established canteens and feeding centers, distributed used clothing and paper roofing to refugees, and inoculated 10,000 people against typhoid and smaller numbers against smallpox and tetanus.

The War Department contributed cots and blankets from Ft. McPherson in Atlanta. More than 3,000 volunteers pitched in, including 120 doctors and 78 nurses.

With his store gone, Delma had no job or income. Thanks to his earlier stint at the Citizen's Military Training Camp, he was able to sign on with the National Guard. He assisted a lieutenant charged with enumerating the casualties. Trucks brought hot food and coffee—and for the first 10 days, water from an artesian well, since the lake water was contaminated— to the disaster crew. Plenty of liquor also was available. When nightfall forced a halt in the search for bodies, the workers—wet, tired, and affected by their macabre task—gathered in hushed groups beside bonfires, took a few drinks, and fell asleep on the ground.

In Pahokee, a recent shipment of lumber, swept into Main Street by the storm, served as the material for rough caskets. Five carpenters from the lumberyard set up an assembly line and turned out a coffin every few minutes. Trucks brought corpses into town and then carried away the full coffins for burial in West Palm Beach or a new cemetery at Port Maraca, where a dragline sliced a long trench in the ground.

One of the funeral pyres on the south shore of Lake Okeechobee, September-October 1928. Courtesy, Lawrence E. Will Museum, City of Belle Glade, Florida.

The assembly line couldn't keep pace with the searchers' gruesome discoveries, and after two days the rescue workers stacked bodies like cordwood at collection points around the lake. Volunteers in small boats skirted the shore and the flooded sawgrass lands south of the lake, looping a rope around the neck of each corpse and returning with a grotesque string of swollen, unrecognizable bodies destined for common graves. Luther Levins, searching in one of the canals, was spooked when the boat's motor dislodged a body trapped underwater. The corpse of a large Black man suddenly shot vertically out of the water a few feet from Levins, giving him the fright of his life.

After two weeks, even burial was out of the question. Workers covered bodies with lime where they lay and erected white flags to mark their location. Others followed to pile the bodies together and douse them with fuel oil for burning. Along the southern shore of the lake, anyone who raised his eyes from the ground could spot white flags and the greasy, black smoke of funeral pyres.

Three quarters of the victims were Blacks, many of them from the migrant labor camps. Zora Neale Hurston, Florida native and key figure of the Harlem Rennaisance, later would celebrate them in her novel, *Their Eyes Were Watching God* (1937).

The authorities suspended clean-up operations during the first week of November. The official count, issued by the State Board of Health early the next month, exceeded 1,100 deaths in the Everglades—more than half in Belle Glade alone—and some 1,833 in all of Florida.

But many victims remained uncounted. In mid-December, a policeman fell into a canal at Chosen and discovered a body tangled in hyacinth vines under the water, and other corpses gradually came to light. Many had washed into sawgrass, where, for decades afterwards, farmers and construction workers periodically discovered the whitened bones of long-forgotten men, women, and children who perished during the night of September 16-17, 1928. The American Red Cross eventually estimated deaths in the lake region at 1,770 to 2,000, but no one considered this figure anything but an approximation. In 2003, the National Hurricane Center revised the official death toll in Florida to 2,500.

A farmer discovers the remains of a victim of the 1928 hurricane, 1930s.
Courtesy, Lawrence E. Will Museum, City of Belle Glade, Florida.

The Great Storm of 1928 ranks as one of the gravest disasters in the history of the United States. Only the hurricane that killed 6,000 at Galveston, Texas in 1900 had a higher death toll. Better-known tragedies claimed fewer lives—the Johnstown flood of 1889, 2,200; Hurricane Katrina in 2005, more than 2,300; the San Francisco earthquake of 1906, 503; and the Chicago fire of 1871, just 250.

Around Lake Okeechobee, survivors of the hurricane would use it for the rest of their lives as the base date for any event. I came to Pahokie three years before the big storm, one would say. Or, My boy was born the year after the hurricane. The listeners would nod their heads knowingly and remember.

Ron Seckinger

DUNCAN DESCENDING

IN HIS FORTIES and still slender, Duncan Fields progressively acquired the farmer's stoop-shouldered look. He affected a drooping moustache and a Stetson hat. Although he sometimes wore ragged overalls or britches, that impeccable white hat always rode his head, as if to proclaim, Here goes somebody.

He often took his children camping and fishing at Coleman's Lake and taught them to swim by tossing them into the water and watching them struggle to shore. One of the older boys usually went along in the boat to paddle so Duncan could concentrate on hooking a catfish or redbreast, but sometimes he took Leila or Romie Delle, gliding over the muddy waters of the Ogeechee River or the placid surface of McKinney's Pond while alligators sunned on the banks.

At home, he sat in a rocker on the front porch in the late afternoon, rolling cigarettes from a pouch of tobacco, surveying his property like some benevolent patriarch while his dogs lay underneath the porch, their sides heaving and their tongues lolling in the dust. Rosa, his favorite child, shaved him with a straight razor. "Rosie, get me a drink," he'd command, and Rosa, who in spite of everything adored her father, would fetch him a glass of corn liquor.

But Duncan, as the locals might say, was all vine and no 'taters. Alcohol brought out his ugly nature. Expletives peppered his speech, and he had a mean streak. Once he took Leila to a funeral at Summertown, and his brother Henry tried to take the reins because Duncan was abusing the mule. His family often fared worse. If he came home in the middle of the night and found the water trough empty, he'd wake the entire household in a rage and send J.D. out to water his horse.

He frequently whipped the boys. Once when Rosa was driving the other girls in the wagon, John A. and Ralph jumped out of the bushes to scare them, causing the mules to bolt. Duncan beat his sons with a belt while the girls stood around bawling as loudly as they had in the runaway wagon. The boys often hid in the barn to avoid crossing their father's path, and the younger children cowered in a corner whenever he entered the house.

Duncan wasn't the only alcoholic in the county, not by a long shot. Many a man came home so drunk he couldn't hit the ground with his hat, but Duncan's appetite for liquor was almost legendary. "Duncan was bad to drink," Callie Fagler recalled decades later, and everyone who knew him marked his excesses.

At the annual county fair, Duncan and his brother Garry B. would park Duncan's Model T outside the fairground and return to it during the day and evening for another snort. Once they crawled into a similar car owned by an African American man who couldn't persuade them they were in the wrong vehicle. Naw, that was their Model T and they weren't getting out. Sheriff Otis Coleman couldn't make them see reason either, and he got so mad everyone thought he might have a heart attack.

One morning, Perry Scott found a hat in the road as he and his sons traveled to an outlying field. "That's Duncan Fields's hat," said Scott. He leaned down from his wagon to pick up the white Stetson, which he placed on a fencepost beside the road. Sometime during the day, Duncan retraced his steps and recovered his prized possession.

He often returned home late at night, accompanied by his drinking and gambling cronies. Reeking of liquor, he rousted the children from their beds and herded them out to the porch to listen to his friends sing. The men, sitting on their horses, worked their way through several songs to humor him, while the children stood there half asleep, the younger ones rubbing their gummy eyes and the older ones burning with shame. The men started up "Goodnight, Irene" as an excuse to leave, but Duncan would have none of it. He insisted they sing another and another, until finally they wheeled their mounts and rode off with a reprise of the tune, leaving the children to stumble back to bed as the words and the hoofbeats faded:

> Goodnight, Irene, goodnight,
> Goodnight, Irene,
> Goodnight, Irene, goodnight,
> I'll see you in my dreams.

Jessie would have nothing to do with Duncan when he'd been drinking, and it fell to Rosa to pull off his boots and put him in bed. On some of those nights, Duncan would recover enough to assault Jessie in the dark, while the younger girls listened fearfully from their beds in the same room. "You're killing me!" Jessie would protest, trying unsuccessfully to fight him off. After Knob's birth in 1925, she suffered two more pregnancies, both ending in miscarriages.

In the mornings, Jessie rifled Duncan's pockets, looking for the money he rarely gave her willingly for sugar, coffee, and other necessities. On more than one occasion, he came out to the fields after finding his cash gone, enraged, carrying a plow line or tree limb with which to beat her. The older boys would intercede, holding him off while trying to duck his blows, slowly coaxing him back to the house. Jessie usually avoided him, particularly when he was drunk and likely to strike her. At least once, when her equanimity failed her, she cracked his head with a piece of firewood.

As the years passed, Duncan spent less and less time at home. Everyone knew about his affair with a married woman on a nearby farm.

As they worked in the fields, Jessie and her children could see the woman's house on a hill, hovering above them like a reproach.

Duncan's health eroded as binge followed binge. One autumn night, when Jessie hadn't returned from a shopping trip to Swainsboro, he suffered a stroke. Leila and Ralph walked through the dark to a relative's home in search of help, and Jessie, delivered home at midnight by Waitus and Margie, found the house in an uproar.

This posed photo of cheating poker players and an armed robber in Stillmore, Emanuel County, ca. 1910, was all in fun. But liquor and guns often turned card games into deadly affairs. Courtesy, Georgia Archives, Vanishing Georgia Collection, emn145.

Ron Seckinger

Duncan recovered but changed not at all. Fishing at Coleman's Lake or McKinney's Pond remained his prime occupation. He camped out with his buddies for a week at a time. At night, they fried fish in a skillet over an open fire, sang a few songs, had a drink of two, and played nickel-and-dime poker by firelight.

Duncan also played cards for higher stakes in barns here and there around the county, and sometimes the carousing turned ugly. One night in 1928, several of his friends burst through the door of Jessie's home, supporting Duncan, who was bleeding profusely. J.D. and Jessie's brother Kermit fainted dead away at the sight of the blood. During a dispute over a poker hand, one of Duncan's companions had pulled a revolver and shot him in the right temple at point-blank range. Miraculously, the bullet had deflected off the skull and traveled under the skin to lodge at the back of his neck. A doctor, summoned from town, extracted the projectile, shaking his head over his patient's survival.

Duncan's recuperation lasted some time, but eventually he rose from his sickbed. With one eye slightly cocked as a result of the shooting, no one could tell exactly where he directed his vision. His love of jug and card table, on the other hand, remained clear to all, and he returned to the business of self-destruction with a vengeance. Duncan had almost completed the job that he'd seemingly set for himself, the ruin not only of his own life but also those of his wife and children. He took a giant step toward its realization by losing the family farm.

The challenges of surviving as a farmer had vanquished better men than Duncan Fields. Any combination of bad weather, bad judgment, and bad luck could bring disaster. Duncan had scraped by for almost two decades, largely because of the hard work of Jessie and her children, while his brothers and many others had come up short.

Like all smallholders, he relied on credit to get him from spring planting to harvest. He borrowed against his property in 1913, 1915, 1916, and 1922, in some cases taking years to pay off the lien. Against all odds, he weathered the recession of 1920 and another decline in cotton prices caused by overproduction in 1925 and 1926. Farmers in general didn't share in the prosperity of the '20s, however, and their vulnerability grew year by year. Having signed three additional notes against his farm in 1928, Duncan was ill prepared to confront the Great Depression that, unknown to all, lay just ahead. Forces beyond his control poised to evict him from the 50 acres given by his father.

Duncan lunged forward to embrace disaster. His descent from land-owner to sharecropper came not from the announcement of a sheriff's sale in the *Forest-Blade* but the laying down of an inferior poker hand in someone's barn, where Duncan forfeited his property by the light of a kerosene lantern amid the smells of horse manure, tobacco smoke, and human sweat. In February 1929, he deeded the property to John A. Bell for $1,575 to cover his gambling debts.

In practical terms, struggling to survive was the same for farmer and sharecropper. But psychologically the change represented a fall from grace. The loss humiliated and frightened Jessie and her children. More than half a century later, Leila and Romie Delle would recall the event with horror-tinted awe, as though the scars hadn't yet healed.

And yet Duncan still hadn't finished. While his family kept working the same land, farming on shares for John A. Bell, Duncan drank. One night in February 1930, he roused the sleeping household when he decided to whip four-year-old Knob for some real or imagined misdeed, while the Fields girls and their visiting cousin Jean Dyson cowered in their beds. Later that night he caused another stir, this time by suffering a stroke—his third. As Jessie and the older children rushed to and fro, the younger ones peeked into Duncan's room and listened to the strange, guttural, snoring sound that emanated from his open mouth.

They moved him to a bed in the parlor, where Dr. C.E. Powell treated him daily for almost a week. Just before midnight on February 15, Jessie woke the children and took them into the parlor to watch their father die by the flickering light of a lantern. His labored breathing ceased with a gurgling noise in his throat as he suffered a massive cerebral hemorrhage and his tongue thrust out of his mouth like a dead chicken's. Leila and Romie Delle felt no emotion.

"I'm better off than I've been in years," said Jessie. "All he caused was pain."

She wired Emmit, who sent $90 from Kentucky to pay for the funeral. On the unseasonably warm day, many of the men were in shirt sleeves. Practically everyone in that part of the county attended the services at Fields Chapel, for Duncan was a popular man. From the chapel, a cortege of automobiles, buggies, and wagons traveled the short distance to Hall's Cemetery, where Duncan's coffin was covered with earth and his soul commended to his Maker. Rosa, the only member of the family to feel any loss at his passing, became hysterical and threw herself on the grave.

Afterwards, many of the mourners returned to the Fields's home, where thoughtful neighbors laid out cakes, pies, and other foods as tangible evidence of their condolences. Dennis Rich and his family, as well as Jessie's relatives and close friends, remained overnight, sitting and talking and consoling Duncan's survivors. In the morning, they said their goodbyes, leaving Jessie in the house she didn't own to continue her fight to make a life for herself and her children.

DREAMER

MAUDE, YOUNGEST of the Stroud children, escaped the drudgery of farming at an early age and never had to accept the hardscrabble realities that made Jessie Fields a tireless worker all her life. Instead, Maude had the luxury of creating her own reality based on daydreams fed by the movies.

By the 1920s, films had become an American institution. Thomas Edison's Kinetoscope, introduced in 1894, touched off the craze. Patrons deposited coins in the machine to view—individually, through eyepieces—brief, primitive moving pictures. Within two years, the invention of the projector turned the experience into a social event that could be shared by hundreds and eventually thousands.

At first, movies played in amusement parks and vaudeville halls, or in traveling exhibits. By 1905, however, the nickelodeon had proliferated across the country. Many communities acquired special, albeit typically Spartan, locales devoted to moving pictures.

The development of film techniques transformed the novelty of motion into an art form and structure for coherent stories, and the movies' growing popularity with the middle classes warranted more elegant surroundings. The studios handled their own distribution and built their own movie houses as a means of ensuring maximum showings of the films they churned out each year. With their ready access to capital, Hollywood moguls financed the construction of hundreds of theaters during the years between the end of the Great War and the onset of the Great Depression, not only in great markets like New York, Chicago, Detroit, and Los Angeles, but also in middle-sized cities and even small towns.

Maude Stroud, before she made the transition to town kid, ca. 1923.

A handful of architects, many of them transplanted from Europe, designed the new temples to fantasy. Just as films plunged moviegoers into strange worlds, so did the theaters themselves. The discovery in 1922 of the tomb of Tutankhamen, the Egyptian boy king, whetted the public's appetite for the exotic, and studio architects hastened to provide it. Each theater typically had a discrete architectural theme—Chinese, Egyptian, East Indian, Babylonian-Persian, Pueblo, Art Deco, Second Empire, Mayan, Spanish Colonial, Tudor, Italian Baroque, Siamese.

Designers intended to lure patrons inside and blunt the annoyance of waiting for the next seating. They pioneered the use of electric signs. The theater's name typically beckoned from a column of flashing lights over an immense marquee heralding the film and its stars. Moviegoers purchased their tickets at a free-standing box office, often made of marble trimmed with brass, and passed through a broad arcade to a palatial lobby where they passed the time on padded benches and savored the sumptuous furnishings. Ladies who retired to the lounge could sit at elegant dressing tables and primp before gilded mirrors. Air conditioning, still a rarity, ensured comfort even for summer matinées. The larger theaters, such as the 6,214-seat Roxy in New York, boasted infirmaries and professionally staffed nurseries.

When the auditorium had emptied from the previous showing, uniformed ushers escorted waiting patrons to numbered seats, frequently upholstered in velvet. Members of the audience gazed with appreciation at the ornate decoration and whispered quietly like worshipers in a Gothic cathedral until the lights dimmed and the show began. Many establishments featured live entertainment before the film, such as a revue by the Fanchon and Marco "Sunkist Beauties" or a performance by a symphony orchestra. Every large theater also had a powerful organ, typically a "Mighty Wurlitzer," which provided musical preludes and accompaniments. At length, the preliminaries concluded, the heavy curtain parted to reveal the silver screen, and the moviegoers, by suspending belief, became participants in high drama or low comedy for a few hours before resuming their relatively humdrum lives.

The Fox Theater in Atlanta ranked as the most famous movie palace in the South. Running into financial difficulties while building a new headquarters on a city block located at Peachtree Street and Ponce de Leon Avenue, the Yaarab Temple of the Ancient Arabic Order of the Nobles of the Mystic Shrine agreed to include a movie auditorium for lease by Fox Studios. The exterior of the building resembled an Islamic mosque, with arches, minarets, geometric designs, and onion-shaped domes. The movie house, designed largely by Oliver J. Vinour, echoed the Middle Eastern theme. Blue-tiled goldfish pools lined the arcade, and the lobby featured ornate chairs, vases, floor lamps, and carpets, as well as bas-reliefs of Egyptian kings, scarabs, lions, and other motifs.

Atlanta's Fox Theater, ca. 1929. Courtesy, Atlanta Historical Society.

The auditorium itself, with almost 5,000 seats, replicated an Arabian courtyard. Towering parapets and turrets running the width of the 140-foot stage dwarfed the screen. An enormous striped canopy hung above the top balcony. The room appeared open to the night sky, for faux stars twinkled overhead and, in the greatest engineering feat of the enterprise, clouds seemed to drift across the expanse above the audience. Inaugurated on Christmas Day, 1929, the Fox immediately became a Mecca for movie-goers and curiosity-seekers all over the South.

Maude had no doubt attended a movie in a tent or small-town theater, but her fascination with motion pictures began in Detroit. One can imagine the awe the nine-year-old felt on entering for the first time the vaulted foyer of the State Theater, with its multiple chandeliers and Empire-style decorative painting, or the 2,800-seat Grand Riviera, which evoked an Italian garden.

Although the quality of the movies didn't match the buildings, the flimsy plots captivated Maude, transporting her to Arabia, medieval France, the Wild West, or the pirate-infested Caribbean. Films shaped her view of the world, and as a teenager and adult she seemed to think of herself as a celluloid heroine, battered by fate but possessing the grit to triumph in the last reel.

The "It" girl, Clara Bow, 1920s. Public domain.

Maude's fascination with motion pictures accompanied her to Swainsboro in 1926, although the Grand Theater near the courthouse square hardly compared with the cinema houses of Detroit. She and Alice, along with their friends, usually took in at least one film each week. Maude particularly liked westerns but wouldn't turn up her nose at any kind of movie. One that impressed the young women of Swainsboro—and, indeed, audiences across the country—was "It," the 1927 silent featuring Clara Bow.

Bow, born into poverty in Brooklyn, had won a screen test by sending her photograph to a fan magazine. Arriving in Hollywood in 1923 at the age of 17, she appeared in 26 films before the end of 1925, emerging as one of the foremost stars of the era. Often cast as a wealthy and headstrong young woman, Bow personified the flapper of the '20s.

Elinor Glyn, a British novelist and screenwriter, anointed the Brooklyn native as a paragon of "It." This concept, as developed by Glyn, referred to a personal magnetism based on utter self-confidence coupled with a complete lack of concern for one's effect on others. The movie of the same name starred Bow as a gold-digging shopgirl who sets her cap for her employer. Dozens of films of the era relied on similar plots, featuring young women who capitalized on their femininity to win the good life.

Maude idolized movie stars and the characters they portrayed on the screen. She bought 10-cent fan publications like *Photoplay* and *Balaban & Katz Magazine*, writing away for publicity shots of her favorite actors. On the wall of the room she and Alice shared at Margie's hung photo-portraits of Bow, Norma Shearer, Richard Dix, and other Hollywood notables.

By the time her 15th birthday approached in 1929, Maude had blossomed into a young lady. Slender and attractive, about five-feet-five, she took pains with her appearance. Her dark hair always just so, she began using lipstick and light make-up long before any of her friends dared. Once Maude plucked Gladys Waller's eyebrows into thin lines like her own, and Gladys's father forbade his daughter to see her friend for a week.

Maude's friend Nesbit Rogers recalled her reserved manner 60 years later:

> Maude was quiet and proud. If someone criticized or spoke crossly to her at home, she would calmly go to her own room. She was a very, very private person, to a great degree. And you never knew, really, what she was thinking about sometimes. She just seemed like … her mind was far away or something. And she was not loud

and boisterous like some of us. She was very quiet. A
very quiet person.

Nesbit's forbidden romance appealed to Maude like the latest
Constance Talmadge film. Nesbit had fallen in love with Johnny Christian,
a suitor totally unacceptable to her parents because he was divorced and,
at 25, 10 years her senior. Johnny, who worked in a service station, drove
to the high school each day at recess so he and Nesbit could stand beside
his car and chat. Maude and Gladys gloried in the conspiracy, conveying
messages between the sweethearts to facilitate their clandestine meetings.
They notified Johnny when the three planned to attend the movies, and the
older man would join them in the back rows of the Grand Theater. Garland
Sherrod, cousin to both Nesbit and Maude, also played a role in the melodrama, serving as Nesbit's escort to parties and other events where Johnny
suddenly would materialize.

Secret sweethearts Johnny Christian and Nesbit Rogers, ca. 1930.

Maude seemed to care little for men. Gladys considered her uncle,
R.J. Waller, a most handsome man, and she fantasized that he and her
friend might fall in love. To this end, she invited Maude to a family reunion

near Blundale one Saturday. Even though R.J. took Maude for a ride in his car, Gladys's plans for their life together came to naught.

None of the men in Emanuel County, no matter how handsome, could satisfy Maude's ambition, for the youngest of the Stroud children had her eyes set on more distant horizons. As Gladys described Maude years later:

> She was a dreamer and talked a lot about when she could leave Swainsboro and get a job. She didn't seem very happy being in Swainsboro. Her dream was just to get away and get a job so she could be independent … She was interested in romance and beautiful clothes and money to spend.

Alice and Maude Stroud about the time they departed Swainsboro for Miami, 1931.

Two of the classmates who scrawled messages in Maude's scrapbook alluded to her daydreams. "I'm sorry we didn't get to take our trip to Hollywood this summer," Jeannette Youmans wrote in October 1929. "Maybe we will get to go sometime, eh? I hope so." The following February, S.R. Curl added his comment: "I hope that you get that millionaire you want."

Others, with the sunny optimism of the young, penned their best wishes for future happiness or offered instructions in life. "May misfortune always follow, but never overtake you," several wrote. "To strive, to seek, to find and not to yield," quoted another. And Lucille Scott: "Let nothing discourage you. Never give up. Maude I think if you always remember the above motto you will come out all right."

Alice graduated high school, the first of her family to do so, in June 1929. She took a job as clerk in the United 5 & 10 on the courthouse square and continued to live with Margie and Waitus.

Maude wanted more than that. The dreamer got her chance to leave Swainsboro in August 1931, when Denver agreed to help his two youngest sisters find jobs in Miami. Just nine months away from completing high school, Maude probably had few regrets as she and Alice boarded a bus for Florida. At last, she was on her way.

Ron Seckinger

EVERGLADES

BEFORE THE FUNERAL PYRES had cooled on the shores of Lake Okeechobee, Nell and Delma Hooks resumed their trip to Georgia. In late 1928, they returned to Florida with Delma's father, now recovered from his accident with a barrel of pine sap. In January 1929, Delma's brother Audie brought their mother, their sister Hazel and family, and Jewel Stroud Hooks's daughter Freddie, along with their meager possessions, to Canal Point. This exodus left Hooks Crossing in Emanuel County practically depopulated.

The lake area still hadn't recovered from the storm of September 1928. Most buildings lay in ruins, and the canal and adjacent fields bore evidence of the devastation. The Red Cross had just closed the two tent cities—one for Whites, one for Blacks—it had set up in Canal Point for homeless survivors of the storm.

In far-off Washington, the wheels of government had begun to grind. On the first day of the new Congressional session, Florida's senators introduced a bill to provide flood control for the Lake Okeechobee region. President-elect Herbert Hoover, scheduled to take office in March, had carried Palm Beach County and the entire state in November, bolstering chances of passage.

Freddie Hooks, 1926-1927.

On February 15-16, 1929, Hoover toured the disaster area, along with the governor, the chief of the Army Engineers, and a Congressman who headed the House of Representatives' flood-control committee. The party passed through Canal Point twice, once en route to Okeechobee and again on the way to Clewiston. Delma Hooks watched and listened as Hoover spoke from the back of a truck, dispensing a politician's promises of a new day for his constituents.

In Clewiston, industrialist Henry Ford and his friend, the inventor Thomas Edison—who maintained a laboratory in Fort Myers on Florida's Gulf Coast—joined the president-elect's group. The Canal Point *Everglades News* reported "tears in Mr. Hoover's eyes as he received the flowers and vegetables pressed on him by children at Pahokee," while the locals asked themselves whether anything would come of the visit. The state's flood-control program had garnered strong criticism after the destructive storm of 1926, and now the residents of the lake region petitioned the federal government to assume responsibility.

Hoover, a mining engineer, supported the notion, and Congress approved building a levee along the southern lakeshore as part of a project to improve the trans-state waterway via the St. Lucie Canal, Lake Okeechobee, and the Caloosahatchee River. In November 1930, the Army Engineers began work on what would become a permanent flood-control effort designed to avert a repetition of the disaster of 1928. The experience had deeply marked the local residents, and for many years to come every report of an impending hurricane touched off a frantic flight to higher ground.

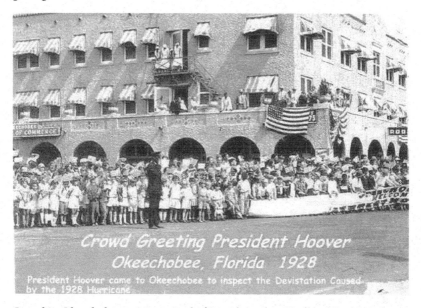

Crowd in Okeechobee awaits arrival of President-elect Herbert Hoover, February 15, 1929. Courtesy, Lawrence E. Will Museum, City of Belle Glade, Florida.

Meanwhile, Delma set out to rebuild the life smashed by the storm. With a partner, he bought the Lakeview Restaurant in February 1929, and in May, he reopened his grocery store at a new location on the lakefront road. R.G. Dun and Company gave the grocery a fair credit rating and estimated its stock at $2,000 to $3,000.

The Depression eroded living standards in the lake area, but perhaps less than in many regions of the country. Although the Southern Sugar Company went into receivership in July 1930, a new enterprise, the

United States Sugar Corporation, absorbed its operations and boosted raw sugar production to 36,000 tons during the 1932-1933 season. Canal Point claimed 2,500 residents, and Delma's restaurant did a brisk trade by feeding busloads of tourists, businessmen, and fortune-seekers from West Palm Beach and Okeechobee for boat connections to Clewiston. Local families strapped for funds could supplement their diet with free fish from the lake, and the cost of living was substantially lower than in West Palm Beach. At Delma's store a dozen eggs cost 33 cents; a 24-pound bag of flour, 84 cents; an eight-pound can of Jewel lard, $1; and a gallon of Bonita syrup, 95 cents.

President-elect Herbert Hoover visited with Henry Ford, Thomas Edison, and Harvey Firestone in Fort Myers after touring the devastated Okeechobee region in February 1929. Courtesy, State Archives of Florida.

Over the ensuing years, Delma did well enough with his restaurant and grocery store to accumulate substantial properties on the south side of town. Lillian and Freddie lived in a building that Delma and four other men had originally constructed as a church, and Hazel and her family resided across the street in another of Delma's houses. For the first time, Freddie and Lillian had indoor plumbing.

Lillian had brought her stand-up piano from Emanuel County, but she soon sold it to a jook joint owned by an African American man. In October 1931, she opened her own establishment, the All-American Restaurant, near the tollgate on the Old Conners Highway on the north side of Canal Point.

Canal Point, Florida, December 10, 1938. Courtesy, National Records and Records Administration.

Other members of the Hooks clan followed the trail to Florida, including Jewel's three remaining daughters. Mae, a stunning blonde, came to Canal Point in 1929 after her suspension from a nursing school in Dublin, Georgia because she and several other students had gone for an auto ride with two young men. Thelma joined the others later the same year, and Melema, a decade later.

The lake area, however, would never be the same, notwithstanding the creation of Everglades National Park in 1947.

The Hoover Dike, the massive levee on the southern shore of Lake Okeechobee, protected local communities from rising waters, but it also severed the lake from its natural outlet, the Everglades. Rather than feed the wetlands to the south, the overflow ran through canals to the Atlantic, damaging the ecology of the coast and leaving former swamp bottoms to dry out and blow away. Expanding sugar plantations poisoned the land and water with fertilizer runoff.

Today, the magnificent Everglades teeters on the brink of utter destruction.

MIAMI

DENVER STROUD had little to complain about in 1929. A skilled die-maker in an auto plant, he made more money than most Americans, and his wife and daughter had rejoined him in Detroit. No, life treated him well—until the stock market crash of October 1929 began the unraveling of the national economy and ushered in the Great Depression. Success suddenly seemed precarious.

Denver felt the impact as the auto companies, like manufacturers throughout the nation, laid off workers by the thousands. In Michigan alone, some 750,000 men found themselves unemployed, and the lucky ones who retained their jobs saw their wages decline by 40 percent. Long queues of men, women, and children lined the sidewalks each day, faces marked by shame and despair, awaiting their turn to feed on free meals in dreary soup kitchens or to file for a place on the government dole. On every street corner, it seemed, jobless men peddled apples—distributed on credit by the International Apple Shippers Association—for five cents each.

At the time of the national census in April 1930, Denver still resided in Detroit, listing himself as a diesinker in an auto factory. But he must have lost his job shortly afterwards, for he soon struck out in search of better prospects in Florida.

Looking west on Flagler Street from Northeast 3rd Avenue, Miami, 1933-1934. Courtesy, Miami-Dade Public Library, Romer Collection.

Although the land boom responsible for Miami's rapid growth in the early 1920s had long since burst, Denver managed to find work. First, he took a job as housepainter, settling his family in a home on Southwest 7th Street. By the beginning of 1932, he'd signed on with Standard Oil, driving a truck and delivering propane gas tanks. He moved Bernice and Lillian to Northwest 15th Street and then to a small home on a pleasant street in the 3200 block of Northwest 16th Terrace, in the sprawling suburbs west of the city.

They took to Miami's tropical climate, palm-lined streets, and beautiful beaches. Neighbors and acquaintances told stories of the hurricanes of 1926 and 1928, but occasional dangers seemed a small price for regular work and the city's delightful environment.

When Emmit wrote in August 1931, suggesting that he help Alice and Maude, Denver quickly agreed, as long as his youngest sister didn't clash with his wife again.

Ron Seckinger

I have just read your two letters was glad to hear from you. Well Send Maude and Alice down here. I will see what I can do for them. I think they may be able to get work this winter. I will be able to feed them if I keep on working. And I think my job is steady ... Yes I am willing to take the kids here with me if we can get along without any fusses ... This is a right good-size town and I believe they can get some thing to do.

Maude and Alice arrived soon afterwards. They lived with Denver and his family until they found jobs working for Claude and Lillian High on Northwest 49th Street. Claude sold automobile tires, and his wife operated Lillian's Beauty Shop. Alice kept their four children and helped out at the salon, giving shampoos, cleaning the brushes, and sweeping up. Maude became a hair stylist.

Alice Stroud with three of the High children, Miami, 1931. From left: Mary Margaret ("Bach"), Thomas R. ("Bob"), and Jean Marie.

More than Alice, Maude had a flair for beautician's work, thanks to her careful attention to her own appearance. ("Never let your eyebrows grow out," one of her high-school classmates had written in her scrapbook.) She enjoyed the camaraderie of the shop and took pride in her work. She wore her own hair short and permed, just like Claudette Colbert and other movie stars.

The two girls often saw Denver and his family. But not for long. On June 18, 1933, while loading propane tanks on his truck, he suffered a cerebral hemorrhage and died instantly, four months shy of his 34th birthday.

Denver's wife Bernice notified Waitus and Margie in Swainsboro, and Waitus phoned Emmit. Kermit and Maude left Fitzgerald in Emmit's Ford. They arrived at Bernice's home in Miami at 1:30 on June 20, an hour before the funeral. Maude asked Bernice to hold the procession until they had bathed and dressed, but at 2:40 they found the house deserted. At the Philbrick Funeral Home, they learned the cortege had departed promptly at 2:30. A man offered to drive them to the cemetery, and they hurtled through the streets of Miami at 50 to 65 miles an hour on what Maude would call "the wildest ride I have every taken or hope to take."

Maude Stroud, ca. 1932.

On the southwest side of the city, they caught up with the procession at Woodlawn Park Cemetery, where flat grave markers stretched in all directions. Flushed and anxious from the frenzied trip, they stood with the other mourners as the Reverend George Hyman, chaplain at Denver's American Legion post, presided over the funeral services. Slim olive trees

Ron Seckinger

provided scant shade, but—despite a heat wave that afflicted much of the country—the temperature in Miami barely reached 80 degrees.

Maude swallowed her resentment at Bernice's having left them behind and embraced the widow and her daughter Lillian. Because Maude and Kermit had had no opportunity to view the body at the funeral parlor, the mortician's crew offered to open the casket, in violation of city ordinances, if the two would stay behind.

"He looked pretty natural," Maude would write Margie a few days later, "but not near like the Denver I used to know. He was so very much thinner and older looking."

At length the crew closed the casket again and lowered it into the ground. As shovelfuls of the sandy soil rained down on the lid, Maude and Kermit drove away and, with a final glance through the rear window, bid farewell to their brother.

COLLEGE BOY

FEW OF JESSIE and Duncan Fields's children could aspire to education and good jobs. Rosa, John A., and Ralph dropped out after the sixth or seventh grade to work full-time on the farm. J.D., the eldest, had the opportunity to stay in school thanks to his athletic prowess. In his father's Model T, he drove the younger children to Summertown School, where he starred on the football and baseball fields and played center on the all-district basketball team in 1927.

Because Summertown had only 10 grades, J.D. transferred to Swainsboro in the fall of 1927 for his senior year. He anchored the football squad that crushed Stillmore 58-0 and was elected captain of the basketball team. Adoring girls surrounded the handsome sports hero with blue eyes and brown hair. In May 1928, he became the first in the Fields family to graduate high school, albeit at 21, four years older than most of his classmates. A sports scholarship provided his ticket to Georgia State Teachers College—now Georgia Southern University—in Statesboro in the fall.

For a farm boy, college presented a new and daunting world. Suddenly thrust among classmates who had enjoyed a more urbane upbringing, J.D. traded his overalls and brogans for blazer and white trousers. He somehow made the transition, acquiring the nickname "Granny" and the acceptance of his fellow students. The editors of his sophomore yearbook identified him with the quotation, "Life is what you make it. Make it worth while," and he seemed dedicated to improving himself. He joined the Stephens Literary Society, the Bachelors Club, the Varsity Club, the Science Club, and the Young Men's Christian Association.

J.D. Fields, high school football star, ca. 1929.

He made his mark in sports. Although thin and enfeebled after contracting typhoid fever while selling Bibles in North Carolina in the summer of 1928 or 1929, he recovered and went on to star in football—his teammates elected him captain in 1930—and basketball, and he managed the baseball team. Everyone agreed that J.D. had a bright future.

But at the end of his third year, J.D. suddenly eloped with another student. Jessie, who heard the news at a Fourth of July barbecue, was devastated, fearing her son might have thrown away his chance to escape the poverty she knew so well. She couldn't help but like his wife, however. A relatively sophisticated town girl from another county who dressed well and owned a car, she charmed the entire family during a visit to the farm. J.D.'s younger sisters felt as though they'd entered the presence of a fairy princess.

J.D. Fields at Georgia State Teachers College, 1930-1931.

Withdrawing from college after completing the spring quarter in 1931, Jessie's oldest son went to live with his in-laws and worked on their farm for a while. But his bride's parents opposed the union, and eventually they sent J.D. home.

Back in Emanuel County, J.D. licked his wounds and filed for divorce. He began courting Ouida Kirkland, born out of wedlock, now a plump woman four years older than he. On Christmas Eve, 1934, they ran off to Midville to get married. The bride insisted the ceremony be performed by a preacher rather than a justice of the peace, and, when they discovered that the pastor in Midville had left town for the holidays, they drove on to Waynesboro. There they located the home of a preacher and exchanged vows in his study, decorated for Christmas. Ouida turned 30 the following day.

J.D. moved into the old house on Ouida's 50-acre farm near Blun, inherited from her uncle, Fess Kirkland. The land was heavily encumbered by debt, but J.D.'s business savvy, combined with President Franklin Roosevelt's New Deal policies, would fix that.

J.D. and Ouida Fields, ca. 1935-1936.

The Agricultural Adjustment Administration (AAA), created barely two months after Roosevelt's inauguration in March 1933, set out to relieve the farmer's plight by providing parity payments in exchange for voluntary reductions in the acreage of seven basic commodities, including cotton. More immediately, the government planned to raise cotton prices by keeping a portion of the bumper crop ripening in the fields from reaching market. Using the county extension agents, the AAA began to plow under the stalks on more than 10 million acres.

Those who made their living from the land were aghast at such destruction, even when promised compensation. But they quickly learned the advantage of receiving government subsidies for not planting cotton, particularly when they could use the land thus freed for other cash crops, such as peanuts. Some 25 percent of the crop fell under the plow in Emanuel County that year, and growers adjusted to the system of allotments that determined their shares of cotton and tobacco production.

To be sure, not everyone saw justice in the size of his allotment. In the early hours of a Sunday morning in October 1935, disgruntled farmers torched the home of Emanuel County Agent J.W. Stephenson. Narrowly escaping the blazing building with his wife and children, Stephenson hurried to his farm bell to arouse his neighbors but found the cord thrown over the roof of the smokehouse so he couldn't reach it. Soon afterwards, the unfortunate agent obtained a transfer to Hall County without finishing out the year.

Like the AAA, other New Deal agencies became an integral part of Southern life. Farmers obtained price-support loans from the Commodity Credit Corporation and assistance from the Soil Conservation Service for crop rotation, terracing, and the introduction of legumes such as soybeans, kudzu, and lespedeza. Many farm boys earned a little cash in the Civilian Conservation Corps (CCC), which improved national parks and croplands, and the Works Progress Administration (WPA), which served as employer of last resort for the entire nation.

Ron Seckinger

The New Deal rescued Southern agriculture for the landowners, but at substantial cost to tenants. The relatively well-to-do served on the county committees that worked with the AAA and the extension agents, and they reaped most of the benefits of the new order. Throughout the South, parity payments and federally subsidized credit allowed landowners to evict their tenants, hire day laborers, and over time buy machinery that further reduced the need for manual labor.

In December 1934, the extension agent for Emanuel County cited the difficulties of persuading landowners to deal fairly with and not evict sharecroppers. Tenancy declined rapidly after 1935. Sharecroppers and renters flooded the towns and cities in search of jobs. Their traces littered the countryside: crumbling shacks torched by arsonists, leaving tall, brick chimneys like sentinels beside the fields.

Parity payments on Ouida's croplands allowed J.D. to retire the debts on the farm in short order. He held a seat on the county committee and took a job as manager of the Coleman Gin and Fertilizer Company in Swainsboro. Even without the college degree that would've meant so much to Jessie, he'd go on to become a successful businessman and pillar of the community.

PATRIARCH

THE MANTEL OF family head had settled easily on Emmit Stroud's shoulders following his father's death. Vulnerable to periodic layoffs and by no means wealthy, he still had more resources than the others and showed a broad streak of generosity. He provided what Christmas Jessie's children knew, paid for the funerals of relatives, and took care of Alice's clothing and incidental expenses. Once, when J.D. wrecked his father's Model T, Emmit sent money for repairs in response to Jessie's plea. As long as he had a job, Emmit helped his siblings.

But he wouldn't always have a job. As the Depression deepened, employment became uncertain even for railroad workers. Operating revenues plummeted. Payrolls declined from 1.7 million employees in 1929 to 1.2 million in 1931, and 500,000 of those worked part time. Even the ones lucky enough to retain their jobs suffered declining income, for an industry-wide negotiation led to a 10-percent wage cut in February 1932. Former railroad men were among the hoboes who hitched rides in empty freight cars, constantly on the move, searching for any kind of work—chopping wood, digging ditches, anything that might help feed their families.

Seniority protected Emmit for a while. Save the occasional short-term layoffs—a few days in October 1931 and a few more at yearend, for example—he continued to pound the inside of boilers at the Ferguson shops. But in March 1933, the axe finally fell. In January, he'd sent Kermit to work the farm in Fitzgerald and soon afterwards told Alice and Maude to keep house for him. Now he and Frances sold many of their goods and set off with Hilma to join the others. Using their last railroad passes, the Strouds hurtled over the rails past hobo jungles as Franklin Roosevelt took office and declared a bank holiday.

Having shared generously with his relatives, Emmit had but $500 in savings. Most recently he'd financed a six-month beautician training course for Alice and Maude, who wanted to open their own shop. With Emmit's promise of support, in mid-1932, the two sisters had headed for Atlanta, the economic heart of the Southeast.

A vibrant commercial life defined "the Atlanta spirit." The city's industries included textiles, ironworks, carriages, farm goods, furniture, paper bags, and Coca-Cola. First sold as a patent medicine by druggist Asa Candler, the soft drink by the 1890s had become nationally known. The founding of the Georgia Technological Institute in 1886 assured a constant stream of engineers for Atlanta's booming industries.

By the time Alice and Maude arrived at the height of the Great Depression, Atlanta claimed more than 270,000 inhabitants. Many of them had no employment and relied on soup kitchens and other charities for survival. An organization known as the Black Shirts in the early 1930s had intimidated many businesses into replacing their Black workers— hotel bellhops, for example—with Whites. Behind the progressive images fostered by the boosters lay the city's seamy side. Speakeasies, brothels, and gambling suffered little interference from the corrupt police force. Thousands of citizens played "the bug," as the numbers racket was called; others shot craps on street corners, and bookies openly took bets in the bleachers at Ponce de Leon Park during baseball games.

Alice and Maude saw little of Atlanta's underside. They boarded with a family on Memorial Drive in the southeastern part of the city. For the first time in her life, Maude had a boyfriend, a man named Waters. Alice, who never had dates of her own, sometimes went along with the couple to have a bite to eat or to a movie at the Fox Theater or elsewhere.

Each morning, the sisters rode a west-bound streetcar to the American School of Beauty Culture on Whitehall, which in the next block became Atlanta's fabled Peachtree Street. By day, the girls learned their craft, each with a different specialty, among the strong smells of chemicals used for permanents and other hair treatments. Soon they were among the students allowed to take care of customers in search of a bargain. In the depths of the Depression, many women had to entrust their looks to the unskilled hands of student beauticians, and Alice honed her talents by giving inexpensive haircuts.

When Alice and Maude completed the course in January 1933, Emmit came from Kentucky to buy equipment and help them set up a shop. Only then did he learn that Georgia law required beauticians to spend six months as apprentices before they could operate their own salons. Emmit sent them to the farm in Fitzgerald while he considered what they should do next.

Now, just two months later, he found himself near destitute, responsible for the welfare not only of a wife and daughter but also of three siblings. Much of his savings went to purchase furniture, cattle, two mules, and a beat-up Ford for the farm. The stress overwhelmed his generosity, and he became a penny-pincher. His quick temper festered into a permanent ill humor. Anxiety didn't drive him to drink, at least no more than usual, but he struck out verbally at those closest to him as he contemplated a future without steady employment.

Alice soon left for Miami, and Kermit moved out after a bitter quarrel with Emmit. Kermit had borrowed Emmit's touring car to take his girlfriend for a drive and failed to secure the new canvas top, which dragged behind the vehicle in the dirt. "Emmit liked to have forty fits," Frances recalled years later, "so mad he couldn't see straight."

Soon afterward. the two brothers came to blows. Hilma, sitting on the back steps, took fright when she saw her father and uncle wrestling on the ground and trying to throttle each other until Frances managed to separate them. Denver had already sold his share of the farm to Emmit for $10 in February. In July, Kermit signed over his share to repay Emmit some $300 in loans and moved out.

In a letter to Margie that same month, Maude, who'd gone to Miami to attend Denver's funeral, described her oldest brother as a spiteful, selfish tyrant rather than the benevolent patriarch of happier days:

> Marjorie, I don't know what is wrong with them at Fitzgerald. But from what I can hear I think every thing has gone wrong. I know I shouldn't say this after all Emmitt has done for me, but honest Marjorie I think he has gone completely crazy. He has been trying for a long time to force Kermit to leave the farm, and now he has succeeded. Not satisfied with that he has gotten Kermit's share of the farm. Kermit did that to try to pay back the money he has gotten from him. After Kermit stayed there all this year and practically made the crop, he had to leave that and only got a few dollars out of it. When I heard from Kermit last week he was with a friend. He does not know what he will do now. Every time I think about it I get so mad that I can't help crying. Kermit has worked hard enough to get a better break than what he has been getting.
>
> Marjorie, do you know why Emmitt <u>would not</u> come to Denver's funeral? Merely because he was afraid he would have to pay his funeral expenses. That night after Waitus called up, he sat out on the porch and talked about the money his family owed him that he would never get back. Threw it up to us about having to pay for Papa,

Mama, Jewel's, Duncan's and Frances's father's funeral expenses, as if Kermit, Frances and I were to blame. He said every thing hateful that nite that he could think of. He wasn't thinking of poor Denver laying down there dead with none of his family around except Alice, but of his own selfish self and his money.

Money that we owe him and the things he has done for his family is all that I have heard since we all got back to the farm. As for him saying a kind word to his family that is something he doesn't do. I can't remember him saying a kind word to me

Poor Frances was almost crazy when I left. She told me several times that she had stood almost as much as she could and that sooner or later she was going to end it all. Frances is too darn good to have to live like she does, but what can she do? She has no one else to go to. But to me death would be sweet compared with the life she is having to lead.

Oh I could sit here all night and write about the nasty things he has done and said, but what's the use? It only makes me think less of him when I shouldn't. May God help me, so that I don't get to hate my own brother.

Emmit, realizing he and Frances couldn't work the farm by themselves, rented it out after gathering the crop. While Frances visited her ailing grandmother in Somerset, he vacated the farmhouse and moved their few belongings into a small, one-room shack his father had operated as a country store. When Frances returned, she found the shack had become their home.

Ron Seckinger

Emmit spent his time repairing the dilapidated dwelling, raising calves, tending a vegetable garden, and gathering pecans to sell. On Saturdays they went to Fitzgerald with the other farmers to socialize and buy a few groceries. Keeping track of every dime, they stayed away from the movie theater and entertained themselves by walking the streets.

At least Hilma enjoyed the farm. Both of her parents were reserved and undemonstrative, and Frances criticized her daughter's every act. Hilma's bout with scarlet fever following an appendectomy in 1931 or 1932 had made Frances and Emmit even more overprotective. In Somerset, they didn't allow her to leave the yard, and other children seldom came to play. She had little to do save frolic with her kitten "Bluey" and read from the Big Little Books series.

Emmit moved his family into this shack when he rented out his Fitzgerald farm, 1933.

In earlier years the annual trip to Fitzgerald for a week in the summer had excited Hilma more than anything. Now, living there year 'round, she had the run of the farm. She roamed through the pines, watched the hogs and other animals, and sometimes played with other children. On Mondays, once Frances finished with the wash, Hilma and some of the Black kids who lived nearby climbed into the large tin tub and splashed in the rinse water.

While Kermit lived on the farm, Hilma followed her uncle around like a puppy, climbed on his lap, and looked to him for the affection her father gave only sparingly. She eagerly anticipated Saturday nights, when Kermit's radio, powered by a car battery, provided the family's only entertainment—"National Barn Dance," broadcast live from WLM in Chicago. During the rest of the week, the massive console radio sat silent against the wall, its battery too precious to use frequently.

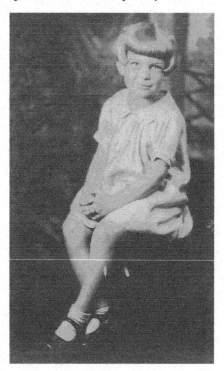

Hilma Stroud, ca 1931.

After a year in Fitzgerald, a friend sent word of a job at a shipyard in Brooklyn, and in April 1934, Emmit left for New York. As often as possible, he sent money to Frances, some for expenses and the rest to save for a trip north. She and Hilma joined Emmit a few months later.

They lived in a fourth-floor walk-up on 49th Street in Brooklyn, near the East River. Hilma, now almost nine, attended a public school a few blocks away. She hated the dark building surrounded by a wall, a far cry from the tree-shaded school in Somerset. She spent hours sitting on the fire escape at home, watching tugboats, skiffs, and ocean-going ships pass majestically on the river.

Winter blew in on a bitter wind. They had no warm clothing and suffered from the cold, Emmit most of all since he often worked outdoors. In November, they quit Brooklyn and returned to Fitzgerald to escape the weather. Only two weeks later, word came that the Southern was hiring again, and they quickly resumed their lives in Somerset.

With steady work over the next several years, Emmit regained some of his equanimity. Even so, he fretted about money. The night before each payday, Frances totaled their bills and calculated how much they needed for the next two weeks. Emmit paid his debts in cash, and any extra income went into a savings account, insurance against the sickening sense of helplessness he'd felt in 1933. He welcomed the introduction of Social Security in 1935 and insisted Hilma apply for a card long before she was old enough to hold even a part-time job.

The cumulative effects of the boilermaker's trade had begun to erode Emmit's health. One day Frances went to the Ferguson shops to get her husband's signature on a legal document. "Where's Emmit?" she asked one of his co-workers.

"That's him," replied the man, indicating a locomotive from which the most awful banging ensued.

The constant pounding on metal plates within confined spaces had by this time damaged his hearing, although Emmit stubbornly insisted that he failed to hear only because Frances spoke too softly. Worse, he often suffered debilitating headaches. Seeing him walking up from the depot, Frances could tell immediately if a migraine had wrapped its coils around his skull. On those evenings, she placed cold compresses on his forehead and admonished him to keep quiet as he lay on the sofa in agony. Even so, he always returned to work the next day, perhaps fearing that taking sick leave might make him more vulnerable to another layoff.

For the rest of his life, Emmit bore the Depression's scars. He and his family had managed to escape the nomadic, hobo-jungle fate that befell millions of others. But they'd come close enough. Never again would he take the future for granted.

SHARECROPPERS

JESSIE FIELDS AND her children remained on the land they no longer owned for one more season before Jessie asked Warren Kea, a relative by marriage, to let her farm one of his properties near Modoc. Instead, Kea contacted R.A. ("Ell") Flanders, president of the Central Bank in Swainsboro and related to the Fields through his wife, Duncan's aunt. Flanders set Jessie and her brood up as sharecroppers on one of his properties on the Old Wadley Road, just two miles north of Swainsboro. They moved to the new location in late 1930 or early 1931 and began working the land with an African American tenant family, Mamie and Deusie Green and their children.

Jessie's plight could hardly have been starker. In the space of a year, she had lost her farm and her husband, and between the two events the country had entered the worst economic crisis in its history. She responded the only way she knew how—with an attitude that was not exactly fatalism but rather realism so solid it admitted no pretense. She faced adversity like a mule harnessed to a plow, looking to neither side, plodding forward, ever forward, to no destiny other than a turn and the beginning of another furrow.

With her children, Jessie took her place in Ell Flanders's cotton fields, and when Knob or Wynelle complained, "My back hurts," she answered, "You don't have a back." She'd pick from their rows to help them keep up while maintaining her own row even with the other adults. If one of them kept complaining, she'd pull up a cotton stalk and lash the whiner across the shoulders with the comment, "Now it hurts." It was a cruel but effective means of focusing the child's attention on the task at hand rather than the unavoidable discomfort of field work.

Picking cotton on the Flanders farm, ca. 1937.

With the collapse of cotton prices--from almost 17 cents a pound in 1929 to less than seven in 1932--this back-breaking, mind-numbing labor yielded even smaller rewards than during the '20s. After clearing the books, Jessie usually earned less than $100 for the year.

Surprisingly, she occasionally told her neighbor Callie Fagler that she missed Duncan. He'd taken care of some of the tasks that now fell to her, she explained, and my, that man could shoot quail.

On the Flanders farm, Jessie and her children occupied a "dog trot" house with an open hall down the middle and rooms on either side. A tall windmill pumped water from the well to a spigot on the back porch, where they washed their hands and faces from a basin and threw the dirty water into the yard. Behind the house were the barn, syrup shed, and two-seat privy.

For the first time the family had an icebox, which rested on the porch. Jessie bought a 100-pound block from the ice truck that came from Swainsboro once or twice a week, and one of the boys would chip off slivers for iced tea.

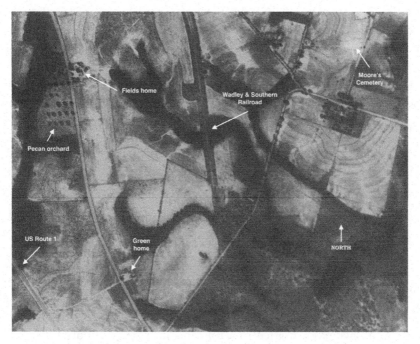

The Flanders farm and surrounding area, September 16, 1937.
Courtesy, National Archives and Administration.

Unlike their old farm, Uncle Ell's was located on one of the main roads. People passing in cars or wagons waved and frequently stopped to chat. Drummers visited regularly, trying to sell pots, pans, brooms, brushes, or other household items. Jessie rarely had cash for such goods, although she usually managed to purchase black pepper and vanilla extract from the Watkins salesman.

The family reaped few direct benefits from the New Deal. The Rural Electrification Administration, which extended power lines into the countryside, brought light to the unpainted farmhouse about 1936. Jessie and the children had commitments elsewhere on the day workmen linked them to the grid, but they drove past at night just to see the building lit up for the first time. For a while, they tugged on a pull-chain just to see the bare bulb magically turn incandescent, but soon they learned to take the new technology for granted. John A. earned a little cash in Civilian Conservation Corps camps or laboring on Works Progress Administration (WPA) projects, but otherwise President Roosevelt's programs helped only by boosting cotton prices and slowly bringing economic recovery. By and large, farm life continued as before.

With no capital to purchase a tractor or other labor-saving devices, Jessie relied on human and animal power. In the spring, John A. and Ralph broke the soil in the traditional way, behind single-blade plows hitched to mules. Jessie and the younger ones planted by hand, nourished the plants with manure, chopped cotton, tended the garden, and handled the livestock. Cotton and corn were their only cash crops, and they stocked the larder with home-canned goods and cured meat rather than store-bought food.

Leila, Romie Delle, Wynelle, and Knob transferred to the school in nearby Swainsboro. Feeling that the town kids looked down on them, they were embarrassed to eat their lunches—usually vegetables and a biscuit with a sausage patty, carried in a tin can—in front of children who had sandwiches made with sliced white bread. Knob, humiliated by his baggy, mustard-colored WPA britches, didn't take to studying and would've quit but for his mother's insistence. Romie Delle and Wynelle, on the other hand, loved school despite their classmates' condescension. Romie Delle learned to ride a bicycle on the school grounds and went on class excursions. Once she went by train to participate in a parade in Augusta, and her new shoes hurt so badly she took them off and marched barefoot.

Despite the loss of the farm and the onset of the Depression, they were happier. Duncan's brooding presence no longer darkened the household, and the children had no fear that he would spoil visits by their friends.

Ron Seckinger

Also, Jessie could keep the fruits of her labor. Instead of making clothing from flour sacks, she bought fabrics from Ehrlich's Department Store at 10 cents a yard. Sometimes she bought an entire bolt and made identical dresses for the girls and shirts for the boys. The saleswomen at Ehrlich's also gave her scraps, including sample swathes of leather or men's suits, which she used to make patchwork garments.

On Saturdays, J.D. took his mother and sisters to town. Embarrassed by his shabby car, the girls insisted he let them out on a side street so they could walk to the courthouse square. They often sat with Aunt Margie, who held court from her auto parked outside Scott's Barber Shop. When Uncle Waitus could take a break from his customers, he'd bring Coca-Colas for the girls. If one of the girls had a nickel, she could buy a triple-scoop ice cream cone or agonize over every item in the toy section of the Five and Ten. During the harvest, Jessie paid her children a dime each for picking cotton all Saturday morning, and their earnings might go for a matinée at the Grand Theater.

Late in the night, as farmers and their families slowly abandoned the streets, J.D. returned to carry Jessie and her girls home from the best day of the week.

JEALOUSY

DUNCAN FIELDS'S younger brother Garry B., born in 1894, grew up to become a man who carried a pistol in each boot. Like all of the Fields men, he drank heavily. He worked as a turpentine runner but never amounted to anything. "He didn't like to work too much, not too hard," his daughter would recall decades later.

His wife, née Annie Viola Robinson, eventually tired of their hand-to-mouth life. About 1926, she fled their rented house near Sardis Church and made off to Augusta with their three children. Two years later, Garry B. stole the kids, who lived with him until Annie stole them back. This traffic went on for a few more years and might've lasted longer save for Garry B.'s untimely death.

In 1935, Garry B., then 41, was dating a 21-year-old divorcée and single mother named Odessa Jones. On Saturday night, March 16, he was shooting pool with Will McMillan in a hall over a drug store in Swainsboro. Someone came in and whispered to Garry B., who turned to Will and said, "We'll wind up the game later on, Mac."

Garry B. walked out, rented a Model A Ford from Henry Rich, and drove to Nunn's Tourist Inn, a jook joint on Route 80, five miles outside town. Despite the repeal of national Prohibition with the 21st Amendment in 1933, the sale of alcohol remained illegal in Georgia and several other states, but "blind tigers" and other illicit saloons continued to thrive.

Ron Seckinger

Garry B. Fields, ca. 1912.

As usual on a Saturday night, a boisterous, hard-drinking crowd filled the Nunn place. Fourteen-year-old Lynwood Screws, who'd arrived earlier with a friend on a motorcycle to buy Coca-Colas, witnessed Garry B.'s arrival and what followed. Dorothy Trapnell later testified that the Nunn family had hired her and Odessa as hostesses "to dance and dine and entertain" the patrons. As he stepped onto the dance floor, Garry B. fired a shot through a Victrola record player, halting the dancing and gaining everyone's attention.

He walked up to Odessa and said, "Well, it's all over now," and shot her three times in the abdomen. He ignored her dance partner, who, some said later, didn't stop running till he reached Statesboro.

Outside, as Garry B. returned to his rented car, the proprietors' son Harry Nunn confronted him, and Garry B. shot him, too. Then a shot from the building struck Garry B. in the head—fired by Harry's mother, so the gossips said. Garry B. died immediately on the side of the road, and his two victims bled out en route to the hospital.

By the time Sheriff P. L. Youmans and Night Marshal Willie Fields—Garry B.'s cousin—arrived on the scene, most of the witnesses had scattered. A coroner's jury, convened the following morning, ruled that Garry B. had shot Odessa and that Garry B. and Harry had come to their deaths "at the hands of parties unknown."

Mourners attended the funerals of Garry B. Fields and Odessa Jones at Hall's Cemetery on Sunday, March 17—hers at 11:00 and his at 3:00 so the two families might not be tempted to continue the altercation at graveside.

Judge R.N. Hardeman, still on the bench 18 years after ruling on whether Swainsboro schoolchildren could attend the movies on weeknights, issued a restraining order against the Nunns' roadhouse in response to a petition from Willie Fields, Central Bank President Ell Flanders, a former county sheriff, and the chairman of the county board of health. The petition accused the proprietors of operating "several slot machines, which are games of chance and prohibited by law." Moreover, the document went on breathlessly, at Nunn's Tourist Inn,

> alcoholic liquors, spirituous liquors, whiskey, moonshine liquor, and intoxicating liquors and beverages are kept to be drunk upon or about said premises by persons going there for that purpose

—which, most folks would argue, was the very essence of such an establishment.

On April 8 Hardeman made the injunction permanent, citing not only the jook's unsavory reputation but also the recent indictment of Harry Nunn's father and brother for assault with intent to murder a patron earlier that year.

Ron Seckinger

The self-described "decent people" of Swainsboro seemingly had won a small victory over the dark forces of dissipation and sin. But just a month after Judge Hardeman's injunction, the citizens of Georgia voted to do away with the state dry law. The repeal carried Emanuel County by a wide margin.

KERMIT

EXCEPT FOR the faint smile, Kermit Stroud might have been a casting director's choice for the role of a sinister gypsy. An exotic and handsome man, he had a swarthy complexion, jet black hair, a slight build, and a face as thin as an axe blade. In a family noted for taciturnity, he proved the most close-mouthed of all. While Jessie, Emmit, and Denver approached life like prizefighters, slugging it out toe to toe, Kermit watched from ringside. Basically passive, he wasn't the kind of man who controlled his own destiny but rather the kind to whom things happened.

Nothing seemed to stick. He followed Denver to Detroit but never found steady work, so he'd labor on Jessie's farm or stay awhile with Margie and Waitus in Swainsboro. Sent to work the farm in Fitzgerald at the beginning of 1933, he sold his share to Emmit within six months and again had no roof.

During the spring, he'd met Rosa Lee Jean Walker, a strikingly beautiful 16-year-old who lived with her parents on the adjoining farm. Breaking soil behind a plow in the early mornings, Kermit would stop when she walked up the road to catch the school bus. They chatted by the fence while she waited, and, as she recalled more than half a century later, "We hit it off."

Kermit Stroud, ca. 1938.

Rose, as everyone called her, liked the older man's looks and set her cap for him, looking forward to seeing him in the mornings, or on Sundays at Bethlehem Baptist Church, or at community social events. And Kermit, who until now had shown himself immune to women's charms, returned her interest.

Emmit and Frances disapproved of the Walker family and tried to dissuade Kermit. Rose's mother, Frances Walker, also opposed the couple's plans. As much as she liked Kermit, then 27 years old, she considered her daughter too young for marriage.

Rose often missed days at school because she had to work in the fields or could not finish her chores—she had to fill a lard can with fresh milk in the dark each morning—in time to walk the mile and a half to the bus stop by 7:30. Held back several times, in June 1934, she finally graduated from grammar school and passed to the eighth grade, just a month before her 17th birthday. Frances Walker thus forbade any talk of marriage.

Rose Walker Stroud, ca. 1938.

Kermit and Rose didn't talk openly about a wedding but went ahead with their plans anyway. Kermit obtained a marriage license on August 3, after returning from Denver's funeral in Miami, and the two awaited their opportunity. When Frances Walker announced that she was driving into Fitzgerald on August 8, Rose said she wanted to go and sent word to Kermit. The conspirators, breathless with excitement, met at the courthouse, where the Clerk of the Ordinary performed the ceremony uniting them as man and wife.

When they returned to the farm to inform Frances Walker, the old lady capitulated graciously. "You know you're too young to get married," she told her daughter, "but that's what you wanted to do, I reckon."

"Yes'm," murmured Rose.

Too late in the year to plant their own crop, they eked out a livelihood by hiring out as day laborers, picking cotton, pulling corn, and shucking peanuts for other farmers. Daily pay for each amounted to 50 or 55 cents, or 65 on a particularly good day, plus the noon meal.

Ron Seckinger

Rose's mother let them use a three-room shack on her property and helped accumulate furniture. The shack lay some distance from the Walker home, and a pigback road—two ruts constantly in danger of being swallowed by weeds and scrub growth—provided the only access through the woods.

Rose and Kermit, ca, 1934.

With just the two of them and a single mule, they could manage to farm only a few dozen acres on shares the following year. Rose worked in the fields beside her husband, planting cotton, peanuts, corn, and a little tobacco. She also tried to brighten the yard with zinnias, marigolds, and petunias, although the chickens usually scratched up the seeds before they germinated.

Rose became pregnant in the second year of their marriage. Like most poor country women, she continued working in the fields and visited a physician only two or three times during the course of the pregnancy. As she came to term in the early autumn of 1935, she suffered from "sick headaches," or migraines. The doctor delivered the baby by forceps in October. Rose faded in and out, and eventually Kermit moved her and the baby,

Carolyn Jean, to Frances Walker's home, more easily accessible in the event of further complications.

"Whatever you do," the doctor told Rose, "don't get pregnant again. I don't want you to have another child. I don't feel like you can."

Rose doted on the baby, and despite their precautions she and Kermit conceived another child late the following year. Fortunately, the second pregnancy went smoothly. Their son, Denver Julian, came in July 1937.

Rose and Kermit Stroud with Jean and Julian, ca. 1940.

Ron Seckinger

A sharecropper family had worked Emmit's farm since his return to Kentucky, but when the family left that summer, Emmit and his brother made up after four years of silence. Kermit moved his family back to the farm once owned by Jim and Sudie Stroud.

Relations between Kermit and Rose steadily soured. The personality differences that had enflamed their mutual attraction soon became irritants, and their passion faded as they confronted the drudgery of the sharecropper's life.

In many ways, Kermit was an exemplary husband. Unlike most men, he shared the housework, drying dishes, scrubbing floors, drawing water, washing clothes. He adored his children. Only once did he spank Jean, when she toppled the firewood he'd just stacked. He worked hard, didn't gamble, confined his drinking to Saturdays, and never disappeared for days on end.

But his passivity rankled Rose. If anything annoyed him—if the cows, for example, proved uncooperative when he drove them to the barn—he displaced his anger onto his wife, pouting and refusing to talk. When Rose pressed him for an explanation, he'd deny any unhappiness and become contrite and sweet. But he couldn't rid himself of the trait, and inevitably he'd withdraw again.

Even when in a good mood, Kermit was quiet and sedentary. He could sit in a room full of people for hours without initiating a conversation or responding to questions with more than the bare minimum. Sitting in a straight-backed chair, he smoked cigarette after cigarette, leaning forward to rest his elbows on his knees and, as the smoke drifted lazily toward the ceiling, broke his silence with his smoker's cough, which deepened and became more frequent with each passing year. A few drinks would loosen his tongue, but normally he remained encased in his solitude.

Slowly, he and Rose drifted apart.

MAUDE

MAUDE STROUD had always hated life in the country, and returning to her father's farm near Fitzgerald 10 years after her escape seemed a cruel trick. Emmit demanded that everyone pitch in, and, as much as she preferred Miami or Atlanta, she had no other option. As they chopped cotton one day in May, Maude claimed illness and left the others in the fields. Emmit groused, believing his sister a loafer.

In reality, Maude was pregnant, as she confided to Alice. Had she given herself, or had someone seduced or forced her? Alice, reluctantly recounting her scant knowledge half a century later, had no details. Maude was terrified. How would she face Emmit and the puritanical Frances once she began to show?

In mid-June 1933, she received a letter from a woman offering her a job in Miami—Maude may have written to ask—and at almost the same time news arrived of Denver's death. Maude seized the opportunity and traveled to Florida with Kermit. Keeping her pregnancy from her relatives in Georgia, she somehow managed to support herself until she came to term in November.

On entering the home for unwed mothers, Maude intended to surrender her baby for adoption. But when she held him and saw his tiny hands and mouth, she couldn't bring herself to let him go to someone else.

Ron Seckinger

She gave him the name George but called him Billy. He might have no father, but he would know his mother.

Her decision had serious consequences. Only Alice and Bernice, Denver's widow, knew of Maude's pregnancy. Had she given up the child for adoption, Maude could've kept her misadventure hidden from the rest of her family and her old friends in Swainsboro. Instead, she marked herself as, in the parlance of the day, a "fallen woman." She didn't have to wear a scarlet letter, but many would treat her as though she did.

In February 1934, Maude sent a telegram asking Kermit to meet her at the train station in Tifton, explaining that the stay-over for a transfer to Fitzgerald would be too long for the baby.

"What baby?" Kermit and Rose asked themselves. But they borrowed her father's car and dutifully met Maude in Tifton, where they learned of their nephew's existence.

Maude and Billy remained with Kermit for six to eight months, during which time she tended the baby and hardly contributed to the household chores. She attended Bethlehem Church with Kermit and Rose, but things went badly. One night, her sister-in-law Frances berated her in front of the entire congregation for having borne a child out of wedlock, and the two never spoke again. She dated a local man named Woodrow, and gossipers whispered that he had fathered the boy. He came on foot through the woods to Kermit and Rose's home to visit, and sometimes he and Maude went for walks.

Margie Scott came from Swainsboro for a visit and saw what was coming. "Rosa, whatever you do," she said, "don't take that baby." Indeed, toward the end of the summer Maude asked Rose to keep Billy while she returned to Miami to get a job. Even though Rose had become attached to the boy, she decided Margie was right.

Kermit, wanting to help his younger sister, got angry, but Rose told him, "That's all right, too, but I'm not taking no baby." And so Billy, just beginning to take his first steps, returned to Florida with his mother.

The lot of working women during the Great Depression was difficult, and that of a single mother even harder. One of every four women
belonged to the workforce in 1930, almost all of them restricted to certain occupations and earning on average half the salary paid to men. Many
girls who left farms for the cities couldn't earn a living wage and eventually
returned to the country.

Maude, determined to avoid that fate, supported herself in a variety
of jobs. For a while, she worked in a hamburger restaurant, according to a
bit of doggerel penned in her scrapbook by Harry Aronow in 1933:

> Here is to Maude,
> Who thinks she's just grand,
> She works at the White Tower,
> The Barbecue Stand.

Usually, she labored as a domestic. Even though the ratio of servants
to total population had declined sharply since 1890, in 1930, domestic service still provided employment for three of every 10 working women in
the United States. Maude earned a little spending money, in addition to
her room and board, at the cost of living with her son. Employers wanted
her attention on their own children, and so Billy had to reside elsewhere.
Alice, now beginning her own family, kept him for almost two years while
Maude cleaned other women's houses and cared for their children in
Miami, Tampa, and Lakeland.

Maude tried to stay in touch with her high-school friends in
Swainsboro. Nesbit Rogers replied to one letter but then fell silent, and
Maude eventually stopped writing to her. Years later, Nesbit discovered that
her mother had intercepted and destroyed Maude's letters. Correspondence
with Gladys Waller proved more rewarding. Maude wrote of parties in
Miami and all the people she knew. Once she told of attending a dance,
how much she'd enjoyed the music, and how she'd met a man she liked.

Maude Stroud in Miami, ca. 1935.

Twenty-three years old in 1936, Maude remained a dreamer. Two women that year must have appealed to her fantasies. The first was the fictional Scarlett O'Hara, the hot-blooded protagonist of Margaret Mitchell's epic work, *Gone with the Wind*. Maude loved books, and Alice vaguely remembered years later that her sister, like much of the nation, had read Mitchell's novel. A best-seller from the day of its publication on June 30, the book sold 1 million copies in the United States within seven months and won Mitchell the Pulitzer Prize the following year.

One of the most popular novels of all time, *Gone with the Wind* had an extraordinary impact. Its mythic rendering of Southern history resonated with young White Southerners like Maude, raised to accept the nobility of the Lost Cause, and the drama of its heroine's life captivated readers around the world. Scarlett's early life as a plantation belle and her subsequent, stormy marriage to Captain Rhett Butler were the stuff of a Southern girl's daydreams.

The second woman was a native of Emanuel County. At the age of 18, Marie Phillips left her mother's turkey farm near Nunez, a small community south of Swainsboro, to pursue a dancing career in New York City. Taking the stage name Lillian Duval, she found a job as a showgirl in a Broadway cabaret and achieved some notoriety back in Emanuel County. Once or twice a year, she returned to Swainsboro, where she visited the beauty parlor and got a write-up in the *Forest-Blade*.

Then, after three years on Broadway, her big break arrived in the person of Paul G. Curley. A graduate of Georgetown University, Curley was a radio announcer and the son of Governor James M. Curley of Massachusetts. He pursued Marie for months. She eventually accepted his suit, and they married on Christmas Eve in 1936, announcing that they would settle in Boston. "It's safe to say 'no more show business' for Marie," the bride's mother told the press. "She wants to be a house wife." (The storybook romance was ill-fated. Paul Curley was an alcoholic, and the marriage soon failed.)

Maude seemingly had her own shot at happiness in that same year of 1936, when she found a husband. How she met Archie Moreno, the son of a Cuban-born cigar maker in Key West, is unknown. On July 16, Maude and the 28-year-old Moreno, who worked as an auto mechanic at Meltzer Motors in Miami, applied for a marriage license at the Dade County Courthouse. The clerk who typed the application entered the laconic comment: "This girl 5 mos. pregnant." That same day a justice of the peace performed the ceremony.

The marriage might have represented a fresh start for Maude, an opportunity to establish a stable home for Billy and overcome the stigma of being a "ruined woman." Instead, she and Archie remained together only until August 1, according to Archie's subsequent testimony, and the union was dissolved in less than a year.

Ron Seckinger

According to the bill of complaint Archie filed the following April—he'd moved to Tampa in late 1936—Maude was a vicious shrew. Testifying in court that he had provided her with "a very comfortable home with gas, hot and cold water ... a very decent place to live, lights, telephone and so forth," Archie described the treatment he received in return:

> It was mean, she was nagging all the time, and would not cook and wanted money all the time, to go out and eat in restaurants, and kept dressed up all day going to picture shows and running around in automobiles and burning up gas and never swept up the home or washed the dishes, and she had gotten to where she would call up and interfere with my work, interfere with my foreman, and my foreman warned me to have her stay away and she said she would not, and she had some cross words with the foreman, and he said, if she does not stay away he would have to fire me, and she would not stay away and in a few days she came back again and he fired me and then I stayed around the house, and she said she would not stay away from that place and she would not cook for me and finally the foreman put me back to work again, and then she said she would not come around, but she did, and she came around there the second time and I was fired again.

He often had to work until late at night, Archie said, and Maude accused him of running around with other women. One night, she confronted him with an ice pick in her hand and said "if I did not come home earlier she would kill me with an ice pick. That was about ten thirty. She said she would kill me and I was afraid to go to sleep. I was afraid she would kill me with the ice pick."

A childhood friend from Key West substantiated portions of his testimony. Ralph Camus told the court he had seen the couple three times, and on every occasion, Maude hectored her husband. Once when Archie invited him for dinner, Maude refused to cook, Camus said, and at Meltzer Motors he witnessed her demand for money. He also testified that he had heard her call her husband a "damned son of a bitch" and that, when Archie escorted her out of the repair area, she said, "I will kill you for this."

We have no account from Maude, and neither Archie nor his friend Camus can be considered unbiased. Moreover, Archie's claim that all these events transpired within two weeks strains credulity. It's safe to assume some degree of exaggeration and perhaps even fabrication.

Archie's rendering paints his wife as a paragon of petulant self-indulgence, and even if his depiction is only partially true, it's difficult to justify Maude's behavior. Perhaps she viewed marriage as an entrée to the kind of pampered life many of her movie heroines enjoyed, an escape from responsibility, the realization of her teenage dreams. Served with a subpoena on March 25, Maude didn't travel to Tampa to contest the suit. On June 18, 1937, the presiding judge granted Archie's petition for divorce.

Archie's court testimony made no mention of Billy, but Maude gave her son Moreno's last name, which he would bear for the rest of his life. Archie also failed to mention her second pregnancy noted by the clerk who signed their marriage certificate.

After giving birth in the fall of 1936, Maude chose to put the baby up for adoption. In mid-1937, she found herself where she had been a year earlier—alone and without adequate resources to care for her son.

POLITICS

WAITUS SCOTT, like the majority of White Southerners, clung to the Democratic Party. The ouster of Reconstruction governments in the 1870s had led to the creation of the "Solid South," a region unshakably committed to the Democrats, who had sought a negotiated settlement of the Civil War and afterwards futilely resisted the punitive policies of the Radical Republicans who controlled Congress. Triumph in the White Democratic primary equaled victory in the general election. Indeed, the winner often ran unopposed in November, given the shortage of quixotic Republican candidates.

Like many of his customers and neighbors, Waitus admired Franklin Roosevelt and always listened to the president's "fireside chats" on the radio. The Northern patrician and former governor of New York seemed an unlikely hero for the dirt farmers and small-town merchants of Georgia. To be sure, the president had strong links to the state; his mother hailed from Georgia, and he maintained a retreat, nicknamed "the Little White House," at Warm Springs, where he frequently took the waters to strengthen his polio-shriveled legs. More importantly, the common people of Georgia came to see the New Deal as their salvation from the misery of the Depression.

But another Democrat with diametrically opposed views, Eugene Talmadge, also had a strong following in Emanuel County. Unlike

Roosevelt, Talmadge sprang from the Georgia soil. Despite his law degree and Phi Beta Kappa key, the farmer from McRae spoke the commoners' language. Bursting on the scene in 1926, he scored an electoral upset of the powerful state agriculture commissioner by portraying himself as an outsider and champion of "the little man."

For the next two decades, Gene Talmadge strode the political landscape like a titan. In the county seats, no one worked the crowds better than he. Wearing a rumpled white suit, snapping the red galluses that held up his pants, his hair unkempt and his arms gyrating like a windmill, he used earthy speech and crude humor to establish a bond with farmers who still plowed behind mules and defecated in outhouses or in the woods. He played on their resentment of state officials in far-off Atlanta and of banks and all the evil forces that kept the have-nots mired in poverty. "The poor dirt farmer," he would declare, "ain't got but three friends on this earth-- God Almighty, Sears Roebuck, and Gene Talmadge."

Swept into the statehouse in 1932, "the Wild Man from Sugar Creek" won reelection in 1934. The county-unit system abetted his career by awarding all of a county's electoral votes to the candidate who finished first in the balloting. The eight most populous counties had six votes each; the next 30 counties, four votes; and the remaining 121 counties, two votes. The system diluted the strength of large cities and gave disproportionate weight to rural areas, where Talmadge's constituency resided.

An archconservative, the governor during his second term began to distance himself from Roosevelt's policies. Convinced that government "give-aways" sapped citizens' independence, he vehemently opposed crop reduction, WPA or CCC employment, and Social Security, oblivious to the benefits his supporters reaped from New Deal programs. In 1936, Talmadge challenged one of Roosevelt's strongest supporters, Richard B. Russell, for a seat in the United States Senate.

Russell, Talmadge's predecessor in the statehouse, had moved in 1932 to fill the unexpired team of one of Georgia's senators. His devotion to the New Deal was uncompromising, and—thanks in large measure to the way Talmadge framed the issue—voters saw his campaign for reelection in 1936 as a referendum on Roosevelt's policies. The contest therefore required that Georgians like Waitus Scott choose between two of their most cherished icons.

The attachment to leaders of such different philosophies and manners reflected a profound ambivalence among many Georgia voters. On the one hand, they continued to embrace traditional values of self-reliance and limited government, confident of their ability to make their own way if not victimized by banks, railroads, or other institutions they perceived as nefarious. They gloried in their own coarseness and applauded Gene Talmadge for taking their side.

Governor Eugene Talmadge (center, waving his hat) campaigning for the US Senate in the 1936 Democratic primary election. Courtesy, Georgia Archives, Vanishing George Collection, trp301.

On the other hand, the experience of the Depression and the New Deal made them less leery of looking to Washington for help. Proud men reduced to begging for handouts leapt at the opportunity to plant trees or dig ditches for the WPA. Farmers unable to recover their production costs welcomed federal parity payments in exchange for limiting their cotton crop. And the idea of old-age pensions didn't appear as sinisterly socialistic as Talmadge claimed.

Both candidates campaigned in Swainsboro. On August 7, the governor addressed a crowd variously estimated at 2,000 to 10,000. Smarting from Russell's barbs, he tried to defuse a key issue by denying an earlier gaffe: "Anybody who says I said the boys of the CCC camps were a bunch of loafers and bums tells a deliberate lie!" But Talmadge also took the offensive, attacking the New Deal and his opponent with his customary vehemence. He quickly challenged a heckler from out of town, and the locals, captivated by the governor's folksy ways, surged toward the stranger and intimidated him into silence.

On August 18, Russell's turn came. Speaking to some 8,000 to 10,000 persons in the county seat and a larger crowd via radio, the senator blistered his opponent. "Men who have supported Gene Talmadge all down the line have a dazed look on their faces," he declared. "They wonder what's happened to Gene. Gene just got too big ideas in his head. He thought he was running for president!"

In one of Russell's standard campaign stunts, a number of men pushed forward to the speaker's platform and stripped off their red galluses as a symbol of their conversion to the senator's camp. "To you folks listening on the radio," Russell chortled into the microphone, "it's raining suspenders down here in Emanuel County!"

In the Democratic primary election in September, Russell won the popular count by a margin of almost two to one and carried 143 counties to Talmadge's 16. Moreover, Talmadge's candidate to succeed him as governor lost to Russell's protégé, E.D. Rivers. The balloting in Emanuel County mirrored the state results. Russell outpolled his opponent, 2,015 to 1,213, and Rivers easily won the gubernatorial vote.

Talmadge would later overcome his crushing defeat and recapture the statehouse in 1940. But the election of 1936 revealed that the voters of Georgia—for the moment, at least-—were looking forward, not back.

SPEED

AS ELLIE SCOTT GREW, so did his interest in music. At the age of 10, he and a classmate sang "When They're Sparkling" at a school assembly, and he served as interlocutor, or master of ceremonies, in a juvenile minstrel show held at the high school. Always willing to participate in performances of any kind, he circulated among the grammar school classrooms and sang songs, such as "Froggy Went A-Courtin'," as part of the morning's entertainment before studies began.

As a young teenager in the 1930s, Ellie spent a dime each week for a magazine that provided the lyrics of popular songs, which he committed to memory. He counted "Home on the Range" and other Western tunes among his favorites.

Ellie used the savings from his part-time jobs at Nixon's Service Station and Harrison's Drug Store to buy a Blackhawk radio. With his parents and friends, he spent hours listening to programs such as "Amos 'n' Andy" and "Fibber McGee and Molly."

Country music, always popular in the South, had gained a national audience with the advent of radio. "National Barn Dance," broadcast from WLM in Chicago, reached millions of listeners, and Nashville's "Grand Ole Opry," which began in 1925, quickly became the premier showcase for country performers. The Atlanta *Journal* in 1922 founded one of the first stations in Georgia, WSB—the call letters stood for "Welcome South,

Ron Seckinger

Brother!"—which carried the Opry broadcasts and other programs featuring local musicians. Ellie learned to yodel by listening to performers like Jimmie Rodgers, known as "The Singing Brakeman," a former railroad worker from Mississippi who had an enormous impact on the music industry.

The Scott family, ca. 1931.

Team sports had little appeal for Ellie, who left football to friends like Claude McLendon. But he loved diving and swimming, and he had a passion for boxing. He owned two pairs of gloves and was always ready for a sparring match.

Proud of the new Ford he purchased every few years, and no less proud of his son, Waitus took pleasure in watching Ellie learn to master the cumbersome vehicle. By the time he was 15, Ellie could borrow the car for school functions, dates, or simple rides with his friends. When Claude closed his father's gas station and garage at 7:30 or 8:00, Ellie picked him up, and they rode around or took a couple of girls to some speakeasy or restaurant.

Waitus and Margie gave their son plenty of freedom. They went to bed even if he hadn't returned, with only the sound of crickets outside. At 4:00 each morning, the whistle of the Georgia & Florida freight train wakened Margie as it slowly snaked into town from the south. Then she drifted off again as the stillness returned.

Ellie Scott, ca. 1937.

Ellie and his crowd were the small-town equivalents of the "Pinks" and "Jells," the tony teenagers from Atlanta's exclusive Northside, the children of bankers, industrialists, and future governors. Few of the Swainsboro teens lived in large homes or enjoyed generous allowances, but they held a special place in town life. Popular and considered by the teachers as brighter than the children bused in from remote farms, Ellie and his friends won the leads in school plays and took for granted their future as pillars of the community.

Respectful of their elders, and keeping their mischief within acceptable limits, the golden boys and girls of Swainsboro High basked in the benevolent tolerance of the town's grownups when they talked loudly and made jokes at the movies. They thrilled to "Mutiny on the Bounty" with Clark Gable and Charles Laughton when it opened at the Dixie Theater early in 1936, and to "Captain Blood" with Errol Flynn. They shuddered involuntarily when Ronald Coleman walked to the guillotine in "A Tale of Two Cities" and shrieked at a special Halloween showing of "The Bride of Frankenstein." They laughed at the antics of Betty Boop, the Three Stooges, and Spanky and Our Gang, and they eagerly awaited each episode of the "Flash Gordon" serial starring Buster Crabbe.

Schoolmates Ellie Scott, Thomas Brown, and Mary Powell, May 2, 1937.

Like their more glamorous counterparts in Atlanta, they loved to dance. At school functions and private parties, they jitterbugged to the records of the great swing orchestras of Tommy Dorsey, Glenn Miller, and Benny Goodman. The juke box at Bill's Drive In on South Main Street featured the latest hits, and Southern Pines, a club on Route One north of town, provided live music by such groups as Joe Samuels and His Hollywood Orchestra. They practiced the latest steps, the boys learning how to toss their partners into the air and the girls daringly swirling their skirts as they pirouetted on the crowded dance floor. Sometimes they sang the newest hits, locking arms like the characters in an Andy Hardy movie and swaying with the tune.

Handsome and self-confident, Ellie Scott did nothing half-heartedly. Whether dancing, performing at school functions, or driving his daddy's car, he never held back, approaching every activity with the hell-for-leather attitude of an ace pilot.

In the spring of 1937, as the end of his junior year neared, he remained in the thick of teen activities, particularly those that involved music. On April 30, he participated in a competition between the two literary societies at the high school, singing "Down by the Old Millstream" and "In the Evening by the Moonlight" with three girl classmates. Later he joined a glee club.

Ellie's 17th birthday and his senior year loomed in September, with promises of more fun and excitement. Afterwards, he might attend college, and he certainly would choose a wife and a job in the town where he'd spent his whole life, bound to everyone by an intricate web of blood, marriage, and long association.

On Thursday, May 15, Ellie decided to go alligator hunting. His steady girlfriend had left for the annual senior trip to Washington and wouldn't return till Friday night. Will McMillan, Jr., an older boy whose family had a 10-year lease on McKinney's Pond, had promised to show him how to bag a 'gator, and Ellie eagerly looked for others who might like to go along. Claude McLendon declined the invitation, partly because he had little interest in stalking alligators in the dark and partly because he held a job at a relative's trailer court on South Main Street. Fred Daniels also said no.

Ellie and Will picked up Pete Rich, and the three boys drove to Will's house to get his father's shotgun. As they left, Ellie said to the McMillans' Black handyman, "Hardeman, don't say nothing around [Will's] daddy about us carrying this gun off, 'cause he'll be 'fraid his little boy'll get killed."

After stopping to pick up two girls, friends from school, they headed north on the Midville Road in Waitus's Ford as night fell.

As usual, Ellie drove recklessly. On the other side of Summertown, the headlights suddenly revealed a small herd of cattle that had wandered onto the blacktop. Ellie cut the wheel, and the car miraculously swerved through the cows without hitting one. Shaken, Will said, "Ellie, if you don't slow down this car down, I'm gonna git out!" But Ellie just laughed and drove on through the night.

In the darkness at McKinney's Pond, Will located two boats with his flashlight, and they pushed off. In the moonlight they could see little more than the brooding, Spanish moss-laden trees along the shore and a few stumps and limbs sticking out of the dark water. The quiet was broken only by water spilling over the grist mill's raceway, the occasional splash of an alligator, and the whispers of the two girls, who shared one of the boats with Ellie. Pete poled the other while Will stood in the bow, his left hand holding the flashlight and supporting the gun barrel.

Just as a 'gator's eyes greenly reflected the light back at him and Will fingered the trigger, the boat hit a snag, and the boy pitched forward into the shallow water, overturning the boat. He and Pete broke the surface to the sound of the girls' shrieks and the thrashing of the startled alligator.

Will had managed to hold onto the flashlight, but the shotgun now rested in the muck on the pond bottom. After a few fruitless dives, he gave up and marked the spot by sticking a long frog gig into the mud. When Pete tried to climb into the second boat, it capsized as well, throwing Ellie and the two girls into the water. The girls screamed all the louder, but the boys laughed and told them the alligators were even more frightened. Unable to right the boats, they pushed them in front as they splashed their way back to shore.

Soaked to the skin and shivering in the night air, they took a few swallows of whiskey and talked about what to do next. Will found some dry cigarettes in the car and offered them around. Ellie, who smoked only occasionally, took one. As he accepted a light from Will, the match flared up and seared his nose.

Will knew better than to return home without his father's shotgun, and Pete volunteered to say with him till morning. Ellie stripped down to his undershorts, threw his soggy clothes in the back seat, and hustled the girls into the car. Will and Pete waved goodbye and built a fire to dry out. Back in Swainsboro, Margie woke to the whistle of the 4:00 freight and fell asleep again.

Ellie sped to town, where he dropped the girls at their homes on the north side. Instead of going to his own home, he roared down Main Street, apparently heading for the tourist court where Claude worked, intending to borrow some dry clothes. As he raced past the courthouse square, Willie Fields, working the night shift in the police office, heard the straining engine and knew immediately the identity of the driver.

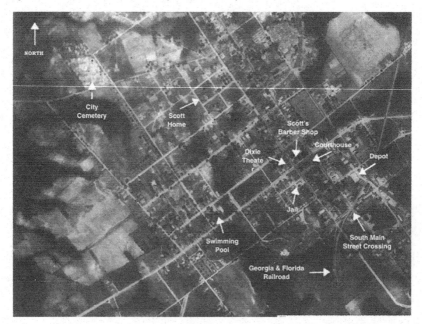

Swainsboro, Georgia, September 16, 1937. The Georgia &
Florida Railroad inaugurated the Auto-Stop Barricade at the
South Main Street crossing nine days after this photo was taken.
Courtesy, National Archives and Records Administration.

Ron Seckinger

The auto was traveling at about 60 miles an hour when it slammed into a railroad flatcar astride South Main Street. At the impact, Ellie's body hurtled forward into the steering wheel and dashboard as the engine was driven into the front seat.

The sound of the crash brought the train crew running, as well as people in their nightclothes from nearby houses. Ellie, clad only in his wet shorts, was still breathing when they pulled him from the wreckage and stretched him on the pavement. But, his chest crushed, he died within minutes.

Back at McKinney's Pond, Will and Pete, who'd dried out beside a bonfire, set out in a boat again at first light. Locating the frog gig, Will clambered into the water and, after a few dives, recovered his father's treasured shotgun. Returning to shore, they waited for a ride back to town. At 10:00, the Coca-Cola delivery truck arrived at the restaurant, and the driver told them of Ellie's death. Stunned, they rode with him in silence, thinking of how—save for the loss of the shotgun—they might have died with their friend.

The news traveled. At the high school, knots of students whispered about the tragedy, many with tears cascading down their cheeks. During the day, some of the boys went to look at the wrecked Ford, which had been moved to Roger Rich's service station. Awed by the destruction the collision had inflicted on the car, they nudged each other to point out the indentations made by Ellie's knees and knuckles when he struck the dashboard. The seniors, effervescent with the excitement of their trip to the nation's capital, were brought up short when they clambered down from the bus at 11:00 that night and heard the story from their waiting schoolmates and parents.

At Jessie Fields's home on the Flanders farm, a passing motorist honked the horn to summon the family to the front porch. "Ellie's been killed!" he shouted. "Oh, my God!" Jessie exclaimed. "It'll kill Margie!"

Mabel Screws arrived at the Scott home hours after the accident to find Margie seated on her bed, oblivious to the murmured condolences of other women, stuffing the end of a bedsheet into her mouth to stifle the screams as she wept unconsolably. The loss of Ellie, the repository of all her love and expectations, seared her with a wound that would never heal. Well-wishers tried to soften the blow by reminding her that she still had Waitus, but Margie would have none of that. 'Oh, yes,' she replied, "but Waitus can't take Ellie's place, and Ellie couldn't take Waitus's place." Her husband, no less devastated, bore his pain stoically, permitting himself no more than misty eyes and deep, ragged sighs.

Cliff Hunnicutt, proprietor of the Swainsboro Funeral Parlor, labored for hours to make Ellie's corpse presentable, using multiple stitches and heavy makeup to cover the wounds and bruises on his face. When the body was brought to Margie's on Saturday, she approached the open casket and, to the horror of her friends and relatives, ran her hands over her son to find out whether he had been mangled or had lost a limb.

The funeral took place on Sunday in Waitus and Margie's home. The casket rested in the parlor at the side of the house, and the mourners could see a bed of lilies through the open window. Heavily sedated, Margie managed to hug each of Ellie's friends. Jessie came from the farm, Kermit and Rose from Fitzgerald, and Emmit and Frances from Somerset, all of the surviving Strouds except Maude, somewhere in Florida. Jessie led 12-year-old Knob to the coffin and whispered, "That's what comes of drinking whiskey." Will McMillan noticed the small burn on Ellie's nose from the cigarette incident three nights before. Three ministers officiated at the service, which included two of Margie's favorite hymns, "The Old Rugged Cross" and "Have Thine Own Way."

Two weeks before Ellie's fateful rendezvous with the flatcar, the Georgia & Florida Railroad had announced in the *Forest-Blade* its intention of building a new type of safety device at the South Main Street crossing. Work began in July, and the Auto-Stop Barricade was completed in September. The device, "the first scientific highway obstruction to be installed in Georgia," included a traffic light, alternating flashing lights, and 270 red reflectors on two warning barriers recessed in the street. An oncoming train would trip a switch, raising the barriers and illuminating the lights. The Georgia & Florida invited Governor E.D. Rivers and some 200 railroad and government officials from five southeastern states to dedication ceremonies, which took place on September 25 with appropriate fanfare.

Had Ellie Scott lived, he well might have attended the event, some 20 days after the celebration of his 17th birthday.

JOOK

LIKE MAUDE, Alice Stroud left the farm in Fitzgerald to return to Miami. The High family welcomed her back, and she resumed her duties in Lillian's Beauty Shop, now located on Northwest 17th Avenue, and in their nearby home. Six-year-old Bobby adored her. Whenever he got in trouble, he'd run to hide behind her skirts or cuddle in her arms, since his mother wouldn't punish him in front of Alice.

Alice soon met a young man who operated a small grocery and ice store a few blocks away. Like Alice, Tom Mitchell hailed from Georgia, born in Spalding County in 1900. Footloose, he'd left home in his teens to roam in search of his fortune. By 1920, he'd drifted to Miami, where he worked as a mail carrier, covering Miami Beach when it was still a rural route. Four years later, he returned to his hometown of Griffin to marry Gussie Douglas, and he subsequently fathered two daughters. As of 1927, Tom labored as foreman for the Creomulsion Company in Griffin while Gussie worked as a hairdresser, but he returned to Miami with his family about two years later. In February 1931, the marriage ended in divorce.

A slim, handsome fellow, Tom Mitchell had dark hair, grey eyes, and a broad smile. At five-feet-eight, he topped Alice by three inches. Until now she'd taken little interest in men, but Tom seemed different. Because he had no car and little money, their dates consisted mostly of walking to the drug store, where they ordered soft drinks and sat at the small, marble-topped tables to chat. Soft-spoken and respectful, Tom talked about himself and told jokes that made the normally serious Alice laugh and laugh.

Alice Stroud, ca. 1933.

When Tom proposed after four months of courtship, Alice accepted. On February 9, 1934, the two went to the Dade County Courthouse, obtained a marriage license, and exchanged vows before a notary public. No relatives or friends attended.

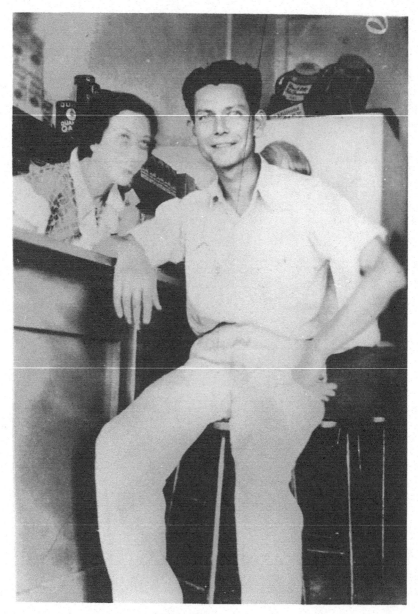

Tom Mitchell, ca. 1933.

Alice left the Highs' home, abandoned her job, and moved her few belongings to Tom's tiny apartment—one room plus a kitchen and bathroom—behind the grocery store. She cooked their meals, kept the apartment clean, and helped Tom wait on customers. His two daughters, who lived with their mother, sometimes came to visit on the weekends. Even better, Alice presented him with a son, Patrick Wise, in November 1934.

But pride in his son didn't cancel Tom's flaws, and Alice quickly regretted her decision to wed. "Marriage wasn't what I thought it would be," she recalled more than half a century later. Tom didn't mistreat her, but he periodically went on drinking binges that depleted their meager savings and sometimes cost him his job. After one such episode, Alice took her infant son and returned to Waitus and Margie's home in Swainsboro, where she resumed her job at the United Five & Ten.

Pat Mitchell and Billy Moreno, ca. 1935.

More than four years after departing Emanuel County to make her own life, Alice found herself once again dependent on the charity of her brother-in-law. Moreover, all of her old friends knew that she'd left her husband.

Uncomfortable with her circumstances, she decided to give Tom another chance when he wrote begging her to come back. Thus began a cycle of reconciliation followed by binge followed by another flight to the sanctuary of Margie's home. This pattern would govern Alice's life for 12 years.

On one of those occasions, in 1938, she and Pat joined Tom in Griffin. He'd drifted back home from Florida and, after working for a while on WPA road projects, began driving a delivery truck for a dairy owned by his uncle. They lived in a tenant shack across the road from the dairy farm.

Alice soon found herself pregnant. Maude, still living in Florida and suffering her own troubles, felt sorry for her sister. In September 1938 she wrote Margie:

> As far as I know, Marjorie, Alice is pregnant. She said that she was when I was up there but has written very little since I came back. I hate to think of her having another child with Tom no more dependable than he is. With just Pat she could manage to make a living for the two of them but with another one she hasn't much of a chance. If she couldn't do anything better, she could do the same as I am [i.e., work as a domestic]. There isn't much money in it but I manage to get by on it. I wish I could do something to help her but I have my hands full at the present time.

When Alice came to term in March 1939, the adults sent four-year-old Pat to the farmhouse across the road. Mystified, he sat outside on a gate with the neighbors' boy until summoned home to meet his sister, Virginia Gail. Tom fairly burst with pride, but as Maude anticipated, he soon went on another bender. Within a few months, Alice again sought refuge in Swainsboro.

Two years had passed since Ellie's death, and Waitus and Margie were delighted to have children in the house once more. They doted on Gail, coaxing smiles and taking pleasure in watching her grow. Alice's next announcement that she intended to rejoin her husband struck the now-childless couple like a thunderbolt. Margie argued that the baby should stay, and Waitus stormed from the room and returned with a shotgun leveled at Alice. Gail was not going.

Alice, Gail, and Pat Mitchell at Waitus and Margie's home in Swainsboro, ca. 1939-1940.

Thereafter, Alice's attempts to pick up her married life came at the cost of separation from her daughter. She and Pat joined Tom in Griffin late in 1939 and again at the end of the following year, each time eventually returning to Swainsboro. In the fall of 1941, they rode the bus to Clewiston, Florida, on the southern shore of Lake Okeechobee, where Tom now worked as timekeeper at the United States Sugar Company's mill.

Clewiston resembled Canal Point in many ways. Still a small town, it nonetheless had grown rapidly over the past 15 years. Facing the lake to the north and surrounded by cane fields on the other three sides, Clewiston served as home to fishermen, hunters, ranchers, railroad men, and most of all to sugar workers. During the harvest, the company's hands numbered in the thousands. Black migrants from the Caribbean did much of the heavy work in the fields, swinging machetes to sever the tall stalks near the ground and then loading cane on railcars for a quick trip to the mill. Other workers handled more specialized chores in the sprawling industrial plant that transformed cane juice into sugar.

Harvesting cane in Clewiston, Florida, 1939. Courtesy, State Archives of Florida.

The Mitchells lived in a company house, nondescript but clean. Pat, then in the second grade, attended classes with the children of other workers. His only playmate had two horses, and the boys often rode bareback along the country roads. When the fields were burned off after the harvest, Tom and the other White men waited with broomsticks by the irrigation ditches and killed rabbits fleeing the flames. They gave some of the animals to their wives for cooking and sold the rest to Black workers.

For a while Alice was content. But eventually Tom wanted a drink, and any number of ramshackle jooks and local moonshiners stood ready to serve him one. Once started, he drank himself into oblivion and missed his

Ron Seckinger

shift at the time clock. Alice again gathered her things and caught the bus to Swainsboro with Pat. Her relatives shook their heads and asked themselves whether she'd finally come to her senses. But she hadn't given up on Tom Mitchell. Not yet.

WORLD'S FAIR

BY 1939, EMMIT Stroud felt secure enough in his job to propose a family vacation. His railroad passes would cover the cost of transportation, and they could save enough for other expenses. He and Frances and Hilma had no trouble deciding on a destination. Where else but the World's Fair?

In late 1934, a New York man named Joseph F. Shadgen proposed a world's fair to mark the 150th anniversary of George Washington's first inauguration, which had taken place in New York. The city's economic and political elites seized on the idea as a way to hasten economic recovery. Chicago, celebrating its centennial, had just completed a two-year exposition, proving that extravaganzas could turn a profit even in the depths of the Depression.

The promoters of the New York fair selected a theme, "Building the World of Tomorrow with the Tools of Today," calculated to generate confidence in the future. By 1936, they had secured enough commitments from city, state, federal, and foreign governments, as well as large corporations, to begin preparing a 1,200-acre site at a swampy landfill in Flushing Meadows, Borough of Queens.

The fair's theme served as a perfect text for President and New Yorker Franklin Roosevelt, who presided over the opening ceremonies on April 30, 1939. For six years he'd devoted his considerable energies to leading his countrymen out of the desert of the Great Depression and into the

Ron Seckinger

promised land of prosperity. With its emphasis on technology and progress, the World's Fair lent him an appropriate soapbox. Even as Europe stumbled toward another conflagration, the President exhorted his listeners to look to a peaceful and prosperous tomorrow.

> All who come to this World's Fair in New York ... will
> find that the eyes of the United States are fixed on the
> future. Our wagon is hitched to a star. But it is a star of
> good will, a star of progress for mankind, a star of greater
> happiness and less hardship, a star of international good
> will, and, above all, a star of peace. May the months to
> come carry us forward in the rays of that hope. I hereby
> dedicate the New York World's Fair of 1939 and declare
> it open to all mankind.

Roosevelt's speech went out to the public not only on radio, already two decades old, but also on the infant medium of television. In the first televised news report ever, the National Broadcasting Company transmitted a fuzzy, streaked image of the event to some 200 receivers within a 50-mile radius, the initial benchmark of a new era in communications. Sales of television sets, which had nine-inch screens and hefty price tags of $200 to $1,000, would soar the following day in New York. Elsewhere, citizens had to settle for newsreel films in their local theaters.

Back in Kentucky, the Strouds scrimped for the big trip. Emmit and Frances had always been frugal—Hilma had never seen a movie until her cousin Ellie Scott took her during a visit to Somerset in the mid-1930s— and the upcoming vacation gave them another reason to pinch pennies. If Hilma asked for a nickel to buy an ice cream cone, her mother answered, "No, no, no, got to have that money for the fair!"

In July, the long-awaited moment finally arrived. Frances bought Hilma three new dresses, the most the 13-year-old had ever received at one time. They boarded the train in Somerset, carrying a box of Frances's fried chicken, and set out for New York.

During a stop at Union Station in Washington, D.C., Frances and Hilma wandered around until the hour Emmit had promised to meet them at a designated spot. Irritated at his delay, Frances looked up and down the hall, growing more anxious as the time for departure approached. Suddenly, she realized that a man lounging nearby was none other than Emmit, who'd purchased a straw boater. Accustomed after so many years to his felt hat or cloth cap, she hadn't recognized him.

A postage stamp celebrated the fair's symbols, the Trylon and Perisphere. Public domain.

Arriving in Brooklyn, they rented a room and unpacked. The next morning, they took the subway to Queens and with throngs of other visitors paid the admission fee—75 cents for adults and 25 for children—and got their first glimpse of the fairgrounds. The Trylon and Perisphere, a 700-foot-high, needlelike pyramid and an accompanying globe, dominated the scene, both bright white under the sun. Together they made the fair's trademark, reproduced on countless magazine covers, postage stamps, and souvenirs.

The three-square-mile area included dozens of buildings in three general areas: government, amusements, and main exhibits. The main exhibit area had seven zones dealing with communications, community interests, transportation, medicine and public health, science and education, food, and production and distribution.

Two of the most popular exhibits presented contrasting views of the future. Every hour some 8,000 visitors paid 25 cents to view the official theme exhibit, "Democracity." They entered the base of the Trylon and ascended long escalators to a ramp that conducted them into the Perisphere, where they stood on two circular platforms rotating slowly above a scale model of a vast metropolis.

Reflecting the collectivist ideal shared by many intellectuals of the 1930s, Democracity was orderly and clean, designed to meet all human needs without any of the randomness or social ills associated with urban life. The city, which existed solely for business and cultural pursuits, had no residences. Its citizens lived in suburban high-rises surrounded by shady parklands and commuted to the city center via broad highways. A stirring musical score and a film projected on the dome overhead enhanced the utopian vision. Radio newscaster H.V. Kaltenborn's deep voice exalted the triumph of the people in building the world of tomorrow as the film showed men and women of all classes united in a jubilant song. The entire experience lasted only five and a half minutes.

"Futurama," the exhibit sponsored by General Motors, evoked a different vision. The seven-acre hall, the fair's largest, featured a scale model of the American countryside as it might appear in 1960. Visitors sat on cushioned armchairs that moved along the exhibit at more than 100 feet per minute while the passing scene was described by loudspeakers. The 15-minute tour carried them past a modern city and rolling farmlands, linked by 14-lane superhighways over which some 10,000 miniature vehicles zipped along. "Futurama" celebrated individualism, as well as the automobile, and proved the most popular exhibit.

The Strouds took in both of these attractions and many others during their three-day visit, buying inexpensive snacks from the concession stands, returning to their rented room in Brooklyn each night, and hurrying back to Flushing Meadows the following morning.

Hilma, wearing one of her new dresses each day, was both awed and skeptical. She considered "Futurama" a hoax. Surely superhighways and fast cars would never come to pass. At the R.C.A. pavilion, Frances turned around to see what everyone was staring at and saw herself on the screen. A speaker told them that someday every home would have a television set, but Hilma didn't believe him. "No, this can't be true," she said to herself.

In the government area they traipsed through the exhibits sponsored by France, Japan, Czechoslovakia, Hungary, Switzerland, Mexico, Norway, Yugoslavia, Sweden, and Belgium, duly recorded in Frances's small notebook. They admired the exterior of the Italian pavilion with its tall waterfall, but Frances ruled out going inside because she understood it contained nude statues. "You will *not* go in there!" she instructed Hilma, even though she couldn't shield her daughter's eyes from the numerous nude female sculptures scattered through the open area of the fair groups. At the General Electric pavilion in the corporate area, they witnessed a demonstration of man-made lightning, 10 million volts flashing across a 30-foot arc in a display that resembled the set from a Hollywood movie about a mad scientist.

Too serious to spend much time in the amusement area, Emmit and Frances passed up the Parachute Jump, a 250-foot descent that cost 40 cents. The most popular ride at the fair, it later moved to Coney Island. And Gypsy Rose Lee's burlesque show was, of course, out of the question. A puppet show and an exhibit called Sun Valley provided Hilma's only chances for frivolity.

Emmit gravitated to the Court of Railways, a 16-acre complex in the transportation zone, where he could examine a John Bull locomotive of 1831, one of the earliest built. Even more interesting, the Pennsylvania Railroad's Engine No. 6100, a sleek, 526-ton steam locomotive, ran continuously at 60 miles per hour on a roller bed in the exhibit's yards. If offered the opportunity, he no doubt would've crawled into the boiler for a look. They saw "Railroads on Parade," a pageant depicting the role of transportation in US development. A cast of 250 performed the spectacle, with a score by noted composer Kurt Weill, on a massive stage. Historic and modern trains passed in review while various boats proceeded along a canal at the rear of the stage. Emmit also checked out all of the other exhibits, including Great Britain's luxury train, the Coronation Scot.

His other preoccupation was sports. Hearing that Jack Dempsey attended the fair that week, Emmit showed more interest in catching a glimpse of the famous boxer than in seeing the marvels of technology. And how could he pass up the chance to see the Bronx Bombers? On the fourth day, Frances went off to shop in Brooklyn while Emmit took Hilma to watch the Yankees, with a young Joe DiMaggio, play the Chicago White Sox. They sat in the upper deck behind home plate, and half a century later Hilma would remember this experience as the highlight of the entire trip.

Yankee Stadium, 1923. Public domain.

After visits to the Statue of Liberty, the Empire State Building, Fifth Avenue, and Coney Island, the Strouds headed for home with their memories and souvenirs, including an orange-and-black plastic salt-and-pepper set in the shape of the Trylon and Perisphere. Exhausted, they decided not to visit the Smithsonian Institution in Washington as originally planned. Instead, they took a northern route home. At the Canadian border they left the train and took a taxi to see Niagara Falls.

Then, the grand adventure over, the rails took them back to Somerset to resume the stable rhythms of their lives in machine shop, school, and the house on Monticello Street.

LETTING GO

JESSIE FIELDS worried about her girls. When they held dances or cake-walks in her parlor, she watched them closely. If one left the party to get a drink from the spigot on the back porch, Jessie would follow in a flash to herd her back to the dance floor. If Leila had a date, Rosa or Romie Delle had to go along as chaperone. Rosa, a chubby young woman with an infectious laugh, once received a visit from a local farmboy named Sprag Scott. While the couple chatted in the parlor, each as nervous as a hog on ice, Jessie circled the house to peer through the windows and make sure her strict standards of conduct were not violated.

"Don't get in any trouble," she told her girls, but for years Romie Delle, despite having shared her parents' bedroom, didn't understand her mother's meaning. Indeed, the absence of any discussion about sex and growing up, even among sisters, was so total that Romie Delle had no fore-knowledge of menstruation until she began bleeding one day at school. Frightened, she ran to one of her teachers, who sent her to her Aunt Margie's home. Margie explained that a woman's period was normal and gave her some sanitary napkins.

Perhaps more than most parents, Jessie wanted her children to have a better life than hers. "Act like you should," she admonished them. "Be somebody." She was determined that Leila, Romie Delle, Wynelle, and Knob finish high school, a luxury that had eluded all of their older siblings except J.D. Jessie feared that one of her daughters might become pregnant and find herself a mother with no husband or, worse yet, forced into marriage with a no-account.

The Fields girls on the Flanders farm, ca. 1938. From left: Wynelle, Romie Delle, Leila, Rosa.

She worried no less about her sons, fearing they might turn out like their father. And her concern wasn't misplaced, for John A. and Ralph took to drink almost as soon as they entered their teens. While shucking corn one day, the two boys nipped from a barrel of fermented cane skimmings, and Jessie raised hell when they came to supper reeking of alcohol. Like their daddy, they bought bootleg liquor from local moonshiners, and their mother's scoldings had no effect. They completed her humiliation when they appeared, tipsy, at Fields Chapel one Sunday. "When they're little, they step on your feet," she often lamented, "and when they're grown, they step on your heart."

Ron Seckinger

Jessie Fields, ca. 1939.

Jessie's children were growing up, and all of her anxieties wouldn't keep them from making their own decisions. Leila, a strapping young woman with her mother's energy and appetite for hard work, left to marry a young man she'd known all of her life. John A., a giant of a man with exceptional strength, found a beautiful bride despite his habit of chewing tobacco and drinking himself into oblivion. Rosa soon left to take her place in a man's house, but as domestic rather than bride. After acting as surrogate mother for her younger siblings for most of her first 30 years, she'd spend the rest of her life caring for other people's families. Ralph married a mill hand's daughter and left farming for life in a South Carolina cotton mill, where he ran a quill machine and laid up fiddling in the loom--eight hours a day, five days a week, for a weekly wage of $13. Romie Delle moved into Swainsboro and took a job in the Agricultural Adjustment Administration office, and Wynelle worked for the Soil Conservation Service in Statesboro. Both soon married.

At the end of 1940, Jessie could no longer make a go of sharecropping, and she and Knob moved in with J.D. and Ouida on their farm in Blun. Active in the 4-H Club, Knob had won seventh place in the fat cattle show in 1939, but he swore to himself that when grown he'd never again pick cotton or velvet beans or pull fodder. Since Summertown High had no football team, he walked or rode his bicycle to Modoc each day to catch the bus to Swainsboro. Tall and scrawny, he suffered from constant tonsillitis and couldn't put on weight, playing lineman at only 135 pounds. After graduating he joined the Navy in November 1943 and shipped out to the Admiralty Islands the following year.

Jessie's principal chore was done. She'd raised her children, losing only one, and had tried to instill in them her own rock-hard determination and upright values. Soon after Knob's departure, she moved into a small, rented house on Lucky Street in Swainsboro. She continued working with the same boundless energy, serving meals in the school cafeteria, sewing, and babysitting.

She was 55 years old, a stooped, wrinkled woman with wire-frame eyeglasses and short, graying hair. For the first time in 36 years, she had no children under her care. And for the first time in her life, her survival didn't depend on making a cotton crop.

TENNESSEE VALLEY

ALICE TRIED again to make a go of it with Tom Mitchell. When she and Pat rejoined him in 1942, he was participating in one of the great economic and social experiments of the era, the Tennessee Valley Authority, or TVA.

The Holston and French Broad Rivers, which drain a section of the western slopes of the Appalachian Mountains in the highest rainfall area in the eastern United States, converge above Knoxville to form the Tennessee. With a volume exceeding that of the Missouri for much of the year, the Tennessee flows southward into northern Alabama, where it drops precipitously at Muscle Shoals, and then meanders northward to join the Ohio at the Kentucky-Ohio border. Settled by pioneers who crossed the mountains in the wake of the American Revolution, the Tennessee River Basin in the early 20th century was inhabited largely by subsistence farmers. At the onset of the Great Depression, the region ranked as one of the poorest, most isolated, and most backward in the entire country.

Muscle Shoals had long inspired development projects such as a canal to facilitate river traffic and, later, exploiting the site's potential for hydroelectric power. President Woodrow Wilson had prodded Congress to authorize the building of a dam to harness the Tennessee's high volume and sharp drop for the electricity needs to produce synthetic nitrates for a domestic munitions industry and chemical fertilizers. No further development took place until the election of Franklin Roosevelt.

*Tom, Alice, and Pat Mitchell at Clingman's Dome on
the Tennessee-North Carolina border, 1942.*

Following a visit to Wilson Dam in January 1933, the President-elect quickly formulated an ambitious plan for the entire Tennessee Valley. In addition to navigation improvements, hydroelectric power, and fertilizer production, his vision included reforestation, flood control, and agricultural and industrial development. The building of a series of dams and reservoirs would provide employment to a depressed region while making electricity available for new industries as well as the isolated homes of poor farmers.

Unprecedented in its regional scope and the extent of federal involvement, the projected authority was entirely consistent with Roosevelt's New Deal, part of an overall blueprint for getting the country moving again. After taking office in March, the new President pushed for immediate action. The bill creating the TVA passed both houses of Congress within two months.

The TVA introduced sweeping changes in the economies and societies of Tennessee, Virginia, North Carolina, Georgia, Alabama, Mississippi, and Kentucky. During the first dozen years of its existence, it would construct 16 dams, providing an impoverished population with employment and new skills. It eliminated the region's annual spring floods, eradicated previously endemic malaria, encouraged unions and collective bargaining, produced and fostered the use of inexpensive fertilizers, attracted new industries, made cheap electricity available in rural areas, built parks, and established lending libraries and some of the best school systems in the valley.

Such advances came at a cost. Thousands of people were displaced, often from ancestral lands, as the waters trapped behind each dam rose and inundated the lowlands and hillsides. And for decades, the TVA ravaged and polluted the environment on a grand scale. Even so, the net effect was overwhelmingly positive, contributing to the national recovery and boosting the standard of living in the South.

Following the Japanese attack on Pearl Harbor, the federal government turned to the TVA to support the war effort. New war industries and the Manhattan Project--the development of an atomic bomb--required increased hydroelectric output. For more than a year, Congress had stalled consideration of a proposed dam on the French Broad River east of Knoxville because the farmers and cannery operators scheduled to lose their lands had more political influence than other residents of the valley. America's entry into the war dislodged the legislation, and groundbreaking ceremonies for Douglas Dam took place in early February 1942.

Despite high labor turnover because of the armed forces' manpower demands, the TVA managed to complete Douglas in a record 13 and a half months. Some 1,800 employees began work just four days after Congress authorized construction, and the labor force swelled to more than 6,000 by the end of June. Multiple shifts kept the work going 24 hours a day, seven days a week, for the entire course of the project. Tom Mitchell had signed on as timekeeper for the work at Douglas Dam, and Alice and Pat joined him there in the spring of 1942.

Most of the workers were locals, but about 700 hailed from else-where and needed housing. The TVA built five dormitories for White men, one for Black men, and a small one for about two dozen White women, as well as a camp of 92 trailers for families. The Mitchells resided in an eight-by-30-foot trailer, Tom and Alice sleeping in a bedroom at one end and Pat on the sofa in the parlor. Other trailers housed community laundry, bath, and toilet facilities.

The Mitchells shopped at a TVA commissary, used the camp library, received medical treatment at the first-aid station and later the hospital, and found their recreation at the community center in the form of sports, games, and entertainment events. Pat rode a bus with the other children to a school in neighboring Jefferson County, where he attended sec-ond-grade classes.

Pat adored his father and enjoyed the time they had together. Having traveled extensively as he knocked around from one job to another, Tom had a wealth of stories about things he'd seen and people he'd met. A natu-ral mimic, he aped the speech of Blacks, hillbillies, and city slickers while his son giggled or hooted in appreciation. Pat watched his father play in softball games, and the two sometimes attended wrestling matches at an outdoor platform in front of the community center.

The seven-year-old boy also tagged along when Tom and his cronies went fox hunting. They would let loose their dogs—Tom had taken in a mangy, stray hound—at night and build a fire, laughing and telling tales as they listened to the dogs' baying in the woods. Pat eventually would find a haystack or soft place on the ground where he could sleep until time to return home to the trailer.

In the summer of 1942, Margie and Gail came by bus to visit—a treat for Alice and even more so for Tom, who'd not seen his daughter since shortly after her birth. The three-year-old girl, no doubt influenced by Margie and Waitus, was somewhat scared of her father, and the few days

Ron Seckinger

at Douglas Dam were to be their last together. She returned to Swainsboro with her aunt, and her mother and brother followed after Tom's next drunk.

Gail and Pat Mitchell with Margie Scott at Douglas Dam, summer 1942.

Alice tried once more to make a go of her marriage. She and Pat were living with Tom in Griffin when the world learned of President Roosevelt's death.

Roosevelt had a long association with Georgia. Stricken with infantile paralysis or polio while vacationing in Maine in 1921, the 39-year-old politician from New York struggled to recover the use of his legs. In 1924 he traveled for the first time to Warm Springs, in western Georgia between Columbus and Griffin, to take the mineral-rich, naturally heated waters. Pleased with the improvement in his withered legs, Roosevelt purchased the shabby resort in April 1926 and transformed it into a health spa. He continued to visit after his election as governor of New York in 1928 and as president in 1932.

After leading the nation through the Depression, and with the Second World War drawing to a close, Roosevelt traveled by train to his Georgia refuge for a much-needed rest, arriving on March 30, 1945. His health had deteriorated badly over the past year, and, on April 12, he suffered a massive and fatal cerebral hemorrhage at the "Little White House," his residence in Warm Springs.

In Griffin as well as in other towns and cities along the route to Washington, schools closed so children could watch the funeral train pass. On a 10-car special, the president's wife and dozens of friends and associates accompanied Roosevelt's coffin. Pat and his classmates stood beside the Southern Railroad tracks and paid their respects as the train rolled past.

Alice and Pat were still in Griffin when Germany surrendered on May 2, and they joined the spontaneous celebration in which motorists honked their horns and everyone shouted and wept with joy. But Alice soon made ready to declare her own private liberation. She and Pat departed Tom's home for the last time and returned to Swainsboro, where six-year-old Gail prepared to begin school.

Although she wouldn't file for divorce until 1949, Alice had had enough of Tom Mitchell, at last choosing the charity of her brother-in-law over the lot of a drunkard's wife. She resumed her place behind the counter at United Five & Ten, among the spools of thread, household gadgets, and gewgaws, and gratefully settled into the security of Waitus and Margie's home.

LIBERTY SHIPS

KERMIT STROUD abandoned his home with Rose in 1942, just as the United States began to tool up its defense industries and provide millions of jobs to skilled workers. Kermit found his opportunity in Savannah, building merchant ships.

Teddy Roosevelt's "Great White Fleet" was but a memory in 1941. The US Navy, which increased seven-fold in 1917-1918, had shrunk during the years following the Great War. After relying on treaties in a fruitless bid to avoid a naval armament race during the 1920s, Washington authorized a large shipbuilding program in 1934 to counter Japan's rise as a major power in the Pacific. Despite the construction of the country's first aircraft carriers during the interwar years, the Navy was unprepared for the life-and-death struggle initiated by Tokyo's surprise attack on Pearl Harbor.

The US merchant fleet had fallen into an even more parlous state. Between 1922 and 1937, US shipyards produced only two dry cargo ships. With the Merchant Marine Act of 1936, Washington embarked on a 10-year program with a target of 50 cargo ships a year, soon quadrupled to 200.

In danger of strangulation by German submarines, Great Britain in 1940 proposed to purchase vessels from American shipyards. Since speed of construction mattered more than elegance of line, US builders adopted and modified an existing British design. The ship, propelled by a three-cycle, 1,500-horsepower engine, had a blunt, awkward appearance that earned it the nickname "ugly duckling," a sobriquet the government attempted to nullify with the more exalted designation of "Liberty ship." The vessel could carry 9,000 tons of cargo at a top speed of 11 knots.

The` simple design, which called for welding rather than riveting, facilitated rapid construction, as did the availability of gantry cranes and the use of standardized parts. The keel of the first Liberty ship, the *Patrick Henry*, was laid at the Bethlehem-Fairfield yard in Baltimore on April 30, 1941, and the launching followed in September.

Once the United States entered the war, the country's shipyards, which by October 1942 would number 60, geared up to increase production for the Allied cause. By 1943, the workforce had risen to 500,000. Men of draft age accounted for almost half of this figure, and turnover was high as large numbers of workers surrendered their tools and reported for military service. As a result, women increasingly took their places, eventually making up a third of the workforce. Workers' living conditions were poor, and the government soon authorized the construction of 100,000 residential units in the shipyards.

In the early months of the conflict, cargo ships proved more critical to the war effort than the Navy's battleships and carriers. Without the food, matériel, and other supplies ferried across the Atlantic, Great Britain might have been starved into submission. Instead, the island held on and ultimately would serve as a platform for the liberation of Europe. The magnificent economy of the United States fed the war machines of Britain and the Soviet Union, thanks to merchantmen like the Liberty ships.

German U-boats made the Atlantic crossing perilous. Soon after the Japanese bombed Pearl Harbor, Adolph Hitler authorized attacks against US shipping and declared war on the United States. His submarine wolfpacks set out to cripple the US merchant fleet. On the high seas they shadowed convoys, picking off stragglers, and they found an abundance of targets while loitering off the east coast. On numerous occasions, a German captain peering through his periscope at night was astonished to spy unprotected freighters silhouetted against bright city lights, despite wartime blackout regulations. All along the coast, citizens saw burning tankers on the horizon and walked beaches littered with debris from destroyed vessels.

During the first six months of 1942, Germany sank almost 400 US vessels and damaged hundreds more on the Atlantic and Gulf coasts and in the Caribbean. For the year, the United States lost dry cargo ships and tankers at the rate of 1 million tons a month; the merchant shipyards turned out only 746 ships representing more than 8 million dead-weight tons that year for a net loss. Not until improved intelligence and advanced techniques of antisubmarine warfare broke the back of the U-boat campaign the following year did the danger recede.

Kermit's contribution to the war effort came at the Southeastern Shipbuilding Corporation, chartered in February 1942 to take over another company that had proved unable to meet the conditions of a contract with the US Maritime Commission. The corporation soon completed a six-slip-way yard at a cost of more than $8.5 million at a site on the Savannah River two miles east of the city. Kermit, with his experience as a machinist in Detroit, joined a workforce that eventually would exceed 15,000. Most of the workers hailed from the vicinity of Savannah, many of them farmers abandoning the soil for the first time. Their number included 3,500 women.

Speed was the watchword. Machinists and boilermakers, making $1.40 an hour, laid a hull, attached cross-struts, and welded on metal plates that had been shaped and fitted together at the Savannah Machine and Foundry. Inefficiency plagued Southeastern, one of two shipyards with an unsatisfactory record as of mid-1943, according to the Senate Special Committee Investigating the National Defense Program, known as the Truman Committee after its chairman, Senator Harry Truman of Missouri, whose excellent performance in the job gave him the national exposure that would lead to his selection as Franklin Roosevelt's running mate in 1944. Absenteeism ranked high among Southeastern's problems. As many as 500 of the 5,000 workers on each of the three shifts might not report on any given day.

The first ship to slide down the ways at Savannah was the *James Oglethorpe*, named after the founder of Georgia. At ceremonies on November 20, 1942, a representative of the board of directors of Southeastern saluted the workers, who watched from the rear of the assembled guests and from perches on cranes and scaffolding. After the wife of Senator Walter F. George of Georgia christened the *Oglethorpe* with a bottle of New York champagne, workers cut free the plates holding the vessel in place, and it moved effortlessly into the water, accompanied by a roar from Kermit Stroud and his fellow laborers. Its fitting-out completed at another yard, the vessel began service in February 1943 and sank as the victim of a U-boat attack in the South Atlantic just four months later.

Ceremonies marking the launching of the SS James Oglethorpe, the first Liberty ship completed by the Southeastern Shipbuilding Corporation in Savannah, November 20, 1942. Some of the yard's 15,000 workers, wearing hard hats, are at the end and left of the slip. Courtesy, Georgia Historical Society, Cordray-Foltz Collection.

Completing the *Oglethorpe* had required nine months and more than $2 million. But experience and experimentation steadily trimmed the time needed to turn out a vessel. In 1943, the shipyard finished a Liberty ship in only 38 days, and 15 months later it set a new record by building an AV1 cargo ship in just 49 days. Costs also declined. In mid-1944, the Truman Commission announced that the average price of a Liberty ship produced by Southeastern had fallen to $800,000.

When the whistle signaled the end of a shift, the workers put down their tools, streamed out of the yard, and boiled up Victory Drive toward Savannah, most of them headed for a bar or jook joint. Jammed into places like Ellis's Barbecue, they drank and talked and danced. The women, enjoying wartime wages and the relaxation of social norms, consumed their share of beer and liquor while flirting with their coworkers.

Kermit had always liked a drink and frequently had too much on Saturdays in Fitzgerald. In Savannah, he had more cash and daily opportunities, and his drinking grew worse. "After he went to the shipyard," Rose recalled 50 years later, "Kermit was altogether a different person. I don't know why that changed him, but it did." He returned to Ben Hill County about once a month. "He never come home that he wasn't drunk. And he stayed drunk the whole time he was here."

Rose had continued to farm Emmit's land for a year with the help of a hired hand, and after he left, she at least took care of the livestock. But soon she moved into Fitzgerald with the two children for a job in a cotton mill.

Relations with Kermit continued to deteriorate, and in 1944, he announced that he wanted a divorce. The two agreed that Rose would file the suit and they would split the legal costs. The deposition Rose gave in June sounded like the dictation of a law clerk:

> The defendant seemed to become dissatisfied with me and he constantly fussed and nagged at me and nothing I ever did seemed to satisfy him. He seemed to be indifferent as to my presence and whether he associated with me or not and never took up any time with me and

the children. Such conduct on his part made me nervous, affected my nervous system and my health and on
account of the same, I separated from him in order to
try to protect my health.

After two juries had found in Rose's favor, the court issued a divorce
decree in January 1945. The dissolution of the marriage was amicable. "We
lived as friends," recalled Rose. "We got along better after we separated."

Kermit continued his work at Southeastern, but trouble was brewing. A strike by 400 machinists closed the yard for two weeks in late July
1945, and Japan's abrupt surrender in August, after the atomic strikes
on Hiroshima and Nagasaki, made the shipbuilding program moot. The
Maritime Commission cancelled orders for eight of the 13 vessels under
construction in late September, and by early November the yard, now
employing only 1,300 workers, prepared to shut down.

In less than four years, the men and women of the Southeastern
Shipbuilding Corporation had produced 88 Liberty ships, 10 AV1s, and
seven other vessels. Enemy action sank only three during the war, and in
1959 all but five of the 105 ships remained in service.

Laid off, Kermit gravitated back to Fitzgerald, where he stayed with
Rose's mother. Depression over the loss of his job or his marriage contributed to his heavy drinking. On a day in late November, he somehow found
his way from town to Frances Walker's home after drinking himself into a
stupor. The household was settling down for bed when Mrs. Walker and
one of her grandsons heard a shot.

Running to Kermit's room, they found him with a pistol in his
hand and a bloody hole in his chest. Kermit had missed his heart, and the
Walkers managed to get him to the hospital before he bled to death.

Rose visited him every afternoon when she finished her shift at
the cotton mill, and the children, scared and apprehensive, came, too.
Discharged after a week, Kermit recuperated at Frances Walker's for 10 days

or so. Shortly before Christmas, Rose's cousin drove him to Swainsboro, where he would stay with Jessie and start a new life.

Ever true to the Strouds' code of silence, he never explained why he had attempted to take his life.

HOMECOMING

FOR TWO YEARS after giving up her second child for adoption, Maude Moreno scraped by as a domestic in Miami. From Swainsboro, Margie Scott helped out from time to time, sending a little money and some clothes for Billy. Periodically, Maude would become dissatisfied with the job, or her employer with her work, and she would pack her few belongings, find a new position, and settle into the maid's quarters at another residence. She maintained contact with Denver's widow Bernice, who had married Vernor Curtis, a 29-year-old US inspector originally from Oklahoma, in July 1934.

Maude continued to date, and one of the men she met may have seemed like a prospective husband, for in July 1938 she wrote the courthouse in Tampa to ask for a copy of her divorce decree. But any hopes of remarrying came to naught.

In a letter to Margie in September, Maude expressed frustration with her 'round-the-clock duties and her inability to make a home for Billy:

> Have just finished putting the kids to bed and will try
> to get a few lines written to you before going to sleep
> myself. I am so tired I don't think I will be able to stay
> up but a few minutes longer. The kids have just about
> driven me crazy today.

How are all of you getting along? Billy and I are fine. I think I could manage all right here and feel swell if I could arrange to take Billy and get out once in awhile. I still have both kids with me whenever I leave the house and that isn't very often. This having them with me day and nite all the time is just a little more than I can stand. I don't know yet just what I am going to do about Bill, Marjorie. No, I'm not going to give him up regardless of what happens. I am just hoping things will be a little different for me in the near future.

Nine months later, Maude had a more positive view of life. Her employer, a Mrs. Hall, had loaned her the family car, "a new Buick with a radio and all the other trimmings," for an outing to the beach with friends. Taking advantage of Mrs. Hall's standing offer, she planned to borrow the Buick again the following Sunday to go fishing in the Florida Keys.

Bernice Register (Stroud) Curtis, Miami Beach, ca. 1935.

"I have already had two afternoons off this week," Maude wrote Margie at the end of July 1939, "and tomorrow is my regular day off and then Sunday I will be out all day. Pretty soon I won't know how to stay at home and work." The sight of the aquamarine waters of Biscayne Bay as she crossed the bridge to Miami Beach, where she could take the sun on the hot sand, did a world of good for her spirits.

Maude was happy with the Halls. "They have been awful sweet to me here and if I can only have Billy with me would like to stay on." Temporarily entrusted to a government-run orphanage, Billy remained her key concern. In response to a question from Margie, she wrote:

> No, I didn't get to see Billy Wednesday but I did go down Sunday. They only allowed me to be with him thirty minutes but it was good to be with him that long. He is much thinner now than he was but he is growing so tall. He is much better satisfied but he said I want to go home with you, Maude. If Mrs. Hall won't let me bring him here then in another month I am going to try to find another place where they will take the two of us. I was down before the judge Mon. and he said they could only keep him for a limited time. If I haven't made some arrangement by that time then I will have to leave him at the home for adoption. But I'll see the bunch of them in hell before I give Billy up. He is the last thing I have got left and I'm going to keep him if I have to scrub floors from morning till night. I am only having to pay two dollars a week for him.

She whispered her defiance into the teeth of a breeze off the Atlantic or silently invoked it as she scrubbed her employers' toilet. But sometimes doubt and fear assailed her, in the solitude of her maid's quarters or as she left the orphanage with Billy's pleas ringing in her ears, and a sense of guilt and helplessness threatened to swamp her. Despite the brave words, Maude's string was playing out.

During a trip to Swainsboro for a funeral, she ran into her old pal, Gladys Waller, who invited Maude to her parents' home. When they sat down to chat, Maude said bitterly that someone had told her she'd never be welcome in the homes of Swainsboro. That's why she had stopped writing to Gladys. Gladys assured her they'd always be friends and she'd always be welcome. But it was the last time the two would meet.

Maude and Billy Moreno, ca. 1939.

Ron Seckinger

By the beginning of December, Maude had left the Halls and begun working for Clifford and Marguerite Holley. Christmas Day would bring her 26th birthday, but she considered her prospects dim and unworthy of celebration. The maxims of her high-school classmates seemed empty words that neither shielded her from discouragement nor persuaded her never to yield. Misfortune had overtaken her after all, and she could find no clemency from the harsh sentence fate seemingly had assigned her.

She was pregnant again, and her latest love affair had proved yet another disappointment. William C. Dracy, a contractor whom she'd been dating, refused to marry her, and the rejection seemed to drain the last remnants of her courage.

Maude Moreno, ca. 1938.

Saturday, December 2, was a typical winter's day in Miami, with a high of 78 degrees and a low of 68. Elsewhere, the Soviet Union was setting up a puppet government in Finland. New York District Attorney Thomas Dewey tossed his hat in the ring for the Republican Party's presidential nomination and the privilege of challenging Franklin Roosevelt's bid for a third term. In Atlanta, preparations continued for the world premiere of "Gone with the Wind" on December 15. More than three dozen debutantes and Junior Leaguers were cinching their waists in corsets to compete for the honor of wearing Scarlett O'Hara's gown to a charity ball.

Oblivious to the rest of mankind, Maude sat in her room at the Holleys' and wrote a brief letter to Margie. She posted it en route to Dracy's residence on the first floor of a two-story stucco house on Northwest 22nd Court in Miami. There she sat on his bed in the gathering darkness and waited, a pistol in her lap, her determination unwavering for this final act.

When Dracy at last pulled his car into the driveway and flashed out the lights, Maude lifted the gun to her breast and pulled the trigger. Hearing the report, Dracy and the upstairs tenants came running to find Maude's body thrown back on the bed, blood staining her dress and the bedclothes, and the pistol on the floor.

The telephone call to the police was relayed to the home of Claude High, who since 1937 had served as deputy sheriff of Dade County and resided in Miami Springs. Claude and his wife Lillian had befriended Alice and Maude Stroud when they first came to Miami in 1931, and both girls had worked in Lillian's beauty parlor. Now, as one of only two officers assigned to Homicide, Claude received calls at all hours of the day and night, and his family was accustomed to his abrupt departures.

But on this night, the High children, awakened by the telephone and their parents' excited voices, were startled to find their mother preparing to accompany her husband. Without offering any explanation, Lillian gave instructions to the children and followed Claude to the car. Alton and Bob stood at the window and watched the vehicle go around the traffic circle and take the Hialeah Bridge toward the northwest sector of Miami.

At the house on Northwest 22nd Court, the Highs beheld the inert form of the young woman who had come to their home as a teenager more than nine years earlier. Maude's suicide letter to Dracy, declaring her love and saying that her action "took a lot of courage," erased any suspicion of foul play, and the upstairs tenant substantiated Dracy's claim that he wasn't present when the shot was fired. The authorities judged no inquest was necessary and released the body to Bess Funeral Home without an autopsy.

Kenneth B. Bess, who apparently obtained Margie Scott's name and address from Dracy or the Highs, sent a night letter to Swainsboro, telling of Maude's death but offering no details. Margie, shocked at the sudden passing of her younger sister, on Sunday arranged for interment and notified the rest of the clan.

In Fitzgerald, Kermit and Rose received a terse telegram: MAUDE PASSED AWAY LAST NIGHT FUNERAL TUESDAY AT SWAINSBORO. They set out for Emanuel County, along with Alice and Pat Mitchell, who were visiting at the time. Emmit and Frances, recipients of a second telegram, took the train from Kentucky. A second night letter from Kenneth Bess advised that he would ship the body on receipt of $234.80, and the coffin did not depart by train until Tuesday.

And so Maude, the youngest, came home. A separate letter from Bess included a clipping from the Miami *Herald*, by which Margie and the others learned that Maude had taken her own life. And all too soon, Margie received more poignant evidence in Maude's own hand, the letter she had mailed the night of December 2 but had not been postmarked until two days later.

> Saturday Nite
> Dear Marjorie,
>
> Before you receive this I imagine you will have heard something in regards to me. I am so terribly tired of the struggle to live that its just no use any longer. There is nothing left for me to live for so I am ending it all tonite. There is only one thing I ask of you. Either you or Emmitt take Billy and raise him for me. Please don't let

him be adopted. I saw him Saturday and he is so sweet. He begged me to let him come home with me. But I have no home now and never will now. Bernice saw to that. She has taken every thing from me that made life worth living for. She wasn't satisfied with just her husband she had to have Bill [Dracy] and so I am leaving him with her. My cloths are at her house, Billys are at Bills and Billys toys and an enlarged picture of me are here at Mrs. Holleys. I guess that is all I own in this world. I beg of you Marjorie take Billy. You wont ever be sorry. I love all of you but my life has been a failure from the start. It is better this way.

Goodbye to you all.
Maude

Although suicide was not uncommon, even in Emanuel County, it invariably stunned everyone. Accidents and disease could be construed as manifestations of God's inscrutable plan, but taking one's own life seemed willful and perverse.

The *Forest-Blade* tactfully attributed Maude's death to "a short illness," and the grownups in the family kept the truth from the children, sharing their pain in private whispers, telling only a few outsiders. As the oldest, Jessie took it badly, as did Kermit, Maude's favorite.

Her old friends also found her last, irrevocable act difficult to comprehend. "I was shocked and even more grieved," Gladys Waller remembered many years later, "because I did not understand what had caused her to commit suicide." Nesbit Rogers had a similar reaction. "That would have been the last thing that I would have thought Maude would have done," she recalled.

Billy Moreno with Knob Fields at the Flanders farm, December 1939.

One final decision remained. What should they do with Billy, just a month past his fifth birthday? Emmit telephoned Miami and arranged for the boy's passage to Emanuel County. A few days after the funeral, the authorities in Miami put Maude's son on a bus for the trip north, but the driver forgot to put him off in Swainsboro and he had to be returned from Savannah.

Dressed in a sailor's suit, the bewildered Billy captured everyone's heart. "Poor little child!" they said, looking at his open and innocent face. "He was the most precious child you ever saw," Leila Fields Scott recalled almost 50 years later.

Margie wanted to keep him. Ellie had been gone for two and a half years, and raising Billy would have partially healed her grief. But Waitus would have none of it. Having lost his only son, he wouldn't risk a second scar on his heart. Margie's pleas couldn't penetrate his stony resolution.

In the end, Alice took the boy. She'd raised him off and on, and she was the only member of the family whom he knew. When she and Pat returned to Griffin, Billy went with them.

He was the only mark Maude had made in her brief life.

EPILOGUE

MUCH OF THE Strouds' world has disappeared. Communities like Blun are no more than signs on county roads. Pine trees cover Duncan Fields's 50 acres, obliterating every vestige of the old farmhouse and barn. Freeway builders tore down the house Denver Stroud and his family inhabited soon after arriving in Miami, although the stucco dwelling where Maude Moreno took her life still stood in the mid-1990s. The Somerset town fathers decided to destroy Crystal Park, where Emmit Stroud courted Frances Bell, to make room for the City Sanitation and Street Department. Agriculture and development have claimed half of the Everglades' 4 million acres, and the rest teeters on the edge of absolute destruction.

The Strouds and almost all of their children are gone, too. Arthritis eventually forced Jessie Fields to abandon the school cafeteria, where she had played surrogate mother to thousands of students. She died in 1977 at the age of 89, beloved "Bigmama" to dozens of grandchildren and great-grandchildren.

Jewel's husband Fred Hooks, after graduating from Moody Bible Institute, served in a number of congregations, notably Second Methodist in Macon, Georgia. He died in 1950.

Emmit and Frances Stroud moved to Danville, Kentucky about 1940 and had a second daughter. He died in 1970. Frances lived until 2001.

Margie and Waitus Scott never recovered from Ellie's death. The gregarious and playful Waitus became somber and reserved, and his visits to the back room of the barbershop for a snort of liquor grew more frequent. Margie took to drinking an alcohol-based tonic. Passers-by frequently saw her sitting beside Ellie's grave in City Cemetery, a solitary figure trying fruitlessly to make sense of her shattered world. Waitus died in 1969, and Margie in 1984.

Kermit Stroud drifted from job to job. He contracted emphysema in the 1960s. In 1971, tired of suffering, he killed himself with a revolver.

Alice Mitchell worked as a salesclerk in Swainsboro and raised her two children in Waitus and Margie's home. She died in 1990, the last of her generation.

Billy Moreno remained with Alice for only a year or so. On one of the occasions when she tried again to resuscitate her relationship with Tom, her husband said Billy couldn't come. And so Emmit took the boy, despite Frances's protests. An unhappy child, he quit school to join the Army at the age of 16. He married a beautiful German woman and was a good father to their two children. He died in 1994.

WRITING EMANUEL'S CHILDREN

THE INDIVIDUALS discussed in *Emanuel's Children* include ruffians and lay-abouts, upstanding citizens and hard-working farmers, men and women both courageous and susceptible to despair. Whether saint or sinner, each of them deserves remembrance as an exemplar of their times.

In 1982, I asked my mother, Ronnie Fields Seckinger, to round up some photos of her family, intending to frame some of them for display in my home. When I arrived at her residence in Concord, North Carolina for a family Thanksgiving celebration, she showed me a few dozen prints. She put names to faces and gave brief life histories for the members of her mother's generation.

The variety of experiences and the pathos of the eight Stroud children stunned me. While familiar with my grandmother, Jessie Stroud Fields, and her descendants, I knew little of my great-aunts and great-uncles, shadowy creatures at the edge of my consciousness. Now their stories seized my attention: abject poverty, two suicides, a death in childbirth, the devastation of an only child's untimely passing, alcoholism, a boy born out of wedlock, crushing despair. Before my mother had even finished talking, I'd decided to write about the Stroud family.

With a doctorate in Latin American history, nine years' teaching experience, and a number of publications to my credit, I had the specialized skills for a professional approach to family tales. But I had to apply them to a different environment and context.

After some preliminary research in census registers, in 1983, I began to interview relatives and friends of the Strouds. Only two of the siblings--Margie Scott and Alice Mitchell--still lived, along with the widows of Emmit and Kermit Stroud. But other kin and associates kindly consented to tell their stories, which proved riveting. Walter Phenious, a natural raconteur and my only African American informant, regaled me with tales of the "devilment" he and playmate J.D. Fields got into as children. Similarly, Annie Lee Hooks, Fred Hooks's second wife, shared her vivid recollections of life in Chicago in the 1920s, including her husband's passing acquaintance with the notorious gangster Dion O'Banion..

I usually spent two weeks each summer, mostly in Georgia and Florida, collecting oral histories and mining issues of the weekly Swainsboro (Ga.) *Forest-Blade* dating back to 1901, as well as similar publications in other towns where the Strouds fetched up. My teenaged son Karl usually went along, displaying tact and immeasurable patience while he listened to aged strangers recount their tales of small-town life and rural poverty. (In compensation, he earned a solid grounding in '50s and '60s music as we listened to my collection of cassettes.) During the rest of the year, I continued to search for archival material and to track down potential informants through phone calls and the US mail in those pre-Internet days.

My initial conception of a collection of photographs with brief life histories soon morphed into a more ambitious goal. I realized that transcribed memories, newspaper accounts, city directories, and courthouse records formed a network of interlocking facts that yielded more information than expected. Moreover, questions about one of the Strouds often opened the way to events unknown to me or added flesh to an otherwise skimpy tale.

For example, I first visited Delmar Hooks in Canal Point, Florida to ask about his sister-in-law, Jewel Stroud Hooks, only to hear his fascinating account of living through the Great Storm of 1928, as well as his brother's association with baseball great Ty Cobb. Similarly, I interviewed Jerry Rich to learn about Ellie Scott, whose death at 16 devastated his parents. As I prepared to leave, I asked Jerry whether he remembered Seab Johnson, an African American man convicted and executed for murder in 1923. To my surprise, he excitedly recounted his friendship with the condemned man during the two years Johnson spent in the Swainsboro jail.

As the project continued to evolve, I decided that understanding the lives of these ordinary people required more context. Readers needed to view them not merely in their daily pursuits but also in the light of contemporaneous events and trends throughout the South and the nation. This required broader research in the historical literature. And so the scope became ever larger.

Oral histories were essential. Only from memories could personalities and specific incidents emerge. Local newspapers provided dates for remembered events and sometimes elaborated on certain experiences. Some of my informants--notably Frances Bell Stroud--had remarkable recall, able to recount the details of even minor incidents. Others' memories proved spottier. I used quotes attributed to themselves or other parties, aware that after decades these would be only approximations of words actually spoken.

Similarly, courthouse records established the timing and circumstances of events. These included birth, marriage, and death registers; arrest and trial records; mortgages; and real estate transfers. Other sources emerged, such as the National Archives' overhead photos, originally taken to monitor New Deal crop-allocation programs, showing the locations of the Fields's farms and the layouts of Swainsboro, Canal Point, Florida, and Somerset, Kentucky. In addition, I have included photos provided by many of my sources and by various institutions.

I derived a great deal of satisfaction from this project. I got to know distant relatives and their associates and to learn about my own origins. I regard the work as a gift to the great-grandchildren and great-great-grand-children of the Strouds so they will have a clearer notion of their family origins and heritage, the bad as well as the good. As an exercise in social history, *Emanuel's Children* demonstrates the feasibility of reconstructing the lives of common folk who left no family or official archives and achieved neither fame nor infamy. Similar studies are possible for later periods, such as the changes to American society experienced following the Second World War.

For me, this project has served as a grand adventure. I hope that others will find themselves equally fascinated by the stories of these ordinary people with extraordinary lives.

ACKNOWLEDGEMENTS

THE KINDNESS AND cooperation of many people made this project possible. Most important were those who shared their memories and answered my questions, often in multiple interviews. Some of these informants also functioned as research assistants, locating photographs or referring me to friends and acquaintances. Most have died since our conversations.

The two surviving members of my grandmother's generation, Marjorie Stroud Scott and Alice Susie Stroud Mitchell of Swainsboro, Georgia, were particularly gracious. Two of their brothers' widows, Rosa Lee Jean Walker (Stroud) Fuller of Fitzgerald, Georgia, and Frances Winwood Bell Stroud of Danville, Kentucky, offered extensive information.

Those of the next generation also proved extremely helpful: Ralph Henry Fields of Langley, South Carolina; Leila Ella Fields Scott of Sylvester, Georgia; Romie Delle ("Ronnie") Fields Seckinger of Concord, North Carolina; Wynelle Rachel Fields Forbes and Patrick Wise Mitchell of Swainsboro; Novis Kenneth Fields of Savannah, Georgia; Freddie Barbara Hooks Sawyer of Avon Park, Florida; Hilma Frances Stroud Boyd of Frankfort, Kentucky; and Jean Stroud Lott of Fitzgerald, Georgia.

Other informants included: Maurice Boatright, Ermie Coleman Durden, Neil Dyson Eberhardt, Callie Gertrude Davis Fagler, Charles Ryal Harmon, Ammie Stroud Hudson, Otis Hudson, Lois Hambly Hunnicutt, Mary Virginia ("Jean") Dyson McGregor, Claude L. McLendon, Will

McMillan, Jr., Jeannette Youmans Neal, Walter Pheanious, Richmond Luther Quick, Jerry Jethro Rich, Aubrey Scott, Lynwood Screws, Mabel Screws, Walter Screws, A.L. ("Al") Seckinger, Daisy Leigh Dunford Smith, Dessie Eugene Stroud, Sr., Greene Y. Underwood, Earl Varner, and Sidney Gladys Waller of Swainsboro; Jack B. Bell, Mary Lee Rich Kea, and Elmo Dennis Rich of Modoc, Georgia; Nesbit Rogers Christian of Waycross, Georgia; Robbie Eileen Scott Temples of Vidalia, Georgia; Ouida Kirkland Fields of Blun, Georgia; Roy Lee Fields of Sterling, Georgia; James Morrison ("Rock") Hall of Arlington, Virginia; Alton B. High and Robert T. High of Miami, Florida; Annie Lee Ducker Hooks of Tice, Florida; Delma Lamar Hooks, Nell Horn Hooks, and Luther Y. Levins of Canal Point, Florida; Grace Pierce Kent of Canoochee, Georgia; Frank Kirkland of Summertown, Georgia; Jack League of Danville, Kentucky; Edna Lois Fields (Cone) (Williams) (Akins) Logue of Augusta, Georgia; Henry Potter of New Port Richey, Florida; Jonathan Carol ("Pete") Rich of McRae, Georgia; Jerell Sawyer of Avon Park, Florida; Carlton Scott of Deland, Florida; Garland Sherrod of Jessup, Georgia; and Tessie Lee Whitehead Stroud of Piney Grove, Georgia.

The staffs at a number of public and private institutions also helped enormously. These include the National Archives and Records Administration and the Library of Congress in Washington, DC; the Georgia Archives, Atlanta; East Georgia College Library, Swainsboro; University of Georgia Library, Athens; Harvard University Library, Cambridge, Massachusetts; Georgia Historical Society, Savannah; Lawrence E. Will Museum, Belle Glade, Florida; Atlanta Historical Center; University of Kentucky Library, Lexington; P. K. Yonge Library of Florida History, University of Florida Library, Gainesville; Alexandria (Virginia) Public Library; Miami-Dade (Florida) Public Library; Belle Glade (Florida) Public Library; New York Public Library; Detroit (Michigan) Public Library; and Chattanooga (Tennessee) Public Library.

Specific individuals who provided assistance include genealogist and historian Becki L. Stroud of Augusta, Georgia; Cheryl Stein of the

Lawrence E. Will Museum, Belle Glade, Florida; Betty Jean Andrews, Office of the Clerk of Superior Court, Swainsboro; Richard Todd Horvatis, Hampton Roads Naval Museum, Norfolk, Virginia; William Dudley, Senior Historian, and John Riley, Naval Historical Center, Washington; Pat Bernard-Ezzell, Cultural Resources Program, Tennessee Valley Authority, Knoxville, Tennessee; and Gail Williamson and Halai Lamb of the Swainsboro *Forest-Blade* and its online service, Emanuel County Live (http://emanuelcounty-live.com).

Other friends and acquaintances who encouraged, supported, or assisted include John Shelton Reed of Chapel Hill, North Carolina; Sheryl B. Vogt of Athens, Georgia; Brenda and Paul Fields of West Palm Beach, Florida; Mary Helen Hooks Harris of North Palm Beach, Florida; Charlotte Waid St. John of Key Biscayne, Florida; Penny Stroud League of Danville, Kentucky; Stanley Hooks of Stuart, Florida; Geraldine Bloodsworth of Lake Butler, Florida; Margaret H. Mosley of Belle Glade, Florida; Robin S. Kent of Great Falls, Virginia; Mary Ellen Johnson of Atlanta; Patricia Sherrod Keith of Waycross, Georgia; Margaret P. Proctor of Dublin, Georgia; Edwin S. James of Rock Hill, South Carolina; Mara Spade of Glen Echo, Maryland; Ralph E. Quay and Lauretta Quay Loar of Toledo, Ohio; Sarah Easham of Bethelridge, Kentucky; and David and Kay Hanson of Hinesville, Georgia.

My nephew Jeff Gable and his wife, Katie Coffey, of Rancho Santa Margarita, California, inspired me to complete this project in book form and contributed substantially to getting it ready for publication. My grandson Scott Seckinger provided frequent IT consultations.

Finally, special thanks not only to my son and road companion Karl but also to my daughter Cristina, who listened to many conversations about family history, and my wife Edie Wilson, who provided constant encouragement and frequent advice.

NOTES

ABBREVIATIONS

ECC	Emanuel County Courthouse, Swainsboro
ED	Enumeration District
ESC	Emanuel Superior Court
NARA	National Archives and Records Administration
OCCC	Office of the Clerk of Circuit Court
OCSC	Office of the Clerk of Superior Court
OPJ	Office of the Probate Judge
RG	Record Group

ORIGINS

Settlement of Georgia frontier: Numan V. Bartley, *The Creation of Modern Georgia* (Athens, Ga., 1983), 11-14.

Emanuel County: James E. Dorsey, *Footprints Along the Hoopee: A History of Emanuel County, 1812-1900* (Spartanburg, S.C., 1978), 17-21.

19th-century Emanuel: Dorsey, *Footprints,* 21-67.

Civil War and postwar Emanuel: Dorsey, *Footprints,* 89-90, 100, 117-21, 231-37; War Department Collection of Confederate Records, Compiled Service Records of Confederate Soldiers from Georgia, Rolls 386, 389, RG 109, NARA.

Raised north of Swainsboro: 10th Census, 1880, Georgia, Emanuel County, ED 51, fl. 11, ED 52, fl. 38, NARA.

Jim becomes sharecropper: Deed Record Book A-J, fls. 217-218, OCSC, ECC, Swainsboro.

Tenancy: Edward L. Ayers, *The Promise of the New South: Life After Reconstruction* (New York, 1992), 195-98; C. Vann Woodward, *Origins of the New South, 1877-1913* (Baton Rouge, La., 1951), 175-85; Gilbert C. Fife, *Cotton Fields No More: Southern Agriculture, 1865-1980* (Lexington, Ky., 1984), 3-6; Robert Preston Brooks, *The Agrarian Revolution in Georgia, 1865-1912* (1914; reprint, Westport, Conn., 1970), 18-36, 55-68; U.S. Bureau of the Census, *Thirteenth Census of the United States Taken in the Year 1910,* 11 vols. (Washington, 1913), VI, 317-18; Bartley, *Creation,* 32-42; Charles Reagan Wilson and William Ferris, eds., *Encyclopedia of Southern Culture* (Chapel Hill, N.C., 1989), 29-31.

Residence in Blun: Interview with Marjorie Scott, July 5, 1983.

School: Interview with Marjorie Scott, July 5, 1983; Swainsboro (Ga.) *Forest-Blade,* June 8, 1911, p. 11. Comment on writing based on limited samples of correspondence.

Poor: Interview with Frances Stroud, May 19, 1985.

Children's activities: Interviews with Alice Mitchell and Marjorie Scott, July 5, 1983.

RUFFIANS

Marriage: Marriage Record Book D, 1904-15, fl. 178, OPJ, ECC; *Forest-Blade,* Apr. 26, 1906, p. 4.

"Tried to": Interview with Tessie Lee Stroud, July 4, 1983.

Fuller and Miles Fields: Bench warrant, Apr. 19, 1895, ms-12, box 2, folder 14, East Georgia State College Library, Swainsboro; Minutes, ESC, Book D. fls. 26, 29, 45, 130, Book I, fl. 505, OCSC, ECC.

Henry Fields: Interviews with Leila Scott, June 20, 1987, Jack Fields, Nov. 28, 1990, and Roy Fields, Nov. 29, 1990; *Forest-Blade,* Oct. 18, 1928, p. 1; Soperton (Ga.) *News,* Oct. 19, 1928, p. 1.

Charges against Duncan: Minutes, ESC, Book H, fl. 405, Book I, fl. 33, Book J, fl. 32, Book K, fl. 47, OCSC, ECC.

Fields farm: White Roster Smith's will, Will Book B, 1857-1907, fls. 210-17, OPJ, and Deed Record Book B-K, fl. 193, OCSC, ECC.

Sheriff: *Forest-Blade,* Jan. 28, 1904, p. 3, Jan. 18, 1906, p. 1.

J.W.'s lands: Deed Record Book A-U, fls. 286, 305, Book A-W, fls. 40, 219, Book B-B, fls. 109, 110, 170, Book B-F, fl. 58, OCSC, ECC.

Duncan: Interviews with Alice Mitchell, July 5, 1983, Ouida Fields, July 7, 1983, Mabel Screws, July 12, 1983, and Garland Sherrod, July 15, 1988.

John Williams: 13th Census, 1910, Georgia, Emanuel County, ED 96, fl. 19B, NARA.

Early years: Interviews with Ronnie Seckinger, Feb. 8, 1983, Leila Scott, July 3, 1983, and Gracie Fields, July 1, 1987.

Relatives: Interviews with Leila Scott, June 20, 1987, and Jack Fields, Nov. 28, 1990. Joe was living with the family in February 1920; 14th Census, 1920, Georgia, Emanuel County, ED 27, fl. 17A, NARA.

PROGRESS

Wiregrass region: Brooks, *Agrarian Revolution,* 102-108; Mark Vickers Wetherington, *The New South Comes to Wiregrass Georgia, 1865-1910* (Knoxville, Tenn., 1994), *passim.*

Foreign-born population: U.S. Bureau of the Census, *Thirteenth Census of the United States Taken in the Year 1910,* 11 vols. (Washington, 1913), II, 367-80.

Railroads in Emanuel County: Dorsey, *Footprints,* 163-67; *Emanuel Memories* (Swainsboro, 1976), 45, 50-51; *Forest-Blade,* July 19, 1906, p. 1, June 16, 1904, p. 8, Feb. 10, 1910, p. 1; Woodward, *Origins,* 379-84. "Pull for Swainsboro": *Forest-Blade,* Dec. 9, 1909, p. 10.

Georgia & Florida Railway: *Forest-Blade,* Feb. 17, 1910, p. 1, July 8, 1910, p. 1, Apr. 7, 1910, p. 5, Jan. 26, 1911, p. 1, Apr. 6, 1911, p. 11; interview with Marjorie Scott, July 5, 1983.

Autos: *Forest-Blade,* July 11, 1907, p. 1, Oct. 13, 1910, p. 10.

Roads: *Forest-Blade,* Apr. 21, 1904, p. 5, Mar. 18, 1909, p. 1, Sept. 8, 1910, p. 6, Mar. 9, 1911, pp. 2, 4; Howard Lawrence Preston, *Dirt Roads to Dixie: Accessibility and Modernization in the South, 1885-1935* (Knoxville, Tenn., 1991), 21-23, 26-28.

Chain-gang system: Dittmer, *Black Georgia,* 86.

Accidents: *Forest-Blade,* July 14, 1910, p. 1, Apr. 13, 1911, p. 8.

BASEBALL

Marriage: Marriage Record Book B, fl. 54, OPJ, Jefferson County Courthouse, Louisville, Ga. Attended school together: *Forest-Blade,* May 20, 1920, p. 1.

John and Lillian Hooks: Interview with Delma Hooks, Feb. 16, 1988; Canal Point (Fla.) *Everglades News,* Mar. 9, 1956.

Ty Cobb: Interviews with Delma Hooks, Feb. 16, 1988, and Annie Lee Hooks, Feb. 17, 1988; Al Stump, *Cobb: A Biography* (Chapel Hill, N.C., 1994), *passim;* Augusta (Ga.) *Chronicle,* 1904-1909, *passim; Forest-Blade,* June 10, 1909, p. 1; Detroit (Mich.) *Free Press,* June 5, 1909, pp. 8-9.

TOWN AND COUNTY

Emanuel County in 1910: R.G. Dun and Company, *Reference Book,* CLXVII (Jan. 1910), Part 1, Georgia, 4-40, *passim.*

Population and cotton statistics: *Thirteenth Census,* II, 380, VI, 302, and *A Compendium of the Ninth Census* (June 1, 1870) (Washington, 1872), 723. Quote about Stillmore: *Forest-Blade,* Sept. 8, 1904, p. 1.

Swainsboro: Swainsboro (Ga.) *Pine Forest,* Mar..7, 1901, p. 3; *Forest-Blade,* 1904-1911, *passim; Emanuel Memories,* 102-104, 174; Dun and Company, *Reference Book,* CLXVII, Part 1, Georgia, 37, 46.

"Belle of cities": *Forest-Blade,* Feb. 10, 1910, p. 1.

Population: Thirteenth Census, II, 347. Statistics on Blacks: *Thirteenth Census,* II, 380-81, VI, 348.

Race relations: Ayers, *Promise,* 132-52, 304-309, 409-11; Dittmer, *Black Georgia,* 94-101; C. Vann Woodward, *The Strange Career of Jim Crow,* 3rd rev. ed. (New York, 1974), 82-93. First White primary in Emanuel: *Forest-Blade*, Apr. 21, 1904, p. 5.

Lynchings: Ayers, *Promise*, 153-59; Dittmer, *Black Georgia*, 131; W. Fitzhugh Brundage, *Lynching in the New South: Georgia and Virginia, 1880-1930* (Urbana, Ill., 1993), 103-39; *Forest-Blade*, Jan. 10, 1907, p. 3 (the issue is misdated 1906).

Ed Pierson: *Forest-Blade*, July 12, 1906, p. 1.

John W. Stroud: *Pine Forest*, June 20, 1901, p. 5; Minutes, ESC, Book E, fls. 452, 471, OCSC, ECC.

WAR

Bryan: Kendrick A. Clements, *William Jennings Bryan: Missionary Isolationist* (Knoxville, Tenn., 1982), 96-122; Fitzgerald (Ga.) *Leader-Enterprise and Press*, Apr. 9, 1917, p. 4.

Draft: Nell Irvin Painter, *Standing at Armageddon: The United States, 1977-1919* (New York, 1987), 330-32.

Duncan and Temples register: James Duncan Fields's and White Temples Fields's draft registration cards M1509, Roll 38, NARA.

Emanuel in the war: *Emanuel Memories, 1776-1976* (Swainsboro, 1976), 99-101.

Emmit and draft: Emmit L. Stroud's draft registration card, M1509, Roll 14, NARA; *Leader-Enterprise and Press*, June 13, 1917, p. 7, July 18, 1917, p. 2, July 23, 1917, p. 1.

Liberty Loans: *Leader-Enterprise and Press*, June 15, 1917, p. 1, Apr. 15, 1918, p. 1, Oct. 4, 1918, p. 1; Painter, *Standing at Armageddon*, 332-333.

Denver and Liberty Loan: *Leader-Enterprise and Press*, Apr. 15, 1918, pp. 1-2.

Hampton Roads: Command History 1918, folder "1918 N.O.B. Command History," Archives, Hampton Roads Naval Museum, Norfolk, Virginia; Paolo E. Dolleta, ed., *United States Navy and Marine Corps Bases, Domestic* (Westport, Conn., 1985), 379-81.

Denver's Navy service: Shipping articles, Enlistments 1919, Serial No. 40, No. 1946284, and service record, National Personnel Records Center, NARA, St. Louis; honorable discharge, Discharge Book 1, fl. 308, Office of the Clerk of Superior Court, Ben Hill County Courthouse, Fitzgerald, Ga.; U.S. Naval History Division, *Dictionary of American Fighting Ships*, 8 vols. (Washington, 1959-81), V, 8, VI, 559-60, VII, 432-33.

Joe Fields: Tombstone, Hall's Cemetery, Emanuel County; interview with Mabel Screws, July 12, 1983.

STRIKE

Postwar troubles: Painter, *Standing at Armageddon*, 346-80.

"Once a railroad man": H. Waldo Hitt, quoted in Clifford M. Kuhn, Harlon E. Joye, and E. Bernard West, *Living Atlanta: An Oral History of the City, 1914-1948* (Athens, Ga., 1990), 86.

Emmit as boilermaker: Interviews with Alice Mitchell, July 5, 1983, and Frances Stroud, May 18, 1985.

1919 shopmen's strike: Atlanta (Ga.) *Constitution*, Aug. 2-Sept. 3, 1919, *passim;* Fitzgerald (Ga.) *Herald*, Aug. 4, 1919, p. 1, Aug. 11, 1919, pp. 1-2, Aug. 14, 1919, p. 1; Mercer Griffin Evans, "The History of the Organized Labor Movement in Georgia" (Ph.D. dissertation, University of Chicago, 1929), 163.

Isolation of shopmen: Walter Licht, *Working for the Railroad: The Organization of Work in the Nineteenth Century* (Princeton, N.J., 1983), 232.

Fitzgerald strike: *Herald*, Oct. 30, 1919, p. 1, Nov. 3, 1919, p. 1; *Constitution*, Oct. 29, 1919, p. 1, Oct. 30, 1919, p. 6, Nov. 2, 1919, p. 4A.

Strouds fired: Interview with Alice Mitchell, July 5, 1983.

JEWEL

Fred's wanderings: Interviews with Delma Hooks, Aug. 5, 1984, and Annie Lee Hooks, Feb. 17, 1988; *Forest-Blade*, Mar. 5, 1914, p. 3, July 4, 1918, p. 4, Nov. 21, 1918, p. 5, May 13, 1920, p. 1.

Watkins Street and boarders: 14th Census, 1920, Georgia, Richmond County, Enumeration District 71, fl. 7A, NARA.

Jewel: Interviews with Alice Mitchell, July 5, 1983, Leila Scott, July 3, 1983, June 20, 1987, Dessie Stroud, July 7, 1983, Delma Hooks, Aug. 5, 1984, Elmo Rich, June 24, 1987, and Henry Potter, Mar. 18, 1991.

Jewel's last pregnancy and death: Interviews with Delma Hooks and Freddie Sawyer, Aug. 5, 1984, and Leila Scott, June 20, 1987; birth certificate no. 47646, Georgia Department of Human Resources; *Forest-Blade*, May 13, 1920, p.1, May 20, 1920, p. 1.

DRY GOODS

Jewish emigration: Ronald Sanders, *Shores of Refuge: A Hundred Years of Jewish Emigration* (New York, 1988), 3-172; Benjamin Kaplan, *The Eternal Stranger: A Study of Jewish Life in the Small Community* (New York, 1957). 30-31.

Ehrliches' arrival and naturalization: 12th Census, 1900, Georgia, Emanuel County, ED 103, fl. 16B, and 14th Census, 1920, Georgia, Emanuel County, ED 26, fl. 5A, NARA.

Peddler: Interview with Frances Rabhan, Sept. 3, 1993. Jewish peddler tradition from Stanley Feldstein, *The Land That I Show You: Three Centuries of Jewish Life in America* (Garden City, N.Y., 1978), 52-59.

Startup capital: Ayers, *Promise*, 92.

Manassas, Millegeville, and Swainsboro: Interview with Frances Rabhan, Sept. 3, 1993; R.G. Dun and Company, *Reference Book*, CXIII, Part 1 (Apr. 1896), Georgia, 25, CXXIV, Part 1 (Jan. 1899), Georgia, 29; 12th Census, 1900, Georgia, Emanuel County, ED 103, fl. 16B, NARA.

Marriage: Marriage Record Book L, fl. 179, Chatham County Courthouse, Savannah, Ga.

Ehrlich's enterprises: Interview with Frances Rabhan, Sept. 3, 1993; *Forest-Blade*, Feb. 8, 1918, p. 1, May 9, 1918, p. 1; R.G. Dun and Company, *Reference Book*, CVII (Oct. 1894), Part 1, Georgia, 37, CXLI (July 1903), Part 1, Georgia, 29. Swainsboro store's capitalization and credit rating from *ibid.*, CXCVI (Mar. 1917), Part 1, Georgia, 42.

War work: Interview with Frances Rabhan, Sept. 3, 1993; *Forest-Blade*, Nov. 16, 1917, p. 1, May 16, 1918, p. 1, Aug. 22, 1918, p. 1.

Ehrlich buys farmland: Deed Record Book B-F, fl. 470, Book B-H, fl. 538, Book B-J, fl. 278, OCSC, EEC.

Screws family: Interview with Mabel Screws, July 12, 1983; 14th Census, 1920, Georgia, Emanuel County, ED 27, fl. 14B, NARA.

Jessie and Lownie Pheanious: Interviews with Ronnie Seckinger, Feb. 9, 1983, Ralph Fields, June 19, 1987, and Leila Scott, June 20, 1987.

Duncan and Blacks: Interviews with Ralph Fields, June 19, 1987, and Leila Scott, June 20, 1987.

RASCALS

J.D. and Walter: Interviews with Walter Pheanious, July 9, 1983, and Mabel Screws, July 12, 1983.

Timing for airplane visit: *Forest-Blade,* Apr. 24, 1919, p. 1.

TOWN AND COUNTY

Margie and Waitus: Interviews with Marjorie Scott, July 5, 1983, and Ouida Fields, July 7, 1983; Marriage Record White Book E 1915-1928, fl. 174, OPJ, ECC.

Amenities: *Forest-Blade,* June 6, 1918, p. 1, Nov. 14, 1918, p. 1, Nov. 28, 1918, p. 1, Mar. 25, 1920, p. 1, June 16, 1921, p. 1, Aug. 25, 1921, p. 2, Dec. 22, 1921, p. 1; R.G. Dun and Company, *Reference Book,* CCVII (Jan. 1920), Part 1, Georgia, 41.

Population: U.S. Bureau of the Census, *Fourteenth Census of the United States. State Compendium, Georgia* (Washington, 1924), 29.

Entertainment: *Forest-Blade,* 1918-1923, *passim.*

Chautauqua: *Forest-Blade,* May 29, 1913, p. 1, and June 19, 1913, p. 5.

Ty Cobb: *Forest-Blade,* Feb 23, 1922, p. 1.

Roller-skating: *Forest-Blade,* Feb. 8, 1923, p. 1.

Movies: *Forest-Blade,* Sept. 22, 1917, p. 1, Mar. 2, 1917, p. 1.

Court case: *Forest-Blade*, Jan. 26, 1917, p. 1, Mar. 2, 1917, p. 1, May 15, 1917, p. 1, Jan. 25, 1918, p. 1; Minutes, Emanuel Superior Court, Book M, fls. 96, 314, OCSC, ECC; Magnum et al. v. Keith, 147 Ga. 603, 95 S.E. 1 (1918).

Senior boys: *Forest-Blade*, Apr. 25, 1918, p. 1, May 23, 1918, p. 1.

Influenza: John M. Barry, *The Great Influenza: The Story of the Deadliest Pandemic in History* (New York, 2004); Forest-Blade, Jan. 16, 1919, p. 1.

Georgia deaths: Augusta (Ga.) *Chronicle*, Jan. 15, 1919, p. 1.

COTTON

Boll weevil: Pete Daniel, *Standing at the Crossroads: Southern Life in the Twentieth Century* (New York, 1986), 11-12; state agent report for 1916, Annual Reports of Extension Service Field Representatives, Georgia, 1909-44 (T-855), roll no. 2, RG 33, Records of the Federal Extension Service, NARA; *Forest-Blade*, Nov. 17, 1916, p. 1.

Extension Service: Jack Temple Kirby, *Rural Worlds Lost: The American South, 1920-1940* (Baton Rouge, La., 1987), 20-22; Georgia state agent report for 1915, roll no. 2, RG 33, NARA.

Salvaging cotton culture: *Forest-Blade*, Oct. 9, 1919, p. 1; Georgia state agent reports for 1915-16, Emanuel County agent reports for 1916-18, rolls nos. 2-3, RG 33, NARA; George B. Tindall, *The Emergence of the South, 1913-1945* (Baton Rouge, La., 1967), 122-25.

Cotton boom: Tindall, *Emergence*, 33-38, 60-61, 66-67; *Forest-Blade*, Oct. 16, 1916, p. 1, June 1, 1917, p. 1; interview with Walter Pheanious, July 9, 1983.

Collapse: Tindall, *Emergence*, 111-13; *Forest-Blade*, Dec. 2, 1920, p. 4, Dec. 9, 1920, p.1.

Watermelons: *Forest-Blade*, July 27, 1917, p. 1.

Tobacco: *Forest-Blade*, Mar. 25, 1920, p. 1, July 29, 1920, p. 1; interviews with Walter Pheanious, July 9, 1983, Mabel Screws, July 12, 1983, and Frances Rabhan, Sept. 3, 1993; Emanuel County agent report for 1931, roll no. 46, RG 33, NARA.

Ron Seckinger

Tobacco prices: Tendall, *Emergence*, 111-12.

RAILROAD MAN

Blacklisted: Interview with Jack League, Apr. 20, 1990.

Residence in Alabama: 14th Census, Alabama, Clay County, ED 52, fl. 4, NARA.

Railroad jobs: Prior Service Control Record, Railroad Retirement Board, accompanying letter from D.A. Turner (Supervisor Pensions, Norfolk Southern Corporation) to Hilda Stroud Boyd, Roanoke, Va., May 6, 1993, in possession of author.

Worked in 45 states: Interview with Frances Stroud, Apr. 20, 1990.

1922 shopmen's strike: Selig Parlman and Philip Taft, *Labor Movements* (New York, 1935), Vol. IV of *History of Labor in the United States, 1896-1932*, ed. John R. Commons (4 vols.; New York, 1918-35), 515-24; Michael Harris, *American Labor* (New Haven, Conn., 1938), 254-63; Mercer Griffin Evans, "History of the Organised Labor Movement in Georgia," 164-65; Gary M. Fink, ed., *Labor Unions* (Westport, Conn., 1977), 36.

Decay of railroads: Albro Martin, *Enterprise Denied: Origins of the Decline of American Railroads, 1897-1917* (New York, 1971), passim; Fink, ed., *Labor Unions*, 36.

Somerset: Alma Owens Timbals, *A History of Pulaski County, Kentucky* (Bagdad, Ky., 1952), 71-72, 81-83; George Tuggle, *Pulaski Revisited* (Lexington, Ky., 1982), 42; U.S. Bureau of the Census, *Fourteenth Census of the United States Taken in the Year 1920* (Washington, 1923), III, 379.

Southern Railway: Burke Davis, *The Southern Railway: Road of the Innovators* (Chapel Hill, N.C. 1985), 26-32.

Railroad men in Somerset: Interview with Frances Stroud, Apr. 20, 1990.

ORPHANS

Douglas: Interviews with Alice Mitchell, July 5, 1983, and June 24, 1987; *Forest-Blade*, July 2, 1914, p. 4; tombstone, Sherrod Cemetery, Summertown, Georgia.

Return to Emanuel: Interviews with Alice Mitchell and Mabel Screws, June 24, 1987.

Move to Fitzgerald: Interviews with Alice Mitchell, July 5, 1983, and Leila Scott, June 20, 1987.

Jim's last years: Interviews with Alice Mitchell and Marjorie Scott, July 5, 1983, and Dessie Stroud, July 7, 1983; Marriage Record Book E, 1915-28, OPJ, ECC.

Jim's death: Interview with Rosa Fuller, Nov. 28, 1990.

HARDSCRABBLE

Blun: Interview with Leila Scott, July 3, 1983, R.G. Dun and Company, *Reference Book*, CCVII (Jan. 1970), Part 1, Georgia, 14.

Lucy: Interview with Leila Scott, July 3, 1983; tombstone, Hall's Cemetery, Emanuel County.

Deliveries: Interview with Ronnie Seckinger, Feb. 8, 1983.

Farm: Interviews with Ronnie Seckinger, Feb. 8, May 29, 1983.

Life on farm: Interviews with Ronnie Seckinger, Feb. 8-9, Apr. 4, May 29, 1983, Leila Scott, July 3, 1983, June 20, 1987, Carlton Scott, July 3, 1983, Ralph Fields, June 19, 1987, Callie Fagler, June 22, 1987, and Hilma Boyd, Apr. 18, 1990; Emanuel County agent report for 1934, roll no. 66, RG 33, NARA.

Average size of Georgia farm: Fife, *Cotton Fields*, 99.

NOOSE

Seab Johnson's background: Minutes, ESC, Book L, fls. 501-502, OCSC) and Marriage Record Colored Book F, 1917-1933, fl. 78, OPJ, ECC; 14th Census, 1920, Georgia, Emanuel County, ED 29, fl. 13B, NARA.

Killing and trial: *Forest-Blade*, June 2, 1921, p. 1, Oct. 20, 1921, p. 1; Minutes, ESC, Book O, fls. 268, 300-301, and Seab Johnson trial records, file "Criminal, Superior Court, 1921-1922-1923," OCSC, ECC.

Johnson in jail: Interview with Jerry Rich, Nov. 25, 1990.

Jerry's and Russell's ages and residences: 14th Census, 1920, Georgia, Emanuel County, ED 26, fl. 4, NARA.

Johnson's appeals: Seab Johnson trial records, file "Criminal Superior Court, 1921-1922-1923," and Minutes, Emanuel Superior Court, Book O, fls. 350, 420-21, 438-39, 466, 468, 495, OCSC, ECC; *Forest-Blade*, Feb. 1, 1923, p. 4, Feb. 8, 1923, p. 1, Feb. 22, 1923, p. 1, Mar. 1, 1923, p. 1; Swainsboro (Ga.), *Emanuel Progress*, Feb. 2, 1923, p. 1; James F. Cook, *Governors of Georgia* (Huntsville, Ala., 1979), 230-235.

Support for Johnson: Folder "Johnson, Seab," 1-40-42, Executive Department, Records Relating to Convicts and Fugitives, Applications for Clemency, Georgia Archives, Atlanta.

Execution: Interviews with Alice Mitchell, July 5, 1983, Jerry Rich, Nov. 25, 1990, and Ernie Durden, Nov. 26, 1990; *Forest-Blade*, Aug. 9, 1923, p. 1, Aug. 16, 1923, p. 1

CHICAGO

Fred and Annie Lee: Interview with Annie Lee Hooks, Feb. 17, 1988; marriage certificate, OPJ, Bamberg County Courthouse, Bamberg, S.C.

Population of Bamberg: U.S. Bureau of the Census, *Fourteenth Census. State Compendium. South Carolina* (Washington, 1924), 17.

Fred's new life: Interview with Annie Lee Hooks, Feb. 17, 1988; letter from Laura S. Hoyal (Ministerial Course of Study, Board of Higher Education and Ministry, United Methodist Church) to author, Apr. 22, 1988; *Forest-Blade*, Aug. 21, 1924, p. 3.

Moody: James F. Findlay, Jr., *Dwight L. Moody: American Evangelist, 1937-1899* (Chicago, 1969), passim; Gene A. Getz, *MBI: The Story of Moody Bible Institute* (Chicago, 1969), 21-46.

Chicago: Interview with Annie Lee Hooks, Feb. 17, 1988; Carl Sandburg, *Complete Poems* (New York, 1950), 3-4; Dominic A. Pacyga and Ellen Skerrett, *Chicago: City of Neighborhoods, Histories & Tours* (Chicago, 1986), 36-50, 198, 513.

Prohibition: Daniel Okrent, *Last Call: The Rise and Fall of Prohibition* (New York, 2010), passim; Andrew Sinclair, *Prohibition: The Era of Excess* (Boston, 1962), 4-5.

O'Banion: Interview with Annie Lee Hooks, Feb. 17, 1988; Chicago (Ill.) *Daily Tribune*, Nov. 11, 1924, pp. 1-2, Nov. 12, 1924, pp. 1-2, Nov. 13, 1924, pp. 1, 4; Herbert Asbury, *Gem of the Prairie: An Informal History of the Chicago Underworld* (1940; reprint, Dekalb, Ill., 1986), 342-52; [Jesse] George Murray, *The Legacy of Al Capone: Portraits and Annals of Chicago's Public Enemies* (New York, 1975), 37-67; Emmett Dedmon, *Fabulous Chicago* (rev. ed., New York, 1981), 292-94; Paul Sann, *The Lawless Decade* (New York, 1957), 105-107.

Annie Lee in Chicago: Interview with Annie Lee Hooks, Feb. 17, 1988.

Fred at Moody: Interview with Annie Lee Looks, Feb. 17, 1988; *Moody Bible Institute Monthly*, XXVII, No. 10 (June 1927), pp. 510-11; letter from Philip Van Wynen (Dean of Enrollment Management/Review, Moody Bible Institute) to author, Jan. 26, 1988.

Return to Emanuel County: Interview with Annie Lee Hooks, Feb. 17, 1988; Waynesboro (Ga.) *True Citizen*, cited in *Forest-Blade*, Aug. 4, 1927, p. 1; *ibid.*, Sept. 23, 1927, p. 1.

KLAN

Original Klan: David M. Chalmers, *Hooded Americanism: The History of the Ku Klux Klan*, 3rd ed. (Durham, N.C., 1987), 8-21.

Dixon and Griffith: *Ibid.*, 22-17; Jack Temple Kirby, *Media-Made Dixie: The South in the American Imagination*, rev. ed. (Athens, Ga., 1986), 1-8.

UDC membership: Wilson and Farris, eds., *Encyclopedia of Southern Culture*, 706.

"Clansman" shoe: *Forest-Blade*, Sept. 12, 1907, p. 5.

"Birth of a Nation" in Augusta and Swainsboro: *Forest-Blade*, Feb. 17, 1916, p. 4, May 25, 1917, p. 1, Apr. 13, 1918, p. 1, Nov. 24, 1921, p. 4, Mar. 10, 1927, p. 1.

Hardeman's comments: *Forest-Blade*, Mar. 2, 1917, p. 1.

Klan revival: Nancy MacLean, *Behind the Mask of Chivalry: The Making of the Second Ku Klux Klan* (New York, 1994), 3-74; Chalmers, *Hooded Americanism*, 28-38, 109-218, 291; Tindall, *Emergence*, 184-96.

Anti-Semitism: Oscar and Mary F. Handlin, "Origins of Anti-Semitism in the United States," in Arnold M. Rose, ed., *Race Prejudice and Discrimination: Readings in Intergroup Relations in the United States* (New York, 1951), 25-34.

Leo Frank: Steve Oney, *And the Dead Shall Rise: The Murder of Mary Phagan and the Lynching of Leo Frank* (New York, 2003); and Leonard Dinnerstein, *The Leo Frank Case* (New York, 1968).

Klan in Emanuel: *Forest-Blade*, Sept. 29, 1921, p. 4, Aug. 30, 1923, p. 1, Nov. 8, 1923, p. 1, Jan. 3, 1924, p. 1.

1924 election: Chalmers, *Hooded Americanism*, 169-70, 198-215; *Forest-Blade*, Mar. 13, 1924, p. 4, Mar. 20, 1924, p. 4.

Klan parades: *Forest-Blade*, Oct. 9, 1924, p. 1, Oct. 30, 1924, p. 1, Nov. 6, 1924, p. 1, Nov. 13, 1924, p. 1, Nov. 12, 1925, p. 1, Oct. 26, 1926, p. 7; interviews with Will McMillan, Jr., June 30, 1987, and Jerry Rich, Nov. 25, 1990.

Jews in Swainsboro: Interviews with Alice Mitchell, July 5, 1983, and Frances Rabhan, Sept. 3, 1993.

Members of Klan: Interviews with Alice Mitchell, July 5, 1983, June 24, 1987, July 14, 1988, Ralph Fields, June 19, 1987, Will McMillan, Jr., June 30, 1987, and Charles Harmon, July 27, 1991.

Decline of Klan: Chalmers, *Hooded Americanism*, 281-305; *Forest-Blade*, Mar. 3, 1927, pp. 1, 4, 5, Mar. 10, 1927, pp. 1, 4, June 16, 1927, p. 4, Aug. 11, 1927, p. 4, Aug. 18, 1927, pp. 1,4, Jan. 7, 1928, p. 7, Jan. 26, 1928, p. 9.

Flanders' connection to *Forest-Blade*: *Forest-Blade*, Aug. 1, 1918, p. 1.

COURTSHIP

Harrison family: Interviews with Frances Stroud, May 18, 1985, and Apr. 20, 1990; 10th Census, 1880, Kentucky, Pulaski County, ED 88, fl. 56A, and 12th Census, 1900, Kentucky, Pulaski County, ED 201, fl. 7A, NARA.

Courtship: Interviews with Frances Stroud, May 18, 1985, and Apr. 20, 1990.

Bertha Bell's death: Somerset (Ky.) *Journal*, Jan. 18, 1925, p. 1.

Farm: Deed Book 288, fls. 115-16, Deed Book 30, fl. 51, and Deed Book 33, fls. 176-77, OCSC, Ben Hill County Courthouse, Fitzgerald, Ga.

Wedding and married life: Interviews with Frances Stroud, May 18, 1985, and Apr. 20, 1990; Somerset (Ky.) *Commonwealth*, Nov. 26, 1924, p. 1; *Journal*, Nov. 28, 1924, p. 1.

MOTOR CITY

Denver and Bernice: Marriage Record Book, 1, fl. 451, OPJ, Ben Hill County Courthouse, Fitzgerald, Ga.; interview with Frances Stroud, May 19, 1985.

Bernice's age: Application for marriage license, Vernor Curtis and Bernice Stroud, July 7, 1934, C.J. No. 12-257, OCCC, Broward County Courthouse, Ft. Lauderdale, Fla.

Northern migration: Carole Marks, *Farewell–We're Good and Gone: The Great Black Migration* (Bloomington, Ind., 1989), *passim*; Kirby, *Rural Worlds Lost*, 309-20. The 9 million Southerners included those departing the former states of the Confederacy--minus Florida--as well as Kentucky, West Virginia, and Oklahoma.

Detroit and automobile manufacturing: Robert Lacey, *Ford: The Men and the Machine* (Boston, Mass., 1986), 18-23, 65-67; John B. Rae, *The American Automobile Industry* (Boston, Mass., 1984), 29-30; Kirby, *Rural Worlds Lost*, 325-26. Three Swainsboro youths: *Forest-Blade*, Jan. 31, 1924, p. 5.

Henry Ford and the Model T: Lacey, *Ford*, 36-109, 169; Rae, *American Automobile Industry*, 35-39; Reynold M. Wik, *Henry Ford and Grass-Roots America* (Ann Arbor, Mich., 1972), 14-33; Michael L. Berger, *The Devil Wagon in God's Country: The Automobile and Social Change in Rural America, 1893-1929* (Hamden, Conn., 1979), *passim*; Philip Van Doren Stern, *Tin Lizzie: The Story of the Fabulous Model T Ford* (New York, 1955).

Price of runabout in 1925: *Forest-Blade*, July 23, 1925, p. 2,

Denver never worked for Ford: Letter from Darleen Flaherty (Archivist, Ford Industrial Archives) to author, Feb. 14, 1989.

Assembly line: Lacey, *Ford*, 127-129.

Five-Dollar Day: *Ibid.*, 117-22; Frank Marquart, *An Auto Worker's Journal: The UAW from Crusade to One-Party Union* (University Park, Penn., 1975), 5-9. Ford's paternalism: Lacey, *Ford*, 122-25.

Labor relations: John Barnard, *Walther Reuther and the Rise of the Auto Workers* (Boston, Mass., 1983), 19-24, 26-27; Marquart, An Auto Worker's Journal, 10-13, 19-25.

Activities in Detroit: Frank Angelo, *Yesterday's Detroit* (Miami, Fla., 1974), *passim*.

Housing shortage: David Allan Levine, *Internal Combustion: The Races in Detroit, 1915-1926* (Westport, Conn., 1976), 14, 37-43.

Stroud residences: *Polk's Detroit (Michigan) City Directory*, 1924-25, pp. 1924-25, 1925-26, p. 1813, 1926-27, p. 1967, 1927-28, p. 2086, 1928-29, p. 1953, 1929-30, p. 1971, 1930-31, p. 1797, 1931-32, p. 1602.

Place and year of Lillian's birth: Application for marriage license, Glen Dale Quay and Lillian Bernice Stroud, Aug. 12, 1943, C.J. No. 18-19B, OCCC, Palm Beach County Courthouse, West Palm Beach, Fla.

BARBERSHOP

Barbershop: *Forest-Blade*, Dec. 4, 1924, p. 1, Oct. 16, 1924, p. 2, Aug. 27, 1931.

Product names: *The Journeyman Barber*, 1924-25, passim.

Waitus: Interviews with Ronnie Seckinger, Apr. 11, 1983, Majorie Scott, July 5, 1983, Alice Mitchell, July 5, 1983, June 24, 1987, Rose Fuller, July 10, 1983, James Hall, June 23, 1984, Frances Stroud, May 18, 1985, Walter Screws, June 24, 1987, Robbie Elkins, July 17, 1988, and Aubrey Scott, Nov. 30, 1990.

Visits to Fields farm: Interviews with Ronnie Seckinger, May 29, 1983, and Marjorie Scott, July 5, 1983; *Forest-Blade*, Apr. 18, 1929, p. 2.

OKEECHOBEE

Delma's baseball career: Interview with Delma Hooks, Aug. 5, 1984. Timing of Camp McClellan visit: *Forest-Blade*, July 3, 1924, p. 5.

Henry Flagler: David Leon Chandler, *Henry Flagler: The Astonishing Life and Times of the Visionary Robber Baron Who Founded Florida* (New York, 1986), *passim*; Michael Grunwald, *The Swamp: The Everglades, Florida and the Politics of Paradise* (New York, 2006), 98-116, 150.

Florida land boom: George B. Tindall, "The Bubble in the Sun," *American Heritage*, XVI, No. 5 (Aug. 1965), pp. 76-83, 109-111; Grunwald, *The Swamp*, 176-80.

Development of Okeechobee region: Alfred Jackson Hanna and Kathryn Abbey Hanna, *Lake Okeechobee: Wellspring of the Everglades* (1948; reprint, Dunwoody, Ga., 1973), 118-72, 185-90, 321; Marjory Stoneman Douglas, *The Everglades: River of Grass*, rev. ed. (Sarasota, Fla., 1986), 294-326; Grunwald, *The Swamp*, 130-70; Will, *Cracker History*, 4-5, 25-26, 93, 120-25, 193.

Move to Florida: Interview with Delma Hooks, Feb. 16, 1988.

Conners Highway: Interview with Delma Hooks, Feb. 16, 1988; Grunwald, *The Swamp*, 166-67, 182; Will, *Cracker History*, 229-34; Canal Point (Fla.) *Everglades News*, July 4, 1924, p. 8, July 11, 1924, p. 1, Nov. 14, 1924, pp. 1, 6.

Arrival in Canal Point: Interviews with Delma Hooks, Aug. 5, 1984, and Feb. 16, 1988.

Lake region: Will, *Cracker History*, 4-6; *Everglades News*, July 11, 1924, p. 1, July 24, 1925, p. 1.

Population figures: U.S. Bureau of the Census, *Fourteenth Census of the United States Taken in the Year 1920* (13 vols.; Washington, 1921-23), III, 193, 197.

Agriculture: Florida, Department of Agriculture, Bureau of Immigration, *All Florida* (Tallahassee, 1926), 162; *Everglades News*, Oct. 17, 1924, pp, 1. 7, May 29, 1925, p. 1, Dec. 30, 1927, p. 1, July 6, 1928, p. 1, Aug. 17, 1928, p. 1, Dec. 28, 1928, p. 1, Jan. 18, 1929, p. 1; J. Carlyle Sitterson, *Sugar Country:*

The Cane Sugar Industry in the South, 1753-1950 (Lexington, Ky., 1953), 361-70.

Life on the lake: Will, *Cracker History*, 218-22; Hanna and Hanna, *Lake Okeechobee*, 235-43, 317-26; *Everglades News*, Feb. 5. 1926, p. 4, Feb. 3, 1928, p. 3; interviews with Delma Hooks, Aug. 5, 1984, Feb. 16, 1988, Jan. 24, 1989, Henry Potter, Mar. 18, 1991, and Luther Levins, May 10, 1987, and Mar. 20, 1991; letter from A.L. Deroo to Lawrence E. Will, Feb. 11, 1969, folder "Canal Point," Lawrence E. Will Museum, Belle Glade, Fla.

Delma and Nell: Interviews with Delma Hooks, Aug. 5, 1984, Feb. 16, 1988, and Nell Hooks, Aug. 5, 1984; *Everglades News*, May 28, 1926, p. 5.

Bought restaurant: *Everglades News*, June 4, 1926, p. 5.

Bought grocery store: Interview with Delma Hooks, Feb.. 16, 1988; *Everglades News*, June 5, 1931, p. 1.

CAVE MAN

Frances in sickbed: Interview with Frances Stroud, Apr. 20, 1990.

Floyd Collins: Robert K. Murray and Roger W. Brucker, *Trapped!* (New York, 1979), *passim.*; Homer Collins, *The Life and Death of Floyd Collins* (St. Louis, Mo., 2001), 129-206; Somerset (Ky.) *Journal*, Feb. 12, 1925, p. 1, Feb. 20, 1925, p. 1, Mar. 20, 1925, p. 1; interview with Frances Stroud, Apr. 20, 1990.

Impact of radio: Alice Goldfarb Marquis, *Hopes and Ashes: The Birth of Modern Times, 1929-1939* (New York, 1986), 15-17.

Musical: https://en.wikipedia.org/wiki/Floyd_Collins-_(musical).

FARM KIDS

Fields Chapel: Interviews with Ronnie Seckinger, Feb. 8-9, 1983, Leila Scott, July 3, 1983, Ouida Fields, July 7, 1983, Lynwood Screws, July 12, 1983, and Edna Akins, Nov. 24, 1990; Deed Record Book C-I, fl. 275, OCSC, ECC.

Cleaning up Hall's Cemetery: Interviews with Ronnie Seckinger, Feb. 9, 1983, and Novis Fields, June 26, 1987.

Holiness Church: Interviews with Nell Eberhart and Jean McGregor, Nov. 26, 1990, and Leila Scott, Nov. 28, 1990; Ayers, *Promise*, 398-408; Wilson and Ferris, eds., *Encyclopedia of Southern Culture*, 1296-97.

Children's activities: Interviews with Ronnie Seckinger, Feb. 8-9, 1983, May 29, 1983, Alice Mitchell, July 5, 1983, Ouida Fields, July 7, 1983, Garland Sherrod, July 15, 1988, Edna Akins, Nov. 24, 1990, Nell Eberhart and Jean McGregor, Nov. 26, 1990, Leila Scott, Nov. 28, 1990, and Roy Fields, Nov. 29, 1990.

Christmas: Interviews with Ronnie Seckinger, Feb. 8-9, Apr. 4, 1983, Leila Scott, July 3, 1983, and Mary Lee Kea, Nov. 27, 1990.

DESPERADOS

Rough life: Alfred Jackson Hanna and Kathryn Abbey Hanna, *Lake Okeechobee: Wellspring of the Everglades* (1948; reprint, Dunwoody, Ga., 1973), 235-43; letter from A.L. Deroo to Lawrence E. Will, Feb. 11, 1969, folder "Canal Point," Lawrence E. Will Museum, Belle Glade, Fla.

Clewiston Inn sign: Florence Fritz, *Unknown Florida* (Coral Gables, Fla., 1963), 149.

Bootlegging and slot machines: Interview with Luther Levins, Mar. 20, 1991; James A. Carter, III, "Florida and Rumrunning during National Prohibition," *Florida Historical Quarterly*, XLVIII, No. 1 (July 1969), 47-56.

Ashley kills DeSoto Tiger: Fort Myers (Fla.) *Weekly Press*, Jan. 4, 1912, p. 6; Miami (Fla.) *Herald*, Jan. 7, 1912, p. 2, Jan. 8, 1912, p. 1, Jan. 10, 1912, pp. 1-2; Hix C. Stuart, *The Notorious Ashley Gang: A Saga of the King and Queen of the Everglades* (Stuart, Fla., 1928), 7-10.

Ashley's age: State of Florida, Bureau of Vital Statistics, Certificate of Death 15598, Nov. 1, 1924.

Surrender and bank job: Stuart, *Notorious Ashley Gang*, 10-15.

Attempted jail break and sentencing: *Ibid.*, 16-20; *Herald*, June 3, 1915, pp. 1-2, June 4, 1915, p. 2; "State of Florida vs. John Ashley, John Doe alias Kid Lowe and Robert Ashley, alias "Bob" Ashley," Nov. 14, 1916, OCCC, Criminal Division, Palm Beach County Courthouse, West Palm Beach, Fla.

Ashley's escape and rearrest, brothers' deaths: Stuart, *Notorious Ashley Gang*, 20-21, 24-26.

Ashley's personal characteristics: *Everglades News*, Nov. 7, 1924, p. 3.

Laura Upthegrove: Stuart, *Notorious Ashley Gang*, 22-23.

Ashley's death, inquest, and funeral: West Palm Beach (Fla.) *Post*, Nov. 2, 1924, pp. 1-2, Nov. 3, 1924, pp. 1-2, 11, Nov. 4, 1924, pp. 1-2, Nov. 6, 1924, pp. 1-2, Nov. 9, 1924, pop. 1-2; *Herald*, Nov. 2, 1924, p. 1, Nov. 3, 1924, pp. 1A-2A, Nov. 4, 1924, p. 5A, Nov. 9, 1924, p. 1F; Miami (Fla.) *Daily News*, Nov. 3, 1924, p. 1; *Everglades News*, Nov. 7, 1924, p. 3, Nov. 14, 1924, p. 8; Stuart, *Notorious Ashley Gang*, 38-46, 67-78; interviews with Delma Hooks, Feb. 16, 1988, and Luther Levins, Mar. 20, 1991.

Laura's death: *Everglades News*, Aug. 12, 1927; Stuart, *Notorious Ashley Gang*, 79-80; interview with Delma Hooks, Feb. 16, 1988.

Joe Tracey: Interview with Delma Hooks, Feb. 16, 1988.

HIGHWAYS

Building roads: John B. Rae, *The Road and the Car in American Life* (Cambridge, Mass., 1971), 36-39; Preston, *Dirt Roads*, 22-64; Berger, *Devil Wagon*, 88-94; David McCullough, *Truman* (New York, 1992), 171; *Forest-Blade*, Nov. 6, 1924, p. 1, Mar. 11, 1926, p. 1, Jan. 12, 1928, p. 4, Apr. 11, 1929, p. 6.

Route One: *Forest-Blade*, July 7, 1927, p. 1, Jan. 19, 1933, p. 7.

Trip to Jacksonville: Interview with Frances Stroud, May 18, 1985.

Street dance and parking ordnance: *Forest-Blade*, Oct. 13, 1927, p. 8, Dec. 15, 1927, p. 1.

Auto camps: Warren James Belasco, *Americans on the Road: From Autocamp to Motel, 1910-1945* (Cambridge, Mass., 1979), 40-142; *Forest-Blade*, Nov. 23, 1922, p. 1, Mar. 5, 1925, p. 6, Dec. 20, 1928, p. 1; *Everglades News*, Dec. 19, 1924, p. 1.

"Buy-It-in-Swainsboro": *Forest-Blade*, Apr. 26, 1934, p. 1.

REUNION

Denver's arrival in Somerset, reunion in Swainsboro: Interviews with Frances Stroud, May 18, 1985, Apr. 20, 1990.

TOWN KIDS

School: Interviews with Alice Mitchell, July 5, 1983, July 14, 1988, Gladys Waller, July 12, 1988, Jerry Rich, Nov. 25, 1990, and Charles Harmon, July 27, 1991; *Forest-Blade*, Dec. 8, 1927, p. 7, May 17, 1928, p. 1, Oct. 2, 1930, p. 5.

Literary societies: Interviews with Gladys Waller, July 12, 1988, Robbie Elkins, July 17, 1988, Jerry Rich, Nov. 25, 1990, and Charles Harmon, July 17, 1991; *Forest-Blade*, May 29, 1929, p. 1, Apr. 10, 1930, p. 6, Nov. 13, 1930, p. 2, Mar. 19, 1931, p. 4.

Margie's second pregnancy: Interview with Marjorie Scott, July 5, 1983.

Swainsboro population in 1925: *Forest-Blade*, June 18, 1925, p. 2.

Tourists: *Forest-Blade*, Sept. 19, 1929, p. 1, Oct. 3, 1929, p. 3.

Boys' entertainments: Interviews with James Hall, June 23, 1983, Will McMillan, Jr., June 30, 1987, Lynwood Screws, June 30, 1987, and Luther Quick, July 12, 1988; *Forest-Blade*, Oct. 26, 1927, p.. 5, Aug. 9, 1928, p. 1, Apr. 4, 1929, p. 1, July 11, 1929, p. 1, Oct. 3, 1929, p. 3; Wilson and Ferris, eds., *Encyclopedia of Southern Culture*, 1019.

Girls' social life: Interviews with Robbie Elkins, July 17, 1988, Nesbit Christian, July 7, 1989, Ruth Temples, July 7, 1989, Mary Lee Kea, Nov. 27, 1990, and Jeannette Neal, Nov. 27, 1990.

Community center: *Forest-Blade*, July 1, 1926, p. 1.

Jefferson Davis's birthday: *Ibid.*, May 30, 1929, p. 1.

Buck dance: Lynne Fauley Emery, *Black Dance from 1619 to Today*, 2nd ed. rev. (Princeton, N.J., 1988), 89-90.

Living at Jessie's: Interviews with Ronnie Seckinger, Apr. 11, 1983, and Alice Mitchell, July 5, 1983.

STORM

1926 hurricanes: Lawrence E. Will, *Okeechobee Hurricane and the Hoover Dike*, 3rd ed. rev. (St. Petersburg, Fla., 1971), 11-46; Grunwald, *The Swamp*, 186-89; interview with Delma Hooks, Mar. 17, 1987; *Everglades News*, July 30, 1926, p. 1, Sept. 24, 1926, p. 1.

Boom: *Everglades News*, July 27, 1928, pp. 1-2, Aug. 17, p. 1.

Vegetable production: American Red Cross, *The West Indies Hurricane Disaster. September,1928* (Washington, [1929]), 73.

Anxiety about storms and floods: *Everglades News*, Aug. 10, 1928, p. 2, Aug. 17, 1928, p. 2, Sept. 7, 1928, pp. 1, 4.

John Hooks loses farm: Interview with Delma Hooks, Aug. 5, 1984; Deed Record Book C-M, fl. 41, OCSC, ECC.

Life of turpentine runner: Interview with Dessie Stroud, July 7, 1983.

1928 hurricane: Interviews with Delma Hooks, Aug. 5, 1984, Mar. 17, 1987, Feb. 16, 1988, and Luther Levins, Mar. 20, 1991; *Everglades News*, Oct. 5, 1928, p. 1, Nov. 2, 1928, pp. 1, 5, 6, Nov. 9, 1928, p. 3, Dec. 7, 1928, p. 1, Dec. 21, 1928, p. 1, Sept. 11, 1931, p. 1; American Red Cross, *West Indies Hurricane Disaster,* 53-77, 87-88; Eliot Kleinbert, *Black Cloud: The Great Florida Hurricane of 1928* (New York, 2003); Robert Mykvle, *Killer 'Cane: The Deadly Hurricane of 1928* (New York, 2002); Will, *Okeechobee Hurricane*, 47-199; Majorie Stonemason Douglas, *Hurricane* (New York, 1958), 167-71; Grunwald, *The Swamp*, 191-94; Belle Glade (Fla.) *Herald*, Sept. 14, 1978, supplement, "The Hurricane of 1928," *passim*; Nixon Smiley, "The Night the Lake Became an Ocean," Miami (Fla.) *Herald*, Tropic Magazine, Sept. 15, 1968, pp. 20-28; St. Petersburg (Fla.) *Times*, Sept. 14, 1986, pp. 1B, 9B; *Forest-Blade*, Sept. 20, 1928, p. 5; report from Homer Dixon and William Meeker, Miami, Sept. 19, 1928, folds DR-284, box 753, RG 200, Records of the American Red Cross, 1917-1934, NARA.

Revised death toll: Kleinberg, *Black Cloud*, xiv.

DUNCAN DESCENDING

Duncan's appearance: Interviews with Carlton Scott, July 3, 1983, Frank Kirkland, Aug. 9, 1984, Ralph Fields, June 19, 1987, and Callie Fagler, June 22, 1987.

Duncan and children: Interviews with Lynwood Screws, July 12, 1983, Ralph Fields, June 19, 1987, Leila Scott, June 20, 1987, Nov. 28, 1990, and Edna Akins, Nov. 24, 1990.

Duncan's drunks: Interviews with Ronnie Seckinger, Feb. 8, 1983, Leila Scott, July 3, 1983, June 20, 1987, Carlton Scott, July 3, 1983, Mabel Screws, July 12, 1983, Linwood Screws, July 12, 1983, Ralph Fields, June 19, 1987, and Callie Fagler, June 22, 1987.

Jessie strikes Duncan: Interviews with Novis Fields, July 10, 1983, and Gracie Fields, July 1, 1987.

Duncan's affair: Interviews with Ronnie Seckinger, Feb. 9, 1983, and Dessie Stroud, July 7, 1983.

Stroke: Interview with Leila Scott, June 20, 1987.

Fishing trips: Interview with Frank Kirkland, Aug. 9, 1984.

Shooting: Interviews with Ronnie Seckinger, Feb. 9, 1983, Leila Scott, July 3, 1983, Ouida Fields, July 7, 1983, and Ralph Fields, June 19, 1987.

Duncan loses farm: Interviews with Ronnie Seckinger, Feb. 8, 1983, Leila Scott, July 3, 1983, and Ralph Fields, June 19, 1987; Deed Record Book B-F, fl. 156, Book B-H, fl. 351, Book B-J, fl. 103, Book B-T, fls. 321, 358, Book C-D, fls. 426-28, 479, 492, 495, Book C-E, fl. 202, OCSC, ECC.

Duncan's death and funeral: Interviews with Ronnie Seckinger, Feb. 8, Apr. 13, 1983, Leila Scott, July 3, 1983, June 20, 1987, Lynwood Screws, July 12, 1983, Wynelle Forbes, July 12, 1983, Garland Sherrod, July 15, 1988, and Jean McGregor and Mary Lee Kea, Nov. 27, 1990; death certificate 30-3435, Feb. 16, 1930, OPJ, ECC; *Forest-Blade*, Feb. 20, 1930.

DREAMER

Movies: Douglas Gomery, *Shared Pleasures: A History of Movie Presentation in the United States* (Madison, Wis., 1992), 3-56; David Naylor, *Great*

American Movie Theaters (Washington, 1967), 15-25, 101-102; John Margolies and Emity Gwathmey, *Ticket to Paradise: American Movie Theaters and How We Had Fun* (Boston, 1991), *passim*; Richard Koszarski, *An Evening's Entertainment: The Age of the Silent Feature Picture* (New York, 1990), 20-25; William Schemmel, *The Fabulous Fox at 50* (Atlanta, 1979).

Movies in Swainsboro: Interviews with Gladys Waller, July 12, 1988, Robbie Elkins, July 17, 1988, and Nesbit Christian, July 7, 1989.

"It": Interview with Alice Mitchell, July 5, 1983; Kowarski, *An Evening's Entertainment*, 307-309; Lewis Jacobs, "Films of the Postwar Decade," in Arthur F. McClure, ed., *The Movies: An American Idiom. Readings in the Social History of the American Motion Picture* (Rutherford, N.J., 1971), 80-81; Joe Morella and Edward Z. Epstein, *The "It" Girl: The Incredible Story of Clara Bow* (New York, 1976), 24-87.

Publicity photos: Interview with Nesbit Christian, July 7, 1989.

Plucked eyebrows: Interview with Gladys Waller, July 12, 1988.

Nesbit and Johnny: Interviews with Gladys Waller, July 12, 1988, and Nesbit Christian, July 7, 1989.

Maude and men: Interviews with Gladys Waller, July 12, 1988, and Nesbit Christian, July 7, 1989.

Alice at the United 5 & 10: Interview with Alice Mitchell, July 9, 1988.

Dreamer: Interview with Gladys Waller, July 12, 1988; Maude's high-school scrapbook, in possession of author.

EVERGLADES

Hooks family moves to Florida: Interviews with Delma Hooks, Aug. 5, 1984, Feb. 16, 1988; *Everglades News*, Jan. 11, 1929, p. 3.

Hoover and levee: *Everglades News*, Nov. 9, 1928, p. 1, Dec. 7, 1928, p. 1, Feb. 22. 1929, p. 1, Mar. 15, 1929, p. 1, Sept. 27, 1929, p. 1; Grunwald, *The Swamp*, 197-200; Will, *Okeechobee Hurricane*, 175-87; interview with Delma Hooks, Mar. 19, 1991.

Delma rebuilds life: *Everglades News,* Feb. 8, 1929, p. 2, May 31, 1929, p. 5, Dec. 5, 1930, p. 5; R.G. Dun and Company, *Reference Book,* CCXLVII (Jan. 1930), Part 1, Florida, 379.

Life in Canal Point: Interviews with Delma Hooks, Aug. 5, 1984, Mar. 17, 1987, Feb. 16, 1988, Jan. 24, 1989, Nell Hooks, Aug. 5, 1984, Freddie Sawyer, Aug. 5, 1984, Feb. 16, 1988; *Everglades News,* Feb. 7, 1930, p. 1, Mar. 28, 1930, p. 2, July 4, 1930, p. 3, Aug. 29, 1930, p. 3, Sept. 5, 1930, p. 3; Sitterson, *Sugar Country,* 370-71.

Population: *Everglades News,* June 12, 1931, p. 1.

Jewel's daughters: Interviews with Delma and Nell Hooks, Aug. 5, 1983.

Degradation of Everglades: Grunwald, *The Swamp,* 200-375, *passim.*

MIAMI

Depression: Robert Lacey, *Ford: The Men and the Machine* (Boston, Mass., 1986), 305; Melvin G. Belli, ed., *Detroit* (New York, 1976), 170-75; Lois Gordon and Alan Gordon, *American Chronicle: Six Decades in American Life, 1920-1980* (New York, 1987), 108.

Residence in 1930: 15th Census, 1930, Michigan, Wayne County, ED 209, Roll 1039, fl. 1B, Image 419.0, NARA.

Denver's move to Miami: *Polk's Miami (Florida) City Directory,* 1931, p. 724, 1932, p. 678.

Willing to help sisters: Letter from Denver Stroud to Emmit Stroud, Miami, Aug. 11, 1931, in possession of author.

Alice and Maude in Miami: Interviews with Alice Mitchell, July 5, 1983, and July 9, 1988.

Denver's death: Death certificate no. 654, June 19, 1933, Office of Vital Statistics, Miami; Miami (Fla.) *Herald,* June 19, 1933, p. 8.

Funeral: Interview with Frances Stroud, Apr. 20, 1990; letter from Maude Stroud to Marjorie Scott, Miami, [June 22, 1933], in possession of author; Miami *Herald,* June 20, 1933, p. 13; Miami (Fla.) *News,* June 20, 1933, p. 6; *WPA Veteran's Grave Registration,* Dade, 43.

Weather: Miami *Herald,* June 21, 1933, p. 1.

COLLEGE BOY

J.D. at College: Georgia State Teachers College, *Reflector*, 1930 [Atlanta, 1930], 32; *ibid.*, 1931 [Atlanta, 1931], 35, 73-74, 77; letter from T. Michael Deal (Associate Registrar, Georgia Southern College) to author, Feb. 2, 1988.

J.D.'s marriages: Interviews with Ronnie Seckinger, Feb. 9, 1983, Leila Scott, July 3, 1983, and Ouida Fields, July 7, 12, 1983; Minutes, ESC, Book Q, fl. 546, OCSC, and Marriage Record White Book G, 1928-40, fl. 245, OPJ, ECC.

New Deal programs: Tindall, *Emergence*, 391-432, 473-85; Kirby, *Rural Worlds Lost*, 51-79; Fife, *Cotton Fields No More*, 128-43; interview with Earl Varner, July 5, 1983; Emanuel County agent reports for 1933-34, rolls nos. 60 and 66, RG 33, NARA.

Stephenson fire: Interview with Earl Varner, July 5, 1983; Swainsboro (Ga.) *Forest-Blade*, Oct. 31, 1935, p. 1, Dec. 19, 1935, p. 1.

J.D.'s success: Interviews with Earl Varner, July 5, 1983, and Ouida Fields, July 7, 1983; *Blazing the 4-H Trail, 1915-1980* (Swainsboro, Ga., 1980), 42.

PATRIARCH

Emmit's generosity: Interviews with Leila Scott, July 3, 1983, and Frances Stroud, May 19, 1985.

Depression: Irving Bernstein, *The Lean Years: A History of the American Worker, 1920-1933* (Boston, 1960), 324-26; Somerset (Ky.) *Journal*, Oct. 2, 1931, p. 1, Jan. 8, 1932, p. 1; John F. Stover, *The Life and Decline of the American Railroad* (New York, 1970), 178; interviews with Frances Stroud, May 18-19, 1985, and Apr. 20, 1990.

Alice and Maude in Atlanta: Don H. Doyle, *New Men, New Cities, New South: Atlanta, Nashville, Charleston, Mobile, 1860-1910* (Chapel Hill, N.C., 1990), 15, 136-58; Kuhn, Joye, and West, eds., *Living Atlanta, passim*; Howard L. Preston, *Automobile Age Atlanta: The Making of a Southern Metropolis, 1900-1935* (Athens, Ga., 1979), 3-6, 45-48, 71-73, 76-94; Franklin M. Garrett, *Yesterday's Atlanta* (Miami, 1974), *passim*; interviews with Alice Mitchell, July 5, 1983, June 24, 1987, July 9, 1988, and Frances

Stroud, May 18-19, 1985, Apr. 22, 1990; *Atlanta City Directory Co.'s Greater Atlanta (Fulton County, Ga.) City Directory*, 1933, pp. 992, 1583.

Emmit and Kermit fight: Interviews with Hilda Boyd, Apr. 18, 1990, and Frances Stroud, Apr. 20, 1990.

Emmit buys out Denver and Kermit: Deed Book 42, fls. 307-308, 329-30, OCSC, Ben Hill County Courthouse, Fitzgerald.

Maude on Emmit: Letter from Maude Stroud to Marjorie Scott, [June 22, 1933], in possession of author.

Life on farm: Interviews with Frances Stroud, May 14, 1985, Apr. 20, 1990, and Hilma Boyd, Apr. 18, 1990.

Brooklyn: Interviews with Frances Stroud, May 18-19, 1985, and Hilma Boyd, Apr. 18, 1990.

Back in Somerset: Interviews with Frances Stroud, May 18-19, 1985, Apr. 20, 1990, and Hilma Boyd, Apr. 18, 1990.

SHARECROPPERS

Flanders farm: Interviews with Ronnie Seckinger, Feb. 8-9, Apr. 13, May 29, 1983, Leila Scott, July 3, 1983, Novis Fields, July 10, 1983, June 26, 1987, Wynelle Forbes, July 12, 1983, Callie Fagler, June 22, 1987, Gracie Fields, July 1, 1987, and Nell Eberhart and Jean McGregor, Nov. 26, 1990.

Cotton prices: Tindall, *Emergence*, 354.

School: Interviews with Ronnie Seckinger, Feb. 8-9, Apr. 13, 1983, Novis Fields, July 10, 1983, June 26, 1987, and Wynelle Forbes, July 12, 1983.

Clothing: Interviews with Ronnie Seckinger, Feb. 8-9, Apr. 4 and 13, and May 29, 1983.

JEALOUSY

Pistol in each boot: Interview with Lynwood Screws, July 12, 1983.

Garry B. and Annie: Interviews with Leila Scott, June 20, 1987, and Edna Akins, Nov. 24, 1990.

Shooting at Nunn's Tourist Inn: Interviews with Lynwood Screws, July 12, 1983, and Will McMillan, June 30, 1987; *Forest-Blade*, Mar. 21, 1935, p. 1.

Funerals: *Forest-Blade*, Mar. 21, 1935, p. 8.

Restraining order and injunction: *Forest-Blade*, Mar. 21, 1935, p. 1, Apr. 11, 1935, p. 1.

Repeal of dry law: *Forest-Blade*, May 16, 1935, p. 1.

MAUDE

Hated farm life: Interview with Ronnie Seckinger, Feb. 9, 1983.

Maude's pregnancy: Interviews with Rosa Fuller, July 10, 1983, Frances Stroud, May 18, 1985, and Alice Mitchell, July 9, 1988.

Return to Miami: Interview with Frances Stroud, May 18, 1985.

Could not give up baby: Interviews with Alice Mitchell, July 9, 1988, and Rosa Fuller, Nov. 28, 1990.

Back in Fitzgerald: Interviews with Rosa Fuller, July 10, 1983, and Nov. 28, 1990.

Plight of working women: Susan Ware, *Holding Their Own: American Women in the 1930s* (Boston, 1982), 1-27; Sara M. Evans, *Born for Liberty: A History of Women in America* (New York, 1989), 197-204.

Working in Miami: Interviews with Alice Mitchell, July 5 and 12, 1983; Maude's scrapbook, in possession of author; Steven Mintz and Susan Kellogg, *Domestic Revolutions: A Social History of American Family Life* (New York, 1988), 124, 129.

Old friends: Interviews with Gladys Waller, July 12, 1988, and Nesbit Christian, July 7, 1989.

***Gone with the Wind*:** Interviews with Alice Mitchell, July 9, 1988, and Nesbit Christian, July 7, 1989.

Sales figures: Darden Asbury Pyron, *Southern Daughter: The Life of Margaret Mitchell* (New York, 1991), 336.

Marie Phillips: *Forest-Blade*, June 4, 1936, p. 1, Aug. 13, 1936, p. 1, Dec. 31, 1936, pp. 1, 5; interview with Nesbit Christian, July 7, 1989; Jack Beatty, *The Rascal King: The Life and Times of James Michael Curley, 1874-1950* (Reading, Mass., 1992), 403, 428.

Maude's marriage: Application for marriage license, Application Book 38, No. 12051, and marriage license, Marriage Book 30, fl. 518, Dade County Courthouse, Miami, Fla.

Archie's background: 13th Census, 1910, Florida, Monroe County, ED 123, fl. 30A, and 14th Census, 1920, Florida, Monroe County, ED 96, fl. 12B, NARA; *Polk's Key West (Florida) City Directory*, 1923, p. 189, 1927-29, p. 170; and *Polk's Miami (Florida) City Directory*, 1935, p. 588.

Divorce: Bill of complaint, Archie Moreno, plaintiff, vs. Maude Moreno, defendant, and divorce final decree 53932-G, OCCC, Hillsborough County Courthouse, Tampa, Fla.

Adoption of second child: Interview with Rose Fuller, Nov. 28, 1990.

POLITICS

Waitus partial to Roosevelt and Talmadge: Interview with Alice Mitchell, July 5, 1983.

Talmadge vs. Russell: William Anderson, *The Man from Sugar Creek: The Political Career of Eugene Talmadge* (Baton Rouge, La., 1975), *passim*; Gilbert C. Fife, *Richard B. Russell, Jr., Senator from Georgia* (Chapel Hill, N.C., 1991), 135-48; Howard N. Mead, "Russell vs. Talmadge: Southern Politics and the New Deal," *Georgia Historical Quarterly*, 65 (1981), 28-45; Tindall, *Emergence*, 615-18; *Forest-Blade*, Aug. 13, 1936, p. 1, Aug. 20, 1936, pp. 1, 4, Sept. 10, 1936, p. 1.

SPEED

Ellie as teenager: Interviews with Margie Scott, July 5, 1983, James Hall, June 23, 1984, Claude McLendon, Aug. 8, 1984, and Jerry Rich, Nov. 25, 1990; *Forest-Blade*, Jan. 30, 1936, p. 8, Mar. 26, 1936, p. 5, Apr. 30, 1936, p. 5, June 11, 1936, p. 3, Oct. 23, 1936, p. 5, Nov. 5, 1936, p. 2, Feb. 25, 1937, p. 1.

Competition, glee club, senior trip: *Forest-Blade*, May 5, 1937, p. 6, May 13, 1937, p. 5.

Ellie's last night: Interviews with Margie Scott, July 5, 1983, Claude McLendon, Aug. 8, 1984, Will McMillan, Jr., June 30, 1987; *Forest-Blade,* May 20, 1937, p. 1; death certificate 12172, May 16, 1937, OPJ, ECC.

Reactions to Ellie's death: Interviews with Mabel Screws, July 12, 1983, Claude McLendon, Aug. 8, 1984, Novis Fields, Aug. 9, 1984, Will McMillan, Jr., June 30, 1987, and Ermie Durden and Otis Hudson, Nov. 26, 1990.

Funeral: Interviews with Rose Fuller, July 10, 1983, Wynelle Forbes, July 12, 1983, Frances Stroud, May 18, 1985, Gladys Waller, July 12, 1988, Robbie Elkins, July 17, 1988, Hilma Boyd, Apr. 18, 1990, and Lois Hunnicutt, July 27, 1991; *Forest-Blade,* May 20, 1937, p. 1; family funeral book, in possession of author.

Safety device: *Forest-Blade,* May 6, 1937, p. 1, July 29, 1937, p. 1, Sept. 23, 1937, p. 1, Sept. 30, 1937, p. 1.

JOOK

Return to Miami: Interviews with Alice Mitchell, July 5, 1983, July 9, 1988, and T. Robert High, Mar. 17, 1991; *Polk's Miami (Florida) City Directory,* 1934, pp. 363, 698.

Tom Mitchell: Interviews with Alice Mitchell, July 5, 1983, and July 9, 1988; 14th Census, 1920, Florida, Dade County, ED 25, fl. 31B, NARA; Marriage Record Book H, fl. 35, Office of the Probate Judge, and divorce record no. 3331, Office of the Clerk of Superior Court, Spalding County Courthouse, Griffin, Ga.; *Miller's Griffin, Georgia City Directory,* 1927-28, pp. 208-209, 1929-30, p. 209.

Marriage: Interview with Alice Mitchell, July 9, 1988; application for marriage license, C.J. No. 7548, and marriage certificate, Marriage Book 28, fl. 135, Clerk of the Circuit and County Court, Dade County Courthouse, Miami.

Married life: Interviews with Alice Mitchell, July 5, 1983, July 12, 1983, and July 9, 1988.

Griffin: Interviews with Alice Mitchell, July 5, 1983, and Pat Mitchell, Nov. 27, 1990.

Maude's letter: Letter from Maude Moreno to Marjorie Scott, [Miami, Sept. 21, 1938], in possession of author.

Confrontation with Waitus: Interview with Alice Mitchell, July 5, 1983, and Pat Mitchell, Nov 27, 1990.

Clewiston: Interview with Pat Mitchell, Nov. 27, 1990.

WORLD'S FAIR

Fair: Marquis, *Hopes and Ashes*, 187-231; Larry Zim, Mel Lerner, and Herbert Rolfe, *The World of Tomorrow: The 1939 New York World's Fair* (New York, 1988), *passim*; Barbara Cohen, Steven Heller, and Seymour Chwast, *Trylon and Perisphere: The 1939 New York World's Fair* (New York, 1989), *passim*; *New York Times*, July 20-31, 1939, *passim*.

Roosevelt quote: Zim et al., *World of Tomorrow*, 9.

Strouds at fair: Interviews with Frances Stroud, May 1985, Apr. 20, 1990, and Hilma Boyd, Apr. 18, 1990; Frances's notebook and various brochures, in possession of author.

LETTING GO

Jessie's anxiety about children: Interviews with Ronnie Seckinger, Feb. 9, Apr. 11, May 29, 1983, Leila Scott, July 3, 1983, Novis Fields, July 10, 1983, Ralph Fields, June 19, 1987, and Gracie Fields, July 1, 1987.

Children leave home: Interviews with Ronnie Seckinger, Feb. 8, Apr. 11, 1983, Leila Scott, July 3, 1983, June 20, 1987, Carlton Scott, July 3, 1983, Wynelle Forbes, July 12, 1983, Ralph Fields, June 19, 1987, Callie Fagler, June 22, 1987, and Gracie Fields, July 1, 1987.

Jessie alone: Interviews with Leila Scott, July 3, 1983, and Novis Fields, July 10, 1983.

TENNESSEE VALLEY

TVA: Paul K. Conkin, "Intellectual and Political Roots," in *TVA: Fifty Years of Grass-Roots Bureaucracy*, eds. Erwin C. Hargrove and Paul K. Conkin (Urbana, Ill., 1983), 3-34; Richard Lowitt, "The TVA, 1933-45," *ibid.*, 35-65; Michael J. McDonald and John Muldowny, *TVA and the Dispossessed: The*

Resettlement of Population in the Norris Dam Area (Knoxville, Tenn., 1982); Wilson and Ferris, eds., *Encyclopedia of Southern Culture*, 355-56.

Douglas Dam: Interviews with Alice Mitchell, July 9, 1988, and Pat Mitchell, Nov. 27, 1990; U.S. Tennessee Valley Authority, *The Douglas Project: A Comprehensive Report on the Planning, Design, Construction, and Initial Operations of the Douglas Project*, Technical Report No. 10 (Washington, 1949), 171-83; Lowitt, "The TVA, 1933-45," 52, 55; Richard A. Couto, "New Seeds at the Grass Roots: The Politics of the TVA Power Program since World War II," *TVA*, eds. Hargrove and Conkin, 231; John H. Kyle, *The Building of TVA: An Illustrated History* (Baton Rouge, La., 1958), 96-97.

Roosevelt: Theo Lippman, Jr., *The Squire of Warm Springs: F.D.R. in Georgia, 1924-1945* (Chicago, 1977), 20-60, 237-41.

Funeral train: Interview with Pat Mitchell, Nov. 27, 1990; Griffin (Ga.) *Daily News*, Apr. 13, 1945, p. 1.

V-E Day: Interview with Pat Mitchell, Nov. 27, 1990.

Divorce: Final judgment and decree, July 25, 1949, Minute Book 1948, fls. 140-41, OCSC, Bulloch County Courthouse, Statesboro, Ga.

LIBERTY SHIPS

Merchant fleet: L.A. Sawyer and W.H. Mitchell, *The Liberty Ships: The History of the 'Emergency' Type Cargo Ships Constructed in the United States during World War II* (Cambridge, Md., 1970), 11-22; A.A. Hoehling, *The Fighting Liberty Ships: A Memoir* (Kent, O., 1990), 29-32; US Congress, Senate Special Committee Investigating the National Defense Program, 78th Congress, 1st Session, Report No. 10, *Additional Report*, Part 8, *Shipbuilding and Shipping* (Washington, 1943), 6-11, 23, 33.

U-boat campaign: Michael Gannon, *Operation Drumbeat: The Dramatic True Story of Germany's First U-Boat Attacks Along the American Coast in World War II* (New York, 1990), 96-100, 378-98; Senate Special Committee Investigating the National Defense Program, Report No. 10, *Additional Report*, Part 8, *Shipbuilding and Shipping*, 23.

Savannah shipyard: Margaret Wayt DeBolt, *Savannah: A Historical Portrait* (Virginia Beach, Va., 1976), 171-77; Senate Special Committee Investigating the National Defense Program, Report No. 10, *Additional Report*, Part 8, *Shipbuilding and Shipping*, 13-14, 33; Sawyer and Mitchell, *The Liberty Ships*, 148-51; interviews with Rose Fuller, Nov. 28, 1990, and Charles Harmon, July 27, 1991; Savannah (Ga.) *Morning News*, Nov. 20, 1942, pp. 5, 12, July 20, 1943, p. 12, Dec. 21, 1943, p. 14, June 24, 1944, p. 9, Feb. 16, 1945, p. 14.

Kermit's drinking: Interview with Rose Fuller, Nov. 28, 1990.

Divorce: Interview with Rose Fuller, Nov. 28, 1990; suit for divorce no. 1959, filed 19 June 1944, Office of the Clerk of the Court, Ben Hill County Courthouse, Fitzgerald, Ga.

Southeastern's last days: *Morning News*, July 25, 1945, pp. 9, 12, Aug. 3, 1945, p. 14, Sept. 30, 1945, p. 32, Nov. 10, 1945, pp. 3, 10.

Kermit's suicide attempt: Interviews with Rose Fuller and Jean Lott, Aug. 30, 1993.

HOMECOMING

Vernor Curtis: Application for marriage license, Vernor Curtis and Bernice Stroud, July 7, 1934, C.J. No. 12-257, and marriage license No. 12209, July 7, 1934, State of Florida, Office of Vital Statistics, Miami.

Request for copy of divorce decree: Letter from Maude Moreno to W.B. Lindsey, Miami, July 10, 1938, in possession of author.

Keeping children: Letter from Maude Moreno to Marjorie Scott, [Miami, Sept. 21, 1938], in possession of author.

Visit with Gladys: Interview with Gladys Waller, July 12, 1988.

December 2: Miami (Fla.) *Herald*, Dec. 2, 1939, p. 1, Dec. 3, 1939, p. 1; Atlanta (Ga.) *Constitution*, Dec. 1, 1939, p. 24, Dec. 2, 1939, pp. 1, 9, Dec. 3, 1939, p. 16A.

Maude's death: Interviews with Rose Fuller, July 10, 1983, Alice Mitchell, July 12, 1983, Frances Stroud, May 18, 1985, and T. Robert High and Alton High, Mar. 17, 1991; *Herald*, Dec. 3, 1939, p. 12A, Dec. 5, 1939, p. 4; death certificate no. 1741, Dec. 2, 1939, Office of Vital Statistics, Miami; letters from Kenneth B. Bess to Mrs. E.W. Scott, Miami, Dec. 3, 1939, and to Swainsboro Funeral Home, Dec. 4, 1939, in possession of author; telegram from Mrs. E.W. Scott to Kermit Stroud, Dec. 3, 1939, in possession of Jean Lott, Fitzgerald, Ga.

Funeral: *Forest-Blade*, Dec. 14, 1939, p. 7; interviews with Ouida Fields and Alice Mitchell, July 12, 1983.

Maude's last letter: Letter from Maude Moreno to Marjorie Scott, [Miami, Dec. 2, 1939], in possession of author.

Reaction to suicide: *Forest-Blade*, Dec. 14 1939, p. 7; interviews with Gladys Waller, July 12, 1988, Nesbit Christian, July 7, 1989, and Jean McGregor, Nov. 26, 1990.

Billy: Interviews with Leila Scott, July 3, 1983, Nov. 28, 1990, Alice Mitchell, July 5, 1983, and Frances Stroud, May 18, 1985.